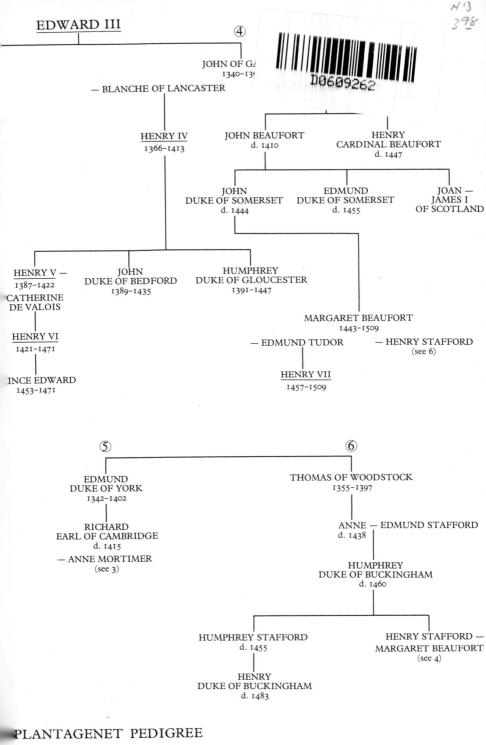

EDWARD III

④

JOHN OF GA[UNT]
1340-13[9]

— BLANCHE OF LANCASTER

HENRY IV
1366-1413

JOHN BEAUFORT
d. 1410

HENRY
CARDINAL BEAUFORT
d. 1447

JOHN
DUKE OF SOMERSET
d. 1444

EDMUND
DUKE OF SOMERSET
d. 1455

JOAN —
JAMES I
OF SCOTLAND

HENRY V —
1387-1422
CATHERINE
DE VALOIS

JOHN
DUKE OF BEDFORD
1389-1435

HUMPHREY
DUKE OF GLOUCESTER
1391-1447

MARGARET BEAUFORT
1443-1509

HENRY VI
1421-1471

— EDMUND TUDOR

— HENRY STAFFORD
(see 6)

[PR]INCE EDWARD
1453-1471

HENRY VII
1457-1509

⑤

⑥

EDMUND
DUKE OF YORK
1342-1402

THOMAS OF WOODSTOCK
1355-1397

RICHARD
EARL OF CAMBRIDGE
d. 1415
— ANNE MORTIMER
(see 3)

ANNE — EDMUND STAFFORD
d. 1438

HUMPHREY
DUKE OF BUCKINGHAM
d. 1460

HUMPHREY STAFFORD
d. 1455

HENRY STAFFORD —
MARGARET BEAUFORT
(see 4)

HENRY
DUKE OF BUCKINGHAM
d. 1483

PLANTAGENET PEDIGREE

NAMES UNDERLINED ARE THOSE
OF REIGNING KINGS OF ENGLAND

THE DRAGON'S BREED

The Dragon's Breed

The Story of the Tudors
from earliest times to 1603

GODFREY TURTON

PETER DAVIES : LONDON

Reprinted by photolithography and bound in Great Britain
by Bookprint Limited, Crawley, Sussex

CONTENTS

Part 1—From Anglesey to the Throne

CHAPTER 1

CHAPTER 2

CHAPTER 3

CHAPTER 4

CHAPTER 5

CHAPTER 6

Part 2—The Dynasty

CHAPTER 7

CHAPTER 8

CHAPTER 9

CHAPTER 10

CHAPTER 11

CHAPTER 12

CHAPTER 13

CHAPTER 14

CHAPTER 15

Part 3—Gloriana

CHAPTER 16

CHAPTER 17

CHAPTER 18

PART I

From Anglesey
to the Throne

CHAPTER I

Wales, the last refuge of British independence when the rest of the country was occupied by Anglo-Saxon invaders, had its revenge some thousand years later with the accession of a Welsh dynasty to the English throne. The Tudors had little if any hereditary right to a place in the line of kings founded by William the Conqueror. A Welsh conquest superseded the Norman, and even if the Welsh monarchs soon became as fully Anglicized as their Norman predecessors they owed success at the outset to the support that they received from their native Wales.

Later pedantry has tried to derive Tudor from the Greek Theodoros, but the name is in fact of Welsh origin and was in fairly common use. In early times there were no surnames in Wales, a patronymic showing father and grandfather was enough to distinguish man from man. Owen son of Meredyth son of Tudor was grandfather to the first Tudor king, Henry VII, and as this Owen spent much of his life at the English court he adopted the English custom and called himself Owen Tudor. He had better reason to be proud of his grandfather than of his father; that seems to be why he chose Tudor and not Meredyth. It was a decision on which more hung than he knew, depriving English history of a Meredyth dynasty, English villages of "ye olde Meredyth tea-shoppe."

The family estates lay in Anglesey at Penmynydd and Trecastell, the latter on the shore of the Menai Straits. Owen's grandfather, the eponymous Tudor, enjoyed considerable dignity there, holding a manorial court and claiming privileges for it which dated from

3

time immemorial so that not even the English occupation was able to upset them. Wales was already a subject nation in his lifetime. Few even of the oldest of his contemporaries were likely to remember Prince Llewelyn, the last champion of Welsh independence, who reigned supreme from one sea to the other, from Flint to Glamorgan. That epoch in Welsh history, a rare interlude of national unity, ended in disaster in 1283 with the decisive victory won by Edward I who invaded with an English army. Llewelyn was killed, and no successor was found able to maintain resistance. In future the only Prince of Wales was the English king's eldest son.

Anglesey was fortunate under the new dispensation. It was among the parts of the country, chiefly in the north, whose administration the English King retained in his own hands. The English system of government was enforced there with little oppression, whereas elsewhere the Royal authority was delegated to the "marcher lords," descendants of the Norman barons who began to penetrate into the Welsh marches soon after the Norman conquest of England, encroaching deeper and deeper as the years went by and planting their castles all over the land. These freebooters were now confirmed in possession, allotted fiefs in which they enjoyed little short of sovereign power. They were foreigners hated by the Welsh, of whose language for the most part they were ignorant. They despised native laws and customs, and the English law which they brought was applied only for the benefit of their English retainers, while the native population felt its punitive force. They were as rapacious in their behaviour to each other as to their subjects. Fief was for ever at war with fief, there was no security for life or property while they waged their interminable feuds. Wales had known anarchy often enough in the past, jealous princes warring against each other before the time of Llewelyn; but at least under native misgovernment a man could appeal with some confidence to the sanctity of tradition and rely on public opinion to support him. The Norman tyrant stripped him of human dignity, the Welshman had no rights.

Seeing what was happening elsewhere the people of Anglesey had reason to be thankful that they owed allegiance directly to the English King, that no marcher lord intervened between them. Much of the work of government here was entrusted to Welshmen, and an official class grew up native by birth, standing midway between prince and people. Tudor of Penmynydd came of a family nurtured in this tradition and serving the English establishment. His grandfather swore fealty to the baby son of Edward I when he was proclaimed Prince of Wales at Carnarvon, and when the boy grew up to reign in England as Edward II he received loyal support from Tudor's father, who fought for him in the English civil war and refused to abandon the Royal cause after the victory of the rebels. When King Edward himself was captured and imprisoned in Berkeley Castle the Welsh formed a league to rescue him; but a traitor informed against them, the plan was thwarted and Edward II murdered.

His son, Edward III, restored Royal authority in England, and the family at Penmynydd was among those whose loyalty to his father he rewarded. Tudor himself visited the English court and took part in the jousting and other entertainments for which it was celebrated. It was probably for the sake of these occasions that he revised his armorial bearings. The device which they flaunted was a trio of bleeding heads, commemorating an exploit performed by an ancestor who killed three English lords in battle, cut off their heads and brought them back to present to the Welsh Prince of Gwynedd. This was an emblem unlikely to earn favour for a guest at a tournament organised by Edward III. So the shield was repainted, the gory nakedness of the heads clothed decently in helmets and visors.

Although the Welshman was ready to make concessions to English pride he stood firm on his dignity. He claimed the title of knight, announced himself at tournaments as Sir Tudor, and when the King asked from whom he received the honour he retorted that he had knighted himself, possessing the three qualifications prescribed by the laws of King Arthur, gentle birth, a hardy spirit and sufficient estate. He added that if anyone disputed his right he was ready to vindicate it in single combat. No one accepted his challenge, he remained Sir Tudor at the English court.

The appeal to King Arthur was of a sort to commend itself to Edward III, a man of enthusiastic temperament and romantic tastes, who built the round tower at Windsor Castle to accommodate an order of knights of the round table founded on the legends of Camelot. There was a fit place here for Sir Tudor, knight of his own creation, with his exotic blazonry and legendary claims. He overstepped even King Edward's indulgence, however, when he sought means with his brother, a clerk in holy orders, to avenge

5

the betrayal of their father's enterprise, the rescue of Edward II from Berkeley Castle. The traitor himself was already dead; but they caught his son in a lonely spot in the hills, attacked and killed him.

The offence against English law could not pass unpunished, and both offenders, the priest and the knight, were committed to prison. They did not stay there long. King Edward was fond of Sir Tudor and could make allowances for an act of violence whose motive showed respect for his own father's memory. Both were soon at large again with their estates intact, the priest to resume his career in the Church, the knight to enjoy the hospitality of a court famous as the gayest and most magnificent in Europe, enriched with the spoils of the French wars and ruled by a genial monarch as insatiable of pleasure as of martial glory.

This was the England in which Chaucer lived and wrote. His *Canterbury Tales* make clear that for many the pleasures were more than balanced by the pains; but the King and his court seemed to exist as carefree as if their revels were hidden in the Venusberg or other secret fastness of romance. Not even the epidemic of plague, the Black Death, which devastated the country towards the end of the reign, could interrupt the profusion of royal festivities, the brilliant society, the banquets, the tournaments where knights showed off their prowess and fashionable young women their charms, even riding into the lists in the interlude in masculine dress of a cut chosen rather to expose than disguise.

Sir Tudor died in 1367, predeceasing Edward III by ten years. He left four sons, Goronwy, Gwilym, Rhys and Meredyth. Goronwy, the eldest, brought by his father to the English court, won the favour of the heir apparent, the Black Prince, followed him on his campaigns in France and was rewarded when the government of Wales was placed in the Prince's hands with the profitable office of Forester of Snowdon, a district covering most of Carnarvon, Merioneth and Anglesey. The Black Prince did not live to succeed to the throne, and his son Richard became King on Edward III's death; but Goronwy suffered no setback in the new reign, Richard II confirmed him in his titles and added that of Constable of Beaumaris Castle, a position held only once before by a Welshman. Goronwy retained it for four days; he died suddenly, drowned in Kent on the Sunday before Lady Day 1382. There can be rough water in the estuary of the Thames in March, but the bards who mourned his loss attributed it to "surfeit of mead."

His brothers, Gwilym and Rhys, failed to rise to his eminence, but were no less ready than he to serve Richard II and found employment as captains in a regiment of archers. Only Meredyth, the youngest, stayed at home in Wales, where he held office in the household of the Bishop of Bangor. He owed it probably to his brother's influence that he obtained preferment later from the King and was appointed escheator of the county of Anglesey, a Royal officer in charge of the estates that reverted by escheat to the Crown. It was Meredyth, the youngest and seemingly the least ambitious of Sir Tudor's sons, who was destined to beget a famous dynasty. His great-grandson became Henry VII, King of England.

In the last decade of the fourteenth century the family enjoyed a position of dignity and influence in Anglesey and North Wales, and lived on good terms with the English overlord. Disturbing events however had begun in England, which put an end there to the stability of the previous reign. Richard II came to the throne at the age of ten; the contemporary author of *Piers Plowman* expressed true forebodings when he deplored the fate of the court where "the cat is a kitten." In appearance at first there was little change, the pleasures of the courtiers, both men and women, were as gay and lavish as ever; but dangerous forces were at work in the country, and the King's uncles who held power during his minority had neither the standing nor the experience effectively to oppose them.

The Black Death had wiped out such numbers of the working population that there was a grave shortage of labour alike on the land and in the towns, and the survivors aware of their own value, of the excess of demand over supply, were no longer content with the low pay and hard conditions of work usual in the past. They took courage to claim a greater measure of social justice. Preachers clerical and lay repeated the couplet:

> When Adam delved and Eve span,
> Who was then a gentleman?

The fruit of these ideas in England was the Peasants' Revolt, which took the form in most parts of the country of disorganised riots; but in the southeast it found a capable leader, Wat Tyler, whose forces stormed the city of London. The famous scene has often been described, how the Royal government offered to parley, how at the meeting arranged a quarrel broke out in which Tyler was killed, and as his followers drew their bows to avenge him the boy Richard—he was fourteen at the time—rode forward alone into their midst, calling to them:

"Sirs, will you shoot your King? I myself will be your captain, you shall have from me all you seek."

It was no fault of his that the promise was not kept. It is probable indeed that much of the severity with which the revolt was suppressed arose from the desire of those in control of the government to put him to shame, to teach him that he was unfit to act on his own judgment. When he grew old enough to assert himself and escape from tutelage the memory of this incident survived to invest him, whether justly or not, with the reputation of a friend of the poor and down-trodden. This was especially true of the remoter parts of the country, where he was least known. In the struggle which filled his reign against the encroachment of baronial power he could count on sympathy in Wales. It was in any case the habit of the Welsh to look to Royal authority for protection from the tyranny of the marcher lords.

Sir Tudor's sons serving in his army followed an example set by many other Welshmen. They were with him on his expedition to Ireland in 1399 to restore order among the native princes there who acknowledged his suzerainty, and they had as companion their cousin Owen, their mother's sister's son, whose father was lord of Glendower, a district of Merioneth lying on the upper waters of the Dee. Owen Glendower, destined to earn lasting fame in Welsh history, was a man of great charm and commanding personality, he won the devoted loyalty of his cousins. They remained closely associated with him till their death.

The Irish expedition was King Richard's undoing. No sooner was he out of England than the most dangerous of his enemies, the Duke of Hereford, seized the opportunity to slip back from exile in France, and other recalcitrant nobles gathered to support him. Hereford was especially to be feared because he was of Royal blood, eldest son of John of Gaunt, the King's uncle. Richard made haste to return, landed at Milford Haven and advanced north along the coast. Hereford's army travelling west to intercept him found him in secure occupation of the strong castle at Conway. Negotiations followed, and the King agreed to terms of peace; but while he was in the company of the rebel lords they overpowered him by treachery and carried him off to Flint, where they forced him to abdicate. He was taken back a prisoner to England, dragged from castle to castle. In a few months' time he was dead, probably strangled. The Duke of Hereford became King as Henry IV.

Owen Glendower was present at Flint, a witness of the scene of abdication. Although the immediate cause of the insurrection which he led soon afterwards to restore Welsh independence arose from the malice of a neighbour, Lord Grey of Ruthin, who made mischief between him and the new King, his success in attracting recruits, in transforming a private quarrel into a national movement owed much to Welsh sympathy for Richard and indignation at his fate. This sentiment was reinforced by ideas gaining strength from the circumstances of the times. The depopulation resulting from the Black Death had its effect in offers of higher pay, less onerous conditions of work, as employers competed with each other for an inadequate supply of labour. The standard of living of the working classes improved, and men no longer engrossed in the task of keeping body and soul together found leisure to exercise their minds on wider interests.

In Wales this rearoused the traditional love of poetry. The bards were active again, and as their themes were drawn mainly from the exploits of national heroes they revived memories of the past, provoked discontent with English domination. Owen Glendower was a generous patron of the bards; his home at Sycharth on the borders of Denbigh and Shropshire became their sanctuary, and the hospitality enjoyed there, the entertainment provided both for the body and for the mind, earned celebration in songs that travelled from one end of Wales to the other.

He himself was a man of cultivated tastes, liberal education. In his youth he read law at Westminster and was called to the bar, and for some years he made a career at the court of Richard II. There was another side, however, to his character, a romantic passion for Wales, its ancient glory, its language and beliefs. Although he had true respect for religion, cherishing the supernatural in his life, he was seldom reluctant in his conduct of the war to plunder and destroy a rich monastery. ·He was less impressed by the sanctity of the monks than of the bards.

Shakespeare draws his portrait with understanding in the first part of *King Henry IV*. Glendower boasts of the portents attending his birth, he is a wonder-worker, a Merlin, something too of a charlatan when he proclaims: "I can call spirits from the vasty deep." Yet when Hotspur jeers at him, makes fun of his pretensions, he keeps his dignity and his temper, refuses to be goaded even by taunts attacking the Welsh language, the Welsh bards. Hotspur is deliberately rude:

> I had rather be a kitten and cry mew
> Than one of these same metre ballad-mongers.

Glendower's reply is to change the subject, return to the political discussion, the purpose of their meeting, for which he needs Hotspur's support. When he leaves the room his son-in-law Mortimer sums him up:

> In faith, he is a worthy gentleman,
> Exceedingly well-read and profited
> In strange concealments, valiant as a lion
> And wondrous affable, and as bountiful
> As mines of India.

His cousins, Gwilym and Rhys ap Tudor, committed themselves wholeheartedly to his cause. While he himself was raising the country farther south they seized Conway Castle on his behalf, choosing their opportunity when the English garrison was at prayers in church to avenge the capture of King Richard. An English army sent under the command of Henry Percy (Shakespeare's Hotspur), heir to the Earl of Northumberland, was unable to dislodge them, and Hotspur disobeying his orders which insisted that he put the rebels to death offered terms for the surrender of the castle, granting Gwilym and Rhys full pardon for their acts of war and restoration of their forfeited property. Soon afterwards the Earl of Northumberland himself broke with the King and rose in rebellion in the north of England. It is likely that this intention was already known when the terms of surrender were offered and accepted at Conway. They left Gwilym and Rhys free in the mountains, with ample resources to promote their campaign on behalf of Owen Glendower.

The rebellion of the Percys led to the secret meeting between Hotspur and Glendower described by Shakespeare in the scene quoted. The third party was Edmund Mortimer, recently promoted by Glendower from prisoner to son-in-law. The three formed an alliance to overthrow Henry IV and divide the country between them, Glendower to hold Wales, Percy the north of England, leaving Mortimer's young nephew, the Earl of March, to be crowned King of what was left of the truncated realm.

The Earl of March had a juster claim to the throne than the usurping Henry, tracing his descent from Lionel Duke of Clarence, Edward III's third son, whose only child Philippa married a Mortimer. Henry IV claimed through his father, the fourth son, John of Gaunt.

The plan miscarried. Hotspur led his men down from the north, expecting to join forces with Glendower at Ludlow; but the King's army pursuing compelled him to retreat to Shrewsbury, where he waited in vain for the Welsh. Glendower in fact had been busy in South Wales, mopping up the marcher lords to protect his rear, and when he set out at last to keep his rendezvous with Hotspur he was delayed by floods. He was too late to support Hotspur at Shrewsbury when the King's army attacked, and the outcome was a crushing defeat in which Hotspur himself was killed. Even so, it is possible that Glendower could have saved the cause if he had pressed on, gathering reinforcements from Mortimer and from Hotspur's survivors. His men were fresh, the King's exhausted by battle. Instead, he turned back into Wales; it was a mistake that cost the Welsh an opportunity never offered again to win lasting independence.

Nevertheless he was still able to maintain the struggle on his own ground with success. The battle of Shrewsbury was fought in 1403, and in the following year he stood at the height of his power, crowned Prince of Wales, setting up his own law courts and even convoking a Welsh Parliament at Machynlleth. He hoped too to found a university, and Welsh scholars flocked to him from Oxford and Cambridge. In England his name inspired a superstitious terror; it was believed that he intended to reconquer the ancient heritage of the Briton from Anglesey to Kent and destroy the English tongue.

In foreign relations he seemed to be no less successful. He received a promise of military help from the regents who governed France in the name of the mad King Charles VI, and he used their influence with the schismatic Pope Benedict XIII at Avignon to win the blessing of the Church. Wales was on the way to recognition as a sovereign nation.

Not for long. English pressure was resumed, and the French achieved little when their promised forces landed at Milford Haven. They advanced into England as far as Worcester, where King Henry awaited them. Neither army was willing to move from the strong position that it occupied, and for eight days they sat watching each other without fighting. The French were the first to tire of this; they slipped away under cover of night, retreated into Wales and re-embarked for France. Glendower was left to carry on the war alone.

From that time his power declined, but for a few years more he was able to make it felt. He had the advantage of fighting in woods and mountains pathless to his enemies but familiar and hospitable to himself, the wilds in which he was at home. He could count too on the favour of the local people, whose poverty he relieved with the spoils and whose centuries of oppression he avenged as he plundered and burnt the castles of the marcher lords. They were unreliable allies, however, tending to melt away home to enjoy the proceeds after a successful raid. To make things worse, they were often on bad terms with one another. The bitterness of internecine feuds not only hindered a common plan of action, it drew many even to collaborate with the enemy.

Others might desert him, but not his cousins, Gwilym and Rhys. They were among his most active supporters, his loyal kinsmen unshaken by reverses and dwindling hopes. He suffered personal bereavement as well as a crushing blow to his cause when in 1412 they were caught by the King's forces, carried off to Chester and beheaded. He himself still kept up the struggle; but he had become a fugitive hiding in caves, from which he broke out at intervals when he could gather a sufficient band of marauders to raid a castle or abbey.

These occasions grew increasingly rare, the reward seldom matched the danger. Henry IV died of leprosy, and his son succeeded as Henry V, a capable general, the future victor of Agincourt, who knew the Welsh marches well, having held command there in his father's lifetime. He had the military skill to suppress any last efforts of resistance, and the subtlety to lure Glendower's following away with tempting offers of pardon to any rebels who submitted.

It was the end of Glendower's dream of Welsh independence. He was a helpless outcast, wandering in disguise about the country, hunted by the English. One night he sought refuge at the abbey of Valle Crucis on the Dee, where the abbot told him that he was born before his time, he should have waited till the next century for a Welshman to conquer England.

He was no longer dangerous. Henry V offered to pardon him if he would give himself up; but his pride would not allow it, he preferred to live on as a hunted rebel, an ineffective ghost in the hills. The last record of him describes how he took leave of his few remaining soldiers, telling them that he was going to France to seek help. It is not known whether he left Wales or stayed and died there. Nothing was ever heard of him again.

When Gwilym and Rhys ap Tudor were executed at Chester all their property was forfeited, and this time no restitution followed. The influential position enjoyed by the family in the reigns of Edward III and Richard II was lost, its members were implicated too deeply in Glendower's rebellion. Only the estate at Penmynydd was saved, the heritage of the eldest brother, Goronwy. At the time of his death by drowning his only son was a child, he was still under age sixteen years later when King Richard abdicated and the trouble in Wales began. He had an elder sister, however, whose husband, the lord of Penrhyn, was on the winning side, a supporter of Henry IV against Glendower. She took possession of Penmynydd, secure under her husband's protection, and managed the estate in her brother's interest, keeping him there with her while he grew up. At last when all was quiet again she gave Penmynydd back to him.

This Tudor ap Goronwy was a man of peace, neither seeking nor attaining eminence. He stood aloof from the turbulent politics of the times, in which another branch of the family played so noteworthy a part. In some records indeed he is described as an imbecile; but this seems to mean no more than that he eschewed public affairs, preferred the obscure and peaceful life of a private citizen. His descendants at Penmynydd followed his example; in so far as their names survive it is in a local context only. Like their cousins they adopted Tudor as a surname, Anglicizing it later in accordance with the prevailing fashion to Theodor. A Richard Theodor held the office of Mayor of Beaumaris under Elizabeth I, another Richard that of Sheriff of Anglesey in 1623. It is a remarkable fact that this branch of the family showed no interest in improving its own fortune even when its cousins wore the crown of England. In spite of the value set by the Welsh on ties of blood there is no evidence that any lord of Penmynydd travelled to seek advantage at the court of a Tudor King.

Before the end of the seventeenth century the male line at Penmynydd died out, and the estate passed by marriage to the Bulkeley family, the last of whom, Francis Bulkeley, in 1722 overwhelmed it in mortgage and shot himself. So ended the senior branch of the Tudors.

Although Meredyth, the youngest of Sir Tudor's sons, was destined to make the greatest contribution to history, less is known of him than of any of his brothers. He owed his start in life to Young, Bishop of Bangor, who gave him a post in his household, and as Young himself was a close friend of Glendower, serving him as chancellor during the brief heyday when Wales had an independent government, it is clear that Meredyth also played an active part in the rebellion. As the chances of victory faded he turned to private brigandage for a livelihood. There is a holy well in Anglesey at the tip of the promontory of Llanddwyn, dedicated to St. Dwynwen, patroness of lovers. Her name means in Welsh the "white goddess"; when Christian piety canonised her the pagan rites of fertility which she promoted shared the blessing, and lovers who enjoyed them testified to their gratitude by generous contributions to her treasury. When Meredyth ap Tudor robbed this sacred hoard his crime provoked angry outcry; he was driven from the country, fled to the mainland to live as an outlaw in a fastness on Snowdon. He was still in hiding there when his son was born, but Glendower remained his friend. The baby was given the name of Owen, and Glendower himself stood godfather.

Owen Tudor, as he called himself when he grew up, was heir to a forfeited estate, son of an outlawed father. The past honours of his family were forgotten, and when his career began to attract remark it was easy for the jealous to throw scorn on him, to represent him as an upstart of obscure, if not disreputable origin. His plight was that of many other Welshmen of good birth compelled to make their way in life with nothing to help them but their own health and strength and the quickness of their wits. Even those who retained some property derived little benefit from it when the buildings were in ruin, the lands untilled and wasted. Glendower's campaigns, the prolonged chaos, the destruction inflicted by his own as well as by the English forces left Wales a wilderness. Fifty years afterwards when the Bishop of Bangor received orders to collect a subsidy from his diocese he replied that it would be a waste of time to appoint collectors, there was nothing to collect.

The hardship was aggravated by the penal laws which Henry IV imposed when the rebellion broke out, and which remained in force till the Tudors themselves revoked them. They degraded the Welsh into a race of helots without rights in their own country. A Welshman was debarred from holding any office under the Crown, from enfranchisement in a borough, from marriage with an Englishwoman, and if an Englishman was charged with an offence he could not be convicted on a Welshman's evidence. There was one law for the Welsh, another in Wales for the English. The marcher lords rebuilt their castles. These were the spirits called by Glendower from the vasty deep.

CHAPTER 2

Leprosy, the horrible disease of which Henry IV died, was regarded in Wales as proof of divine judgment punishing him for his usurpation of the throne, murder of King Richard and persecution of the Welsh. This belief did not prevent Welshmen from accepting his son's offers of clemency, or even from taking service in his army. There were many soldiers bearing Welsh names who fought for Henry V with distinction in his campaigns in France. The alternative, if they stayed at home, was as often as not utter destitution, and they had less reason for patriotic scruples when the battlefield lay beyond the sea, the enemy was a foreigner. The French deserved little gratitude for their half-hearted efforts, the ineffective expedition with which they supported Glendower.

Glendower's own son Meredyth was among those fighting for the English in France, and Owen Tudor, his second cousin, followed his example. The date of his military service is uncertain; but if he was born during Glendower's rebellion he could not have been more than twelve years old at the time of the Battle of Agincourt. It is most unlikely that he was present there.

The plight in which Henry V found himself at Agincourt was very similar to that in store for a later generation of his compatriots at Dunkirk in 1940. He was retreating to Calais to embark for home from a rash adventure on the continent when the French intercepted him with forces greatly outnumbering his own. His lucky victory enabled him to transport his army safely back to England. He waited there for two years till his preparations to renew the invasion were complete. When he returned to France

16

the campaign was prolonged till 1419. If this was when Owen Tudor enlisted, arriving among reinforcements sent from England, he could have taken part in the siege and capture of Rouen and the subsequent advance of the English army to the walls of Paris. Whether by his exploits or his manners he earned favorable attention from the King, who took him into the Royal bodyguard. He rose, however, to no rank above that of esquire, lacking the means needed for knighthood.

In the following year a treaty of peace was signed. Charles VI of France gave Henry his daughter Catherine in marriage and accepted him as his heir to succeed on his own death to the French throne; but his only surviving son, the Dauphin Charles ("Dauphin" is the title borne by the French King's heir apparent), refused to submit to the terms and escaped to Touraine, where he kept up resistance to the English. Henry did not live to succeed his father-in-law. In 1422 he was engaged in operations against the Dauphin's supporters on the Loire; dysentery was prevalent in the army, and he himself fell a victim. He was at Paris for convalescence in the early summer, and Catherine joined him there with their infant son; but in August he received an urgent appeal from his ally, the Duke of Burgundy, who sought help against the forces besieging a Burgundian garrison. His illness still gripped him, he was too weak to ride a horse; but he insisted on taking command in person and set out in a litter. He travelled only a short way; the strain was too much for him, and he was carried back a dying man to the castle of Vincennes.

He died on the last day of August, Charles VI less than two months later on the 21st of October. A child under a year old was left to be the first and only wearer of the crown of the united kingdoms of England and France.

As Catherine de Valois, the child's mother, was to play an important part in the story of the Tudors it is necessary to go back a few years to trace her life from the beginning. She was born in Paris in 1401, daughter of Charles VI and Isabeau of Bavaria, a princess of the house of Wittelsbach. There was a strain of hereditary weakness in the family, three children died in infancy; but at the time of Catherine's birth she had two surviving brothers and four sisters, and some sixteen months later a last brother was born, who, on the death of the two elder in early manhood, grew up to be heir to the throne, the Dauphin Charles.

The younger members of the family had an unhappy childhood.

17

Nine years before Catherine was born the King, her father, suffered the first attack of the mental disorder which afflicted him off and on at intervals for the rest of his life. The misfortune was the more distressing because it was so unexpected. Few could have seemed better fitted than he as a young man to wear the crown, tall, fair-haired, good-looking, an athlete renowned for his prowess at tournaments and in other feats of strength. He won popularity too by his easy manners and affability, the charm that he exerted on all, but especially on women. It is possible indeed that the restless energy with which he sought entertainment, whether in jousting or lovemaking, foreshadowed the weakness destined at last to produce insanity.

The crisis came during a hot August. The King had been unwell, his air of abstraction aroused comment, and often in answer to a question he spoke at random. When a quarrel arose with the Duke of Brittany, and he insisted on leading his army in person, his doctors tried in vain to dissuade him. He reached Le Mans and was riding through a wood when a ragged man in white ran out from the trees, calling to him to stop, warning him of treason. The King drew up sharply, and the page riding behind him, carrying his lance, who was dozing half-asleep, woke with a start, and the lance slipped from his grasp. It fell clattering against the armour of the man next him.

The King, alarmed by the strange intruder's message, assumed from the noise that traitors were already active in the rear, and he drew his sword and shouted. So far his behaviour was natural; but the shock had upset his reason, he lunged fiercely at the Duke of Orleans riding beside him, his brother to whom he was devoted. The Duke evaded the blow, and the King turned on others, striking indiscriminately. Four were killed before a man succeeded in gripping him from behind, pulling him from his horse and disarming him. The access of frenzy ended in coma. He lay as if dead.

Skill and care nursed him back to health, and for a time it seemed that his recovery was complete; but in the following year he suffered a relapse, and others followed inexorably, often with such violence that his life was in danger. Premonitory symptoms announced the approach of each bout; he would be sitting in his council discussing affairs of state when he would leap to his feet and rush to and fro, declaring that a thousand needles transfixed him. He knew very well what it portended, and his distress was so pitiful that those present wept to see him. He was obliged to leave the government of the kingdom to his uncles, of whom the Duke of Burgundy was the most powerful.

This was the shadow under which Catherine grew up, and her mother did little to lighten it for her. Queen Isabeau sought distraction from the troubles of her married life in social gaieties and politics. When the Duke of Burgundy died in 1404 she was able to combine these interests. The leading part in the government was assumed by the King's brother, the Duke of Orleans, in whose company she found great pleasure. He was very like his brother in face and figure and had a charm of manner that recalled his brother's before his illness. In quality of mind and cultivated tastes he surpassed him. His love of literature was inherited by his son, whose name, Charles d'Orléans, holds a place of honour among the poets of France.

Scandal was soon busy with the relations between the Duke of Orleans and the Queen, asking whether it was always business of state that kept them so often alone together. She bought a piece of ground adjoining the property of the Celestine monks in Paris and had a gate inserted in their wall, so that she could pass to and fro in private to attend services in the monastic church. The gate gave access also to the extensive gardens of the monastery, a favourite resort of the Duke.

If she was unfaithful to her mad husband she had given him eleven children of whom many survived, and it was peculiarly galling for her that in his fits of delusion, even when he recognised others, she herself remained a stranger to him. He would ask his attendants who she was, why she pestered him, and implore them to send her away. At last the very sight of her provoked him to violence so that she dared not approach. She was probably glad of the excuse to avoid him; he was unshaven, unwashed, his clothes were seldom changed and his body crawled with vermin. Public opinion laid the blame for this neglect on her and the Duke, accusing them of spending on their pleasure the money intended for his maintenance; but there was reason enough for his squalor in his own refusal to let himself be touched.

A trick is described to which his attendants resorted. They got themselves up as savages with blacked faces, taking care to wear shirts of mail under the disguise to protect them from his blows. When they burst like this into his room he was so dumbfounded with terror that they were able to seize, undress and wash him, dress him again in the clean clothes that they had brought. The charade had to be repeated whenever he was given a bath.

Between a mad father and an intriguing mother the children suffered grave privation. During one of the King's intervals of sanity their nurse went to him and described their plight, that they were ill fed and ill clothed, with few to serve them as they were without the money to pay wages. It was a feature of his illness that when it lifted his reason at once was restored. He listened to her with indignation, shocked especially by the disrespect shown to his eldest son, the Dauphin Louis, heir to the throne, who was eight years old. He sent word to his cousin, the new Duke of Burgundy, asking him to come and take charge. This champion known as John the Fearless (he had distinguished himself in battle against the Saracens) was a personal enemy of the Duke of Orleans.

The Queen was out of town at the time with the Duke of Orleans, visiting her second daughter, Marie, a girl of twelve, at the convent where she had placed her to take the veil. There was a chance of an advantageous marriage for Marie, and the Queen was anxious to persuade her to return to secular life. News reached her there of events in Paris, and in great alarm she sent friends to fetch the Dauphin and bring him to join her before the Duke of Burgundy arrived. The younger children —Catherine aged four, and her brothers John and Charles, the one a little older, the other younger than herself—were left where they were.

The party escorting the Dauphin set off in haste, but they had not gone far when they were caught in a violent thunderstorm and obliged to seek shelter. They spent the night waiting for the weather to improve, and the Duke of Burgundy, riding in pursuit, overtook and found them. He asked the boy whether he wished to go on to his mother or back with him to his father in Paris. Without hesitation the boy chose his mad father and arrangements were made for him, and for the younger children too, to live removed from their mother's influence.

Marie remained with the nuns, refusing to be enticed away; but the Queen had her will with her eldest daughter, Isabel, who at eighteen was already a widow, having been married as a child to the English King Richard, sent to England to live at his court, and recalled to France when he was deposed and murdered. Isabel was inconsolable on her return; she had enjoyed the three years spent in England and was devoted to King Richard, who treated her as a father, content to wait patiently till she was old enough to be his wife in fact. It appalled her when her mother arranged a marriage for her now with the eldest son of the Duke of Orleans. The betrothal did much to restore the Queen's prestige and was a rebuff to the Duke of Burgundy, but Isabel wept bitterly. Her bridegroom, the future poet, was only fourteen, she herself would be nineteen at the end of the year. Her heart pined for King Richard.

The conditions in which the Royal children grew up were little likely to encourage respect for established authority; but worse was in store in the following year when assassins hired by the Duke of Burgundy attacked and killed the Duke of Orleans in a Paris street. The supporters of the murdered man leagued themselves to avenge him, they became known as Armagnacs after the name of their leader. Attempts made to mediate failed, and the country was plunged into civil war. Burgundians and Armagnacs fought, and the common people suffered destruction and pillage. Those who sought justice were told to complain to the "mad King."

Burgundian influence was strong in Paris where the Duke enjoyed great popularity from the belief which he encouraged that he favoured social reform. The more violent of the mob led by the guild of butchers seized the government of the city on his behalf. The scenes which followed were a foretaste of those enacted centuries later during the French Revolution. Led by the butcher Simon Caboche and the apothecary Jean de Troyes, the working population had its revenge for past oppression. There was great disorder; full advantage was taken of the licence to pursue private feuds, hunt down unpopular nobles. It was enough that a man was rich to expose him to the charge of Armagnac sympathies, an offence punished with the headsman's axe unless he saved himself by payment of an enormous fine.

There was the difference between this and later attempts to set up a ruling commune in Paris that the monarchy was not in danger. Caboche and his friends professed allegiance to the King and kept him with them to lend authority to their doings; but he was virtually their prisoner and had no power to oppose them, even when he was sane enough to understand what was happening. They took care to deprive him of his former advisers, imprisoning some and putting others to death.

His children, detained with him, had to endure nothing worse than censorious observation and outspoken rebuke. The new masters of Paris disapproved of moral laxity, whose indulgence encouraged costly festivity at the public expense. The Dauphin, who was fond of pleasure, refused to be intimidated; he persisted in gay entertainments, keeping them up till late into the night. Catherine, nearly thirteen, was old enough to be present on the occasion when their dance was interrupted by a posse of armed men led by Jacqueville, the captain of the militia, who delivered a stern lecture denouncing the Dauphin for his frivolity, his disregard of the welfare of his people. One of the guests replied indignantly on the Dauphin's behalf, protesting at the unseasonable hour chosen for the intrusion and the insolence of the language used. Tempers flared on both sides, and in the heat of the altercation the Dauphin drew his dagger and stabbed Jacqueville in the chest.

A shirt of mail worn under the coat saved Jacqueville from injury, but he was a man of violence accustomed to strike an opponent dead in the street on far smaller provocation. It is evidence of the respect still accorded to royalty that he withdrew, contenting himself with sullen threats. The dance was not resumed, a further shock awaited the guests. The Dauphin's paroxysm of anger brought on a haemorrhage. For three days he spat blood.

Scenes like this were the background to Catherine's life as she grew from childhood to maturity. The Armagnacs returned to power in Paris, taking the town by storm and revenging themselves on the commune with great slaughter; but their victory brought no respite from strife. The Duke of Burgundy gathered fresh forces to oppose them, the civil war continued unabated. At the height of these troubles, while the French were too busy fighting each other to offer effective resistance, the distracted country was invaded by Henry V of England.

Even the shock of the defeat at Agincourt produced no reconciliation at home. France remained as divided as ever, and the rift extended even to the Royal Family. The Dauphin supported the Armagnacs, while the Queen, his mother, favoured the Duke of Burgundy, her former lover's murderer. She was a woman whose head governed her heart; the advantages which she saw in the alliance outweighed any sore feelings. She even overcame the aversion which she professed for the Duke's face, his protruding chin underpinned with rolls of fat.

At the end of the year the Dauphin fell suddenly ill and died. His mother's enemies accused her of poisoning him; but the scene at the dance at Paris with its aftermath of blood-spitting tells its own story. His brother John became Dauphin in his place, but a vicious heredity haunted the family. Before another year was out he too succumbed to a fatal illness. Only one son was left to carry on the Royal line, Catherine's younger brother Charles, who was fourteen.

The pendulum of the civil war swung again. Paris rose against the Armagnacs; many of their leaders were killed in the massacre, the Dauphin Charles himself barely escaped with his life, saved by an officer of his bodyguard who hearing the noise in .the night ran to his room and picked him up in his arms, carried him to the Bastille where he dressed, took horse and fled into the country. Catherine was left in Paris, a girl of vulnerable age among the riot, till the Duke of Burgundy arrived with the Queen, took control and restored order.

The Duke held the capital, but his position was far from secure. The Armagnacs threatened him on the upper, the English on the lower Seine. Only peace could save France, the question was whether to seek it with the domestic or the foreign enemy. He chose the latter and sent envoys to negotiate with King Henry; but the talks made little progress, the English terms were too hard. King Henry had taken Rouen and was advancing already on Paris.

The Duke turned at last to the Armagnacs to try if he could not do better with them. A meeting was arranged between him and the Dauphin at Montereau at the junction of the Seine and the Yonne. He rode on to the bridge over the river, where the Dauphin waited for him with a party of officers. One of these—the same who rescued the Dauphin from the riot in Paris—stepped forward unobserved while the two leaders greeted each other. He stabbed the Duke to death. For a second time the Queen was bereaved by assassination.

The crime was of advantage to the English. The murdered Duke's son who succeeded him sought King Henry's help to avenge his father's blood, and he had the sympathy of many in France who had previously supported the Armagnacs; public opinion was outraged. This was the favourable atmosphere in which King Henry renewed negotiations, and the outcome was a treaty whose terms were those described at the beginning of this chapter. The English King was to marry the princess Catherine and succeed to the French throne on the death of Charles VI. The Dauphin was disinherited.

It was a victory ample enough to satisfy even King Henry's ambition, no matter what the French princess was like; but fortune, as if to fill his cup to overflowing, added a girl whom he ardently desired. He had seen and, according to Shakespeare in *Henry V*, had kissed her in the course of the negotiations; he was impatient to make her his wife. She was eighteen when he married her, and she was known to her contemporaries as "Catherine la Belle." She owed her large eyes but nothing else to her mother, who with prominent features and a poor complexion was no beauty even in youth, before age and eleven pregnancies gave an unbecoming stoutness to her figure. Queen Isabeau, however, made up for a plain face by the lively charm of her manners, which won men's hearts in spite of her appearance. Her daughter had the same fascination, with beauty added.

In character mother and daughter had little in common. Through all the troubled events of her life Queen Isabeau allowed nothing to deflect her from the furtherance of her ambition. She enjoyed the luxurious splendour, the gay festivities of the court; but her pleasures were the means to promote a political purpose, and when her virtue yielded to temptation the motive was political expediency. No carnal desire interfered in her choice of lovers, she found the Duke of Burgundy repulsively ugly. Her singleminded devotion had its reward. Arriving in France a nonentity, an obscure German princess, she picked her way so successfully through the feuds and intrigues of the time that she climbed to the summit of power, governing the kingdom as regent for her mad husband.

Catherine, in contrast, as her story will show, cared greatly for personal affection, little for power and success. It is no evidence to the contrary that she accepted an offer of marriage from the King of England. Shakespeare, following well-established tradition, shows her as much attracted by Henry as he by her. He was a man of striking appearance, a fine athlete, a merry companion, and if he could be a stern, often ruthless opponent there was warmth and great kindness in his friendship. The speech which Shakespeare puts into his mouth, when he kisses her in defiance of French convention, was of a sort to appeal to her:

"Dear Kate, you and I cannot be confined within the weak list of a country's fashion; we are the makers of manners, Kate, and the liberty that follows our places stops the mouth of all find-faults."

They were words which she bore in mind after his death when she was left to make a new life for herself, a stranger in England.

Her brother's supporters were indignant with her for helping the foreign enemy to usurp the crown of France, for celebrating her wedding so gaily with the English King, feasting and dancing, while he sacked and destroyed French cities, put Frenchmen to death. They would have had more right to condemn if they had shown more respect themselves for the lives and property of their fellow countrymen. From childhood she had lived among scenes of civil war, the pitiless feuds of the French nobles. Her English husband offered security such as she had never known. It was no disloyalty to her distracted country if she felt more confident of its welfare in his hands than in those of her rapacious kinsmen or her mad father. Her sister Isabel's stories of her own King Richard encouraged a prejudice in favour of English Kings.

Long before this, however, Isabel herself was dead. She died in childbirth, and the young Duke of Orleans, whom she accepted so reluctantly as her second husband, was by now a prisoner in England, taken on the field of Agincourt. He was held at Ponte-fract Castle, the fortress in which King Richard was murdered. Catherine visited him there when she accompanied Henry to the north. It was during the brief heyday of her married life; the England that was his prison offered her gaiety, novelty and happiness. She could have little sympathy with him in the passionate longing for France inspiring the poetry that he wrote:

> En regardant vers le pays de France,
> Un jour m'avint a Douvre sur la mer
> Qu'il me souvint de la doulce plaisance
> Que je souloye oùdit pays trouver.

The words had more meaning for her later when she was left a widow among strangers who cared nothing for her except to promote their own interests.

Another prisoner to whom she was drawn was King James of Scotland. He was still a young man, little older than herself, but he had already endured more than fifteen years of captivity. The ship on which he was sent as a boy to complete his education in France was intercepted by English sailors on the orders of Henry IV, who kept him as a hostage, and Henry V was no more willing than his father to release him. So on the death of his own father, Robert III, he inherited the Scottish crown as a King in exile, James I. The conditions of his imprisonment were made as easy for him as possible; he had quarters at Windsor Castle and attended most of the entertainments at court, where Catherine met him. In spite of his short stout build he distinguished himself in tournaments and similar feats of skill; but like his fellow prisoner, the Duke of Orleans, he had a taste too for music and letters, composing a long poem in the style of Chaucer to celebrate his love for Lady Jane Beaufort. It is an odd coincidence that there were two Royal captives in England at the time, both of whom were poets.

Catherine and James became close friends; but as she encouraged his passion for Lady Jane, and did her best to promote its success, it is clear that there was nothing amorous in her own feeling for him. His betrothal was in fact announced during the festivities arranged for her coronation, and at the banquet with which they concluded she took advantage of King Henry's genial humour to beg him to set James free. The terms on which the favour was granted show that Henry had other motives to prompt him besides Catherine's charm. He insisted that James should accompany him when he returned to France to crush the Dauphin's supporters. There were Scottish troops fighting on the Dauphin's side, and he hoped that it would dissuade them to know that their King was serving the English.

Soon after the coronation the time came for the undertaking to be fulfilled. Henry had intended to stay in England till his heir was born; but news arriving from France of a grave defeat suffered by his army compelled him to hurry back there at once. James went with him and shared the campaign, and when Catherine's baby was born she too joined them in Paris. After Henry's death at Vincennes it was James who escorted her back to England.

The terms agreed to by Henry V were carried out faithfully by his brother John, Duke of Bedford, acting as guardian for the infant Henry VI. James married Lady Jane Beaufort and was allowed to return with her to Scotland to reign. She was Henry V's first cousin, granddaughter of John of Gaunt, fourth son of Edward III; but a bar sinister blocked her Royal descent as her grandmother, Catherine Swynford, was John of Gaunt's mistress, not his wife. This flaw in the heredity of the Beauforts has a bearing, as events will show, on the story of the Tudors.

Catherine spent Christmas of 1423 with James at Hertford. Early in the following year she attended his wedding, then he and his wife set off for Scotland and she never saw them again. She had been a widow for nearly two years; even now she was only twenty-three, but she was a person of consequence in England as the King's mother. An ample dower was settled on her by Act of Parliament with the lands and houses belonging to English Queens by ancient right. She attended the opening of Parliament in person, sat on the throne in the House of Lords with the little King on her lap. Her presence added much that was decorative, nothing of political importance to the proceedings.

Unlike her mother she was without ambition to dominate public affairs. She had had a surfeit of troubles during her childhood, riots and civil war, a father who suffered recurrent fits of frenzy. In her new life in England she sought peace and seclusion, turned her back on the leaders of society, preferred the friendship of a prisoner like James of Scotland. When he left she filled his place with a companion still less likely to bring advantage; but she had a strong will and no argument could deter her from following it. King Henry himself found this out during their brief marriage. An astrologer told him that Windsor held bad luck for his line, and when he was called to the war he warned her to avoid the place, on no account to let their child be born there. She was fond of the castle and resented the superstition that defamed it. The future King Henry VI was born Henry of Windsor.

Years afterwards, in her dying confession, she expressed repentance for her waywardness, as if she had a presentiment of the misfortunes awaiting her son after her death.

The same stubbornness of character inspired her association with Owen Tudor, her defiance of convention. She enjoyed not only as with James a friendship of kindred minds; Owen won her heart and she gave herself to him, bore him children, and was so contented with their life together that for more than a decade she vanished almost completely from public view. The date when they first became acquainted is uncertain; but if he was serving in the Royal bodyguard it is very probable that on King Henry's death he passed into the establishment of his son, and accompanied the boy-King and the Queen Mother on their return to England. As he was not even a knight, held no rank above that of esquire, he could have little contact with them; but Catherine at twenty-one had a quality that caught the eye, even of those who only admired from a distance.

Two accounts are offered by tradition of the circumstances that made them lovers; they are not incompatible, it is possible that each describes a different stage in the story. The longer and fuller is taken from a Welsh chronicle.* Catherine, it seems, was looking from a window on a summer afternoon at the river flowing beneath the walls of the castle, and she caught sight of a group of young men bathing naked there. As there was no one with her except a maid-of-honour of her own age, a close friend, she did not think it necessary to affect outraged modesty; she pointed instead at the handsomest and asked who he was. The girl told her that his name was Owen Tudor, that he pestered her with his attentions, had obtained a promise from her to meet him that very night, which she bitterly regretted. When Catherine heard this she suggested that she should go herself to keep the assignation, disguised as her own maid-of-honour.

The meeting-place was in the gallery leading to the bedrooms. Owen was waiting there, and as the light was dim he was deceived by her dress and failed to recognise her; but it puzzled him why she kept her face hidden, why her manner was so strange. At last in exasperation he grasped her and thrust her face up to his to be kissed. At that moment they heard footsteps on the stairs, saw a light approaching. He thought that it was the Queen on her way to bed, she herself was no less afraid of being caught there by an intruder. Both moved hastily, and the clasp of his cloak grazed her cheek and scarred it. She fled to her room, he along the gallery in the opposite direction.

On the next day she gave orders that Owen Tudor should serve her at dinner. He came unsuspecting; but when he saw her scarred cheek and recalled the strange behaviour of the girl in his arms he understood and was aghast at the outrage, knelt to implore her forgiveness and offered to go home at once to his native Wales. She forgave him readily, but she denied him leave to depart.

The other story is the better known. There was a dance in the great hall, and she sat on a low settee watching it with her little son, the boy-King, on her knees. Owen having worked himself up with ample draughts of wine was giving an exhibition of a Welsh hornpipe. In the exuberance of his pirouettes, his eldritch

* I have used the translation made by Mr. Howell T. Evans in *Wales and the Wars of the Roses*.

howls, he lost his balance, lurched sprawling into the Queen's lap, catching the child in his arms out of harm's way as he fell. The boy laughed gleefully thinking that it was a game, and Catherine laughed too, so that those who hurried forward to rebuke the presumptuous soldier were checked. The incident provoked much gossip. It was evident that Owen Tudor enjoyed high favour, and many guessed that this was not the first occasion on which it bore fruit.

Some of the older ladies in attendance ventured to remonstrate with Catherine, pointing out that Owen was not only of humble rank but was also a Welshman. The Welsh, they explained, were a race of savages despised by the English, excluded by law from reputable society and any responsible career. She replied that as a Frenchwoman she was unaware of racial distinctions in this island and could not share the prejudices founded on them. She told Owen of these remarks, and they provoked him to great indignation; he gave her an eloquent account of the dignity and achievements of his ancestors in Wales before the English conquest. To rebut calumny and impress her with the excellence of their appearance and manner he even brought two of his kinsmen to meet her, John ap Meredyth and Howell ap Llewelyn of the family of Gwydir, who happened to be in England at the time. There was not much conversation as they spoke no language but Welsh.

On their departure however she described them as "the goodliest dumb creatures I ever saw." The words were intended as a compliment; she included most Englishmen too among "dumb creatures," anyone indeed unable to speak French.

CHAPTER 3

No record has been found to show that Owen Tudor and Catherine were married; but they lived together as man and wife, and he remained devoted to her till her death at the age of thirty-five. If there was a marriage they had good reason to keep it secret. Under the penal laws enacted by Henry IV it was an offence incurring heavy punishment for a Welshman to marry an Englishwoman. Although Catherine was a Frenchwoman by birth she was the widow of an English King.

It has been generally assumed that they went through a religious ceremony lacking legal validity but enjoying the blessing of the Church. If so, it seems to have contented them. In 1432 Owen received a grant of denizenship relieving him from many of the disabilities imposed on the Welsh, but he took no advantage of it to make Catherine his lawful wife. His two elder sons, Edmund and Jasper, were already born. There was little to be gained from calling attention to his private life, much to lose if he aroused the suspicion of enemies. Conditions prevailed at court resembling those at the beginning of Richard II's reign. Once more the cat was a kitten.

The chief authority during the King's minority was exercised by his uncles, John Duke of Bedford and Humphrey Duke of Gloucester. The elder had the qualities needed in a statesman; he was conscientious, capable and humane, understood how to rule men by standing apart from their quarrels, without ambition of his own beyond the successful performance of his duty. If he had been able to devote himself to the government of the country he might have averted the troubles lying in store for his nephew's reign; but his attention was fully occupied by the war persisting in France, where the Dauphin, Catherine's brother, contested the English claim to the throne. Bedford was a competent, but no brilliant general; success veered from one side to the other, and the issue remained in doubt. Meanwhile he left the administration of affairs at home to his brother Humphrey, with equally unsatisfying results.

Duke Humphrey had many talents, but statesmanship was not among them. He was a scholar, a patron of learning, and his name still distinguishes the rooms in the Bodleian Library at Oxford where the collection of books that he presented is stored. He was efficient too in the details of government, firmly maintaining order in the country in spite of the difficulties created by a turbulent nobility and an infant King. His failings however undid much of the value of his public work. He was his own worst enemy, combining an insatiable ambition with ineptitude in the means chosen to promote it. Although he bore the title of Protector during his brother's absence in France his powers were ill defined, excited much jealousy in the council of regency. It was a task demanding great tact to preserve harmony between the Protector and the council. Bedford was capable of it on the rare occasions when he was at home; Humphrey, impulsive and arrogant, left to himself, became involved in a bitter quarrel with the most powerful of the councillors, his uncle, Henry Beaufort, Bishop of Winchester.

The Beauforts, illegitimate descendants of John of Gaunt, have already been mentioned. Lady Jane Beaufort who married King James of Scotland was the Bishop's niece. The family had great influence since an Act of Parliament of Richard II had removed the stigma of bastardy for all purposes except that of succession to the throne. Henry Beaufort was not only a leading dignitary of the Church, soon to be made a Cardinal by the Pope; he was also an exceedingly rich man, on whose moneylending operations the government was dangerously dependent.

It was typical of Duke Humphrey that in the middle of his struggle with the council he succumbed to the charms of Jacqueline, refugee Countess of Hainault, who came to England to seek help to recover her lost inheritance and release her from her forced marriage to the impotent John of Brabant. Hainault lay in territory regarded by the Duke of Burgundy as his private preserve; he allowed no one to meddle there, and as his alliance was vital to the English in the war in France the importunate Jacqueline received no sympathy from Bedford, who was much displeased by his brother's infatuation. No argument however prevailed; Duke Humphrey married his distressed damsel (counting prematurely on a Papal dispensation to acquit him of bigamy) and set off with her and a hastily raised army of his own for Hainault to right her wrongs.

The campaign in Hainault earned no glory; superior forces from Burgundy intervened, and after a succession of reverses Duke Humphrey yielded to his brother's advice and returned to England, abandoning Jacqueline to her former husband's unfruitful embraces. His own affection was straying in any case to her waiting woman, Eleanor Cobham, whom he promoted from mistress to wife.

These events have a bearing on the story of Owen Tudor and Catherine. In the course of the fighting in Hainault, Duke Humphrey called the Duke of Burgundy a liar and received in consequence a challenge to a duel. Bedford, appalled by the quarrel between his brother and his principal ally, did his best to avert this crowning disaster. He persuaded the parties to submit the point of honour to his arbitration and invited his sister-in-law, Catherine, to be his fellow arbiter. The Duke of Burgundy had great regard for her both for King Henry's sake and for her own.

This is the only recorded occasion when as Queen Mother she played an active part in politics. It seems that her good offices were successful, the duel did not take place; but she earned no gratitude from Duke Humphrey, his later conduct suggests that he bore her a grudge.

After this brief glimpse she disappeared again into the country to resume her hidden life with Owen Tudor. Her legitimate son, the King of England, reaching an age for a tutor rather than a nurse, was taken out of her care; but she had two younger sons, Edmund and Jasper Tudor, to comfort her, the former born at Hadham, the latter at Hertford, both in houses of her own where she was safe from observation. It is remarkable how well she kept her secret. If there were suspicions no one gave them voice. Possibly Bedford, her brother-in-law, helped to suppress them; he remained her friend, cherished the memory of her youth when she was King Henry's bride.

He needed the authority of her name in any case to support

his cause in France, where the appearance of the "Maid of Orleans," Joan of Arc, put new heart into the forces fighting for the Dauphin, and the English were threatened on all sides by popular revolt. The course of the war filled him with distress as he saw the work of his brother Henry V undone, and felt that he himself was responsible. Joan of Arc at last was captured, delivered to the Inquisition for trial and sentenced to be burnt to death for witchcraft. Bedford refused to intervene to save her, he described her as "a disciple and limb of the fiend." Yet he was a humane man, easy-tempered and conciliatory in his habitual dealings with people. His behaviour on this occasion is a measure of the embitterment tormenting him as France slipped from his grasp, as if he heard already the reproaches of King Henry's ghost.

Soon afterwards, to reassert English authority, he brought the little King Henry VI over to Paris and had him crowned there. It was a magnificent ceremony; but it made less impression on the French than the rival coronation of the Dauphin as Charles VII, which took place at Rheims three years before.

Catherine did not go to Paris to see her son crowned. No reason need be sought other than her own reluctance to emerge from seclusion in England, revisit the scenes of her troubled childhood. Nothing was known against her; so little was Owen Tudor's position suspected that when Edmund Beaufort, brother of her friend, Lady Jane, was released by the French and came home, having been a prisoner of war since before King Henry's death, he sought her hand in marriage, and Duke Humphrey took great alarm, foreseeing a dangerous accretion of strength to the Cardinal if the Queen Mother became his niece. She was still only thirty, well able to bear Edmund Beaufort an heir.

Duke Humphrey need not have disturbed himself. Catherine neither would nor could accept Beaufort's proposal. Nevertheless a measure was hurried through Parliament imposing severe penalties on anyone who married the Queen Mother without the council's consent. Although Beaufort gave the occasion the prohibition threatened Owen too; he and Catherine had more reason than ever for secrecy. There is some mystery about this Act; the page has been torn out of the Statute Book, the rest renumbered. The assumption is that this was done on the orders of Henry VII to protect his grandmother's reputation and his own legitimacy.

Bedford died in 1435, and in the following year disaster struck the Tudors. Catherine hitherto so careful to hide her pregnancy was taken by surprise on a visit to Westminster, and her third son was born there prematurely. The child was smuggled away as soon as possible to a neighbouring monastery, where the monks looked after him. He was sickly and did not live long. No precautions, however, could prevent the news from spreading.

Catherine herself was removed to the abbey of Bermondsey, and it was given out that she retired there of her own choice; but her children were taken from her and placed in the care of the Abbess of Barking, and although Owen Tudor was left for the present a free man he was not allowed to visit her. It was as if the respite of peace and happiness had been a dream, and she awoke again to the troubles haunting her childhood. The disappointment, the separation from her husband and her sons broke her heart. She died a few months later, in January 1437. She was not yet thirty-six years old.

Her will made provision for her servants and the payment of her debts, but there is no mention in it of sons other than the King. She was buried in state in the Lady Chapel at Westminster Abbey, and her epitaph described her as a widow. When Henry VII demolished the chapel he left the tomb intact, but it received a fresh inscription. He took care that it fitly celebrated his grandfather's name.

Duke Humphrey has been held responsible for Catherine's misfortunes. His brother's death left him the most powerful man in the kingdom, heir to the throne if his nephew, the fifteen-year-old King, died childless. Edmund and Jasper Tudor were without a drop of Plantagenet blood; nevertheless they were the King's brothers, and Duke Humphrey took no risks with them. He kept them out of sight at Barking, allowed neither their mother while she lived nor their father to visit them. At least they came to no harm there. More fortunate than the princes held by a later Duke of Gloucester, they suffered nothing worse than the displeasure of the Lady Abbess, who complained of the inadequate allowance which she received for their support.

Catherine's death deprived Owen of any protection afforded by her name. He was in Warwickshire waiting to see what his enemies would do. There were many charges that could be brought against him, not least that of marrying the Queen Mother in breach of the new Act of Parliament. When he was summoned to appear before the council he refused to obey without a written promise of safe-conduct, and even with that in his pocket he was not reassured. He travelled to London in great secrecy and sought refuge at once at Westminster within the precincts of the sanctuary. It was not in his nature, however, to refuse a convivial invitation, and when former friends urged him to drink with them in the tavern at the gate he fell into the plot laid for him and was arrested.

At his trial a new charge was added to the indictment, that of stirring up rebellion in Wales. He defended himself with spirit, reminding his judges of his loyal service to Henry V in France, protesting that even if he was at fault in associating with the Queen Mother he had lived with her in peaceful domesticity, faithfully guarding her interests. The King, his stepson, present in the council, was greatly impressed by his defence and anxious to let him go back to Wales; but he was not yet of age, and Duke Humphrey prevailed when he insisted that Owen would disturb the fragile peace there, revive the claim to Welsh independence, the cause which Glendower so nearly carried to victory. It added weight to the argument that Owen's father and uncles had been among Glendower's principal lieutenants.

Although Owen had been given safe-conduct to come and go freely it was held that this protected him only from proceedings relating to his marriage, that the new suspicion of treasonable conspiracy in Wales relieved the council of its promise, so that he forfeited his immunity. He was therefore imprisoned at Newgate, where his companions were a Welsh servant and a priest, who had come south with him and refused to leave him. The priest was an old friend, the same, it seems, who performed the ceremony whereby Owen and Catherine became man and wife in the eyes of the Church.

They remained in prison for the best part of a year, then on a winter evening at "searching time," when the turnkey came round to see that all were there, a long concerted plan was put into effect. The priest engaged the man in conversation and while they were talking Owen darted towards the open door. He was not quick enough, the man intercepted him; but the Welsh servant, a brawny mountaineer, joined in the struggle and felled the turnkey to the ground, as the chronicle says, "hurting him foul." They seized the keys and all three escaped into the darkness.

A hue and cry gave chase; they were caught, and a purse containing £89, a very considerable sum in those days, was found on the priest and confiscated. It is likely that they had accomplices in the town who helped them. For the time being, however, the plan miscarried. Owen and his priest were removed to Wallingford Castle, held there in the custody of the Earl of Suffolk. The Abbess of Barking who had charge of Owen's sons was Suffolk's sister.

The outcome was unexpected. The prisoners did not stay long at Wallingford; they were brought back to London, put together again at Newgate in the same cell, and for a second time they escaped. On this occasion the plan went smoothly, no warder was "hurt foul." Owen and the priest rode safely away into Wales. Either they enjoyed remarkable luck or the gaolers were deliberately negligent.

William de la Pole, Earl of Suffolk, was a close friend of Cardinal Beaufort, and there was little love between him and Duke Humphrey. In another year or so indeed they were in open conflict. Suffolk was in favour of peace with France, and with this end in view he advocated the release of the Duke of Orleans and the marriage of the King to the French princess, Margaret of Anjou. These were aims resolutely opposed by Duke Humphrey, who insisted on the English right to the French throne, the claims asserted by his brother, Henry V, and refused to consider any end to the war till the French were defeated. He was in no hurry, either, for the King to take a wife. As things stood, he himself was heir presumptive.

In so far as the boys at Barking, Edmund and Jasper Tudor, were an inconvenience to Duke Humphrey's ambition they could be useful to Suffolk, especially when they were living under his sister's care. It was not to his interest to confine their father too zealously.

At home in Wales, Owen found himself a national hero, the Welshman chosen in preference to English rivals to be the husband of the widow of the English King. Like his father before him he hid from pursuit in the wilds of Snowdon. The bards encouraged by Glendower still flourished there, and the most famous of them, Robin Ddu, "Black Robin," became his friend, celebrating his exploits in his songs and lamenting the persecution of a true son of Wales whose only fault was to have "won the affection of a princess of France."

The outlawry did not last long. Henry VI came of age, took the government into his own hands, and he made it his business as soon as he could to befriend his stepfather, not only restoring him to his rights but also promoting him to honour, appointing him constable of the Royal parks in Denbighland, the cultivated intakes planted among the moors and forest between Denbigh and Snowdon. He was careful too to provide for his brothers, who were growing too old for a nunnery. They received a good education at his expense.

Duke Humphrey's power was declining. He spent more time in his library at Greenwich than in the council chamber, consoling himself with his books which held next place to politics in his affection. Soon afterwards a blow struck him that weakened his position still further. His wife Eleanor, Countess Jacqueline's former waiting woman and supplanter, was accused of practising sorcery, of spells intended to cut short the King's life. It was a damaging charge when her husband stood next in the line of succession, and among the books in his collection covering every field of human knowledge there were indeed a few that dealt with the black art. He was an omnivorous student.

The Duchess was convicted, sentenced to perform public penance with bare head and feet and a lighted taper through the streets of London; she was then imprisoned for life. No one dared to propose like treatment for the Duke, but he suffered great shame.

During the years that followed, while Owen Tudor managed the Royal estates in Denbighland, and Edmund and Jasper grew to manhood, the seeds of political conflict were sown that bred the Wars of the Roses. From earliest youth Henry VI was remarkable for the gentleness of his character, his hatred of cruelty and all violence. He was a scholar, better suited to quiet study than to the rough arts of government, nowhere less at home than on the battlefield where he showed a courage more akin to endurance, as if he were too bewildered to care for his safety. Lack of confidence in his own ability made him rely on the judgment of others in public affairs, and having chosen his advisers he was reluctant from loyalty to change them, however unfortunate the choice proved. In spite of their common taste for learning he was out of sympathy with his uncle, Duke Humphrey, whose arrogant temper and warlike policy were uncongenial to him. The favourites in whom he put faith were the Duke's opponents, Cardinal Beaufort and the Earl of Suffolk.

Both were anxious for peace with France. The first step taken was to release the Duke of Orleans, who for twenty-five years had been eating out his heart in captivity, enjoying every privilege befitting his rank except that of return to his native land:

> Mais non pourtant mon cueur ne se lassoit
> De veoir France, que mon cueur amer doit.

At last his wish was granted, and the English treasury enriched with a heavy ransom.

Negotiations went forward also for the marriage of the King to Margaret of Anjou, whose aunt was wife to the French King, Charles VII. Margaret was sixteen at the time, Henry twenty-three. He had grown up observing an almost monkish chastity. The story is told of a visit to Bath where the scanty bathing drawers worn by some girls filled him with such confusion that he fled from the scene in outraged modesty, exclaiming: "Fie, fie, forsooth, ye be much to blame." Shyness and inexperience, however, in no way deterred him from marrying, they even added enchantment to the prospect. In his instructions to the envoys sent to promote the match he insisted on the loneliness of his condition, his eager desire to "live under the holy sacrament of matrimony." He asked too that an artist be employed to paint Margaret's portrait, and when the work was shown him he was delighted.

Suffolk went in person to treat with the Duke of Anjou, her father. He was charmed when he saw her, much taken both with her appearance and her spirit. The difficulty was that her father could offer no dowry, having been stripped of his possessions by a succession of wars. Even his duchy of Anjou with the adjacent province of Maine was occupied by the English, and he refused to let his daughter marry the English King unless these were restored. Suffolk urged by King Henry to obtain the bride, and susceptible himself to her fascination, was unwilling to return without her. He yielded to her father's demands on condition that for the time being the cession of Anjou and Maine should be kept secret. He knew very well what an outcry it would provoke in England.

The wedding was celebrated at Nancy in February 1445, with Suffolk standing proxy for the bridegroom, Henry VI. When Margaret arrived in London her beauty made a favourable impression, and many people wore bunches of daisies, her emblem, in their hats; but the enthusiasm soon cooled when it became known that she brought no dowry and cost the English Crown two of the richest provinces in France. The only political advantage gained was the conclusion of a truce for two years with the French. The war had been going so badly for the English that even this could be represented as an achievement.

Duke Humphrey approved neither of the truce nor of the bride; but he had lost influence at court since his wife's disgrace. There was an unaccustomed humility in his behaviour, his efforts to conciliate the girl who supplanted him in the King's confidence. His overtures failed to appease her; his enemies, Suffolk in particular, were anxious to complete his downfall before he could make trouble for them over the loss of Anjou and Maine. The old charge was revived of black arts threatening the King's life, others were added of misapplication of public funds, undue severity in the punishment of petty offences. The end came two years later when the King summoned a Parliament at Bury St. Edmunds, and Duke Humphrey, arriving to attend it, was arrested in his lodgings.

He never emerged from them alive. It was given out that the shock was too much for him, that he died of a "palsy"; but rumours were soon busy attributing to more violent means so convenient a death.

His removal left Suffolk and the Beauforts in alliance with Queen Margaret free to pursue their policy of peace with France. Cardinal Beaufort himself was an old man by now, he outlived Duke Humphrey by little more than a year; but the family retained undiminished power when his place was taken by his nephew, Edmund Beaufort, Queen Catherine's former suitor, who had succeeded to the title of Duke of Somerset. Nevertheless, if Duke Humphrey was murdered, the crime was a political error. It was the odd destiny of the House of Lancaster that already the line was in danger of extinction. Henry IV had four sons, all of whom grew to manhood, but only the eldest, Henry V, begot a lawful heir; the others had illegitimate issue, none from their wives. In the third generation there was no one but the young King, Henry VI, to carry on the succession, and hope dwindled as year followed year and his marriage remained unfruitful.

While his uncle, Duke Humphrey, lived, there was at least an immediate successor available, a man indeed not yet too old to beget an heir of his own. His death brought nearer the possibility of a failure of the Royal line; it revived too the argument over Henry IV's usurpation, the question whether his line had any right to reign at all. The effect was to shed a new importance on Richard, Duke of York, who comes forward now into the centre of the stage, the principal opponent of Suffolk and Somerset, a possible heir to the throne itself.

The claims of the rival Houses of York and Lancaster, which led to the Wars of the Roses go back to Edward III and his numerous sons.* The eldest of these, Edward the Black Prince, died before his father, and his only surviving son, Richard II, was murdered in Pontefract Castle, leaving no heir. The second, William of Hatfield, died childless. The third, Lionel, Duke of Clarence, left a daughter, Philippa, but no son; she married Edmund Mortimer, Earl of March, and was grandmother to the Edmund Mortimer who became Glendower's son-in-law. The fourth son, John of Gaunt, was the father of Henry IV, founder of the House of Lancaster. The fifth was Edmund, Duke of York, whose eldest son married Anne Mortimer, granddaughter of Philippa, great-granddaughter of Lionel, Duke of Clarence. Their son, Richard, the Duke of York with whom this story is concerned, traced his descent through his father from Edward III's fifth son, but from the third son through his mother, and as the male line of the Mortimers was extinct he claimed that the female line succeeded.

The claim was not yet directed against Henry VI himself, it was a danger only threatening the House of Lancaster if he died without issue. York professed nothing more than concern for good government, to free the King from harmful influence. In attacking Suffolk and Somerset he could count on powerful support. Duke Humphrey's death, the suspicion of murder, earned them bitter enemies, especially among those engaged in trade and industrial enterprise who respected him for his strict enforcement of the law, his care for the rights of property. Indignation rankled too over the cession of Anjou and Maine. Many of the English garrisons refused to obey when they were ordered to surrender their strongholds. A party of adventurers eager to defy the French crossed the sea in breach of the truce and plundered the town of Fougères. The pressure of opinion in England was such that the government dared not disown them.

The French replied to the provocation by renewing the war. They had made good use of the truce to strengthen their forces, and the English soon had reason to regret their rashness. Disaster followed disaster till Normandy itself was lost, the most cherished

* See genealogical table on front endsheet.

of Henry V's conquests. Although Suffolk was not in command in the field he bore the brunt of the nation's anger, was impeached and committed to the Tower. His enemies demanded a sentence of death, but King Henry always loyal to his friends did what he could to save him and reduced it to a term of banishment.

Before he left the country Suffolk wrote a letter to his son, which has been preserved. It throws a favourable light on Owen Tudor's lax gaoler, Duke Humphrey's alleged murderer. He knew that his career was finished, he did not know how little longer he had to live. There is more, however, than a courtier's prudence, there is sincere warmth of feeling in the earnestness with which he urges his son to be "true liege" to the King, "to whom both ye and I have been so much bound," and charges him, "as father can and may, rather to die than to be the contrary or to know anything that were against the welfare or prosperity of his most Royal person." Henry VI was not always mistaken in the confidence which he placed in his favourites.

Suffolk embarked for Calais, but he was intercepted at sea off Dover by a ship of the Royal Navy, the *Nicholas of the Tower*, which put out a boat to pick him up and take him off. He obeyed more surprised at first than alarmed, the sailors professed to be acting on the King's authority; but as he climbed on board the captain greeted him with the ominous words, "Welcome, traitor." For a day or two he was held prisoner on the ship, then a trial was staged and he was sentenced to death, to suffer execution, as his judges assured him, proper to his rank.

The sailors carried him down again into the boat, made him lie with his head across a thwart, and one of them brought out a sword from the gear in the bilge. It was rusty and blunt, six strokes barely severed his head. Then the boat was cut loose, to drift with his body on to the coast of Kent.

Even if the Duke of York himself was not implicated his partisans were known to have instigated the outrage, bribed the captain and sailors. The guilty, however, went unpunished, the government had enough on its hands to quell the growing unrest in the country. A dangerous insurrection was spreading through Kent and Surrey. The leader, Jack Cade, won support by assuming the name and rank of the Mortimers, the forerunner of a succession of pretenders destined to disturb the peace in years to come with fictitious pedigrees. His followers included many people of wealth and influence, who laid the blame on the government for all the nation's troubles, the scarcity of labour resulting from the Black Death, the decline of agriculture, the disastrous progress of the war in France. It was a favourite argument among the discontented that if only the men in power were changed, the King induced to give up his corrupt and incompetent favourites, every obstacle to prosperity would vanish—a hope little likely to be fulfilled when the jealousy of those who coveted the places of honour was itself among the chief causes of the prevailing distress.

The rebels came near to success when they occupied London; but the citizens rose against them, and the King's forces had time to muster. Cade himself was lucky to be killed fighting, to escape a more painful death. The defeat of the rebellion, however, did not put an end to the demand for a change of government. Cade was dead; but his voice persisted, a clamour more formidable than ever, inspired by the Duke of York.

The King made matters worse by recalling Somerset from France to preside in the council. Like Suffolk he was blamed for the disasters of the French war, and he was unpopular in the country because of the violence of his temper. Years had passed since his unsuccessful proposal of marriage to Queen Catherine, but it may be that the rebuff still rankled. He yielded with reluctance to the King's wishes to allow the betrothal of Edmund Tudor to Margaret Beaufort, his niece. It was a connection much to Edmund's advantage, in spite of the bar preventing the Beauforts from succession to the throne.

Both Edmund and Jasper, being now of full age, were knighted in this year 1450 at a Christmas festival held at Greenwich. Ennoblement followed shortly afterwards, Edmund became Earl of Richmond, Jasper, Earl of Pembroke. The declaration confirming their promotion describes them as the King's "uterine brothers" born in "lawful matrimony"; but no mention is made of their father, the constable of the Royal parks in Denbighland. It is as if the King, or his advisers, were uncertain yet how far public opinion was ready to accept his mother's second marriage. While he insisted on the legitimacy of his brothers he kept his Welsh stepfather in the background. There is a hint of disagreement in the council when the document declares that these titles are conferred of the King's free will, at the instance of no one else. Somerset was unwilling to bear responsibility for the Tudors.

Henceforward Edmund and Jasper began to play a part in

public affairs. They supported their brother, the King, with a loyalty traditional in the family, serving him as devotedly as their grandfather Meredyth, their great-uncles Gwilym and Rhys, served Owen Glendower. They showed no such devotion to Somerset, attached themselves on the contrary to the party of the Duke of York, who professed that he was acting in the King's true interest to rid him of Somerset's influence. York was heir presumptive to the throne, there was no reason yet to suspect him of any ambition to usurp it.

The struggle between the parties was little different from that which persisted earlier in the reign. Somerset stood in the place of his uncle, Cardinal Beaufort, relying on inherited wealth and power and on the dominant influence established by the Cardinal over the impressionable mind of the King. York, like Duke Humphrey, appealed to the merchants, farmers, artisans, who craved for strong government to ensure peace and order and despaired of obtaining it from the present rulers. The issue, however, was confused by local feuds and ambitions; powerful nobles chose the side that offered a temporary advantage. As the rift widened the spirit of the party spread like an infection, ranging men on this side or on that in obedience to a common impulse of dissension. The ardour with which they fell into line is illustrated by the story, whether fact or fiction, of an occasion when Somerset met the Earl of Warwick, York's principal supporter, in the Temple gardens. Somerset picked a red rose from a bush, Warwick a white, and at once every hat in the crowd wore a rose of the appropriate colour. The white rose was always the emblem of the House of York; it is less certain that the red rose belonged to the House of Lancaster, it was worn in Wales long before this by the Tudors.

In the spring of 1453 York's expectations received a heavy blow. It became known that the Queen was pregnant. She had been married to the King for more than eight years, and as the marriage continued childless so long everyone gave up hope of an heir. News of the impending birth let loose a flood of speculation. It was enough for a man to be known as her friend to arouse the suspicion that he was her lover, however ill it accorded with his age or reputation. Her old friendship with Suffolk was recalled, the admiration which he expressed for her. That he was already fifty at the date of her marriage when she herself was sixteen, that his wife was among her most intimate

43

companions, remaining so after his death—no argument of this sort deterred malicious tongues. They would have held the case against him as proved if he had not been dead, a headless corpse, when the child was begotten.

Having made as much mischief as it could with Suffolk's ghost, scandal proceeded to attach itself to Somerset. In spite of every eagerness to impute adultery to the Queen no partner could be found of less than middle age to share the guilt. Queen Margaret was no coquette; ambition and statecraft meant more to her than the courtship of handsome young gallants. Her favourites were mature counsellors, on whom she relied not always wisely for political guidance. Conjugal infidelity was out of keeping with her character. It is much easier to believe that King Henry, living in a world of his own, wedded to principles of chastity, needed eight years to consummate the marriage.

He himself was delighted to hear of her condition, looked forward with pride to become a father; but in July the news arrived from France of a crushing defeat suffered in Guienne, the last of the French provinces left to the English Crown. The army was destroyed on the battlefield, the commander killed. Nothing was left of the domains of the Plantagenets except the town of Calais. When King Henry understood the extent of the disaster, his father's whole work undone, the shock was too much for him. The effect was like that produced on his grandfather, Charles VI of France, by fear of an ambush at Le Mans. The symptoms of madness were less violent, they subsided quickly into coma; but they left him deprived of reason, incapable of any part in affairs.

In October the child was born, a son to inherit the throne; but when the Queen herself took the baby in her arms to show to the King to ask for his blessing she obtained no sign of recognition or understanding. He stared at her in vacant silence, glanced once at the child, then his eyes dropped without a word.

He remained in this state for the rest of the year and most of the next. It was as if the dreams to which he was addicted had grown to possess him entirely, till he no longer inhabited the kingdom in which his body was present. Deprived of his protection Somerset was accused by his enemies of treasonable negligence in his conduct of the war, the loss of both Normandy and Guienne, and he was committed to the Tower to await trial. The Duke of York's party gathered strength and sent an impressive deputation of bishops and nobles to see the King at Windsor, to tell him what confusion his illness created in public affairs and persuade him to delegate his authority. They had to wait till he finished dinner, then the Bishop of Chester made an eloquent speech to which he listened in silence. The Bishop repeated his arguments, still the King said nothing. At last they grew hungry, not having dined themselves; they left him, ate a hasty meal, and came back to renew their pleading, with no better effect than before. They made a last attempt in another room, to which he allowed himself to be led by two attendants. He neither dissented nor assented, smiled blankly. They were arguing with a phantom, someone who was not there.

The council therefore took matters into its own hands, appointed York to be Protector of the realm with similar powers to those held by Duke Humphrey during the King's minority. Even now there was nothing in York's behaviour to arouse suspicion of disloyalty. He was no longer heir presumptive; but he expressed no resentment, declared that he held office only till the King's newborn son, Prince Edward, came of age. It is evidence of the confidence which he still inspired, the ability and wisdom with which he ruled as Protector, that Edmund and Jasper Tudor continued to support him, attending the meetings of the council over which he presided and retaining their position in the King's household, when many of Somerset's friends were sent to join him in prison. The young Tudors had no affection for Somerset, no reason to lament his fall. This produced estrangement from his ardent champion, the Queen; but Jasper was in any case out of favour with her, having been granted with the earldom of Pembroke a number of castles by the King, to which she claimed a title.

In the last days of 1454 the King's sanity was restored. He was like his grandfather, his mind cleared again suddenly. He understood and was filled with joy when the Queen brought his son to him; he told her that he knew nothing of what had happened or where he had been, and was as eager for news as if he had just come home from a long journey. There was great rejoicing at first in the country, thanksgiving was offered for his restoration to health; but enthusiasm was checked when the fresh course of events became known. York at once resigned the office of Protector, and the King yielding to the Queen's insistence annulled the charges against Somerset, released him from prison and promoted him again to favour and power. York and his friends were excluded from positions of importance, and when the King summoned a council to meet at Leicester, to which they were not invited, they took fright and retired to their estates to gather their retainers.

The country was on the verge of civil war, and Somerset was not the man to avert it by conciliation. He raised an army of his own and set out to intercept his enemies as they marched south. His forces were not as large as theirs, but he had the King with him to invest his cause with authority. Edmund Tudor was in Wales, but Jasper accompanied the King. He was willing to support the Duke of York while he acted in the King's name, not when he bore arms against the King's person. His dislike of Somerset was forgotten, his brother's cause came first.

The armies met at St. Albans, and the battle raged to and fro in the streets. York's men prevailed by sheer force of numbers. Somerset took refuge in an inn till the doors were broken down and he led his party out in a desperate sally in which he was killed. The King stood aloof from the fighting, hating the sight of blood, but he made no attempt to move to a place of safety. The air was thick with arrows. Some of his bodyguard were killed round him, others fled. He himself was wounded by an arrow in the neck. The few men left urged him into the shelter of a tanner's shop, and he waited there, lost and bewildered, till York and Warwick arrived together and found him. They knelt to him in homage; but he was their prisoner, and they conducted him to the abbey to join the other prisoners of importance confined there.

A contemporary ballad puts the words into his mouth:

I followed after, I wist never why.

It is a true decription of Henry VI in the Wars of the Roses.

CHAPTER 4

Although the battle of St. Albans is usually taken as the first of the Wars of the Roses its immediate result was nothing more startling than a change of ministers in the King's government. Somerset's death left the highest office vacant in any case, and York himself filled it. He still professed allegiance to King Henry, still recognised the little Prince Edward as heir apparent, insisting only on the removal of his opponents from the council and their replacement with trustworthy followers of his own. He was not vindictive towards his former enemies, he was content to accept their submission and deprive them of power. Both parties were ashamed of the bloodshed at St. Albans, anxious to belittle its importance. The nation shrank from the prospect of civil war. It was generally agreed to lay the blame on Somerset, who was dead and unable to reply.

Edmund Tudor was already in Wales, given the task of pacifying the country whose chronic anarchy was aggravated by the political trouble in England. He was well fitted to succeed, esteemed for his Welsh ancestry and in particular as the son of Owen Tudor, whose exploits, his love for a French princess, a Queen of England, and his flight into Wales for safety from his persecutors, filled the songs of bards. York's victory left Edmund there undisturbed, and no obstacle was put in his way when he married Margaret Beaufort later in the year. The marriage strengthened his position, linked him more closely with Royal blood, if only with an illegitimate branch and in the female line.

Margaret was an only child, daughter of Somerset's elder brother

47

who died while she was a baby. Although her uncle became head of the family she was given Suffolk as her guardian, and it was his wish to betroth her to his son. Wards seldom opposed what their guardians wished, but when Margaret reached the age of nine she declared that St. Nicholas had told her in a dream that Edmund Tudor was her destined husband. It is unlikely that Suffolk would have let the saint have his way if mundane pressure had not been added, probably by the King himself, always active in his brother's interest. She was married when she was fourteen, and by that time Suffolk was dead. So too was Somerset, her uncle. There was no one left to cast doubt on St. Nicholas.

The story of her vision reached Wales, where it aroused burning enthusiasm. Her husband's courtly manners, his father's fame, the tradition that traced his ancestry from ancient heroes of Welsh history and legend—all combined to foster the belief that this was a marriage of happy omen, destined to give birth to a second King Arthur, a saviour of Wales. Owen's friend, the bard Robin Ddu, risked his reputation on the prophecy, and when Edmund died suddenly of a fever in November 1456, within a year of his marriage, and left no son, the disappointment and indignation were such that Robin Ddu was thrown into prison. Two months later the Countess of Richmond gave birth to a posthumous child, and the prophet triumphantly vindicated was released. He hurried off to Pembroke Castle to greet the promised heir with an ode composed in advance during his imprisonment.

The boy was at first called Owen after his grandfather, but his mother changed the name to Henry in deference to English sentiment. English history acquired Henry VII instead of Owen I.

On Edmund's death Jasper took his place in Wales. There was no abatement here of the struggle between the parties. The Duke of York, heir through his mother to the Mortimers, controlled their huge estates in the eastern marches extending almost without interruption from the upper waters of the Severn to the mouth of the Usk. The House of Lancaster had its stronghold in the west, in the old principality of Gwynedd comprising Anglesey, Carnarvon and Merioneth and in the southern promontory of Pembroke and Carmarthen. There was much territory between the two, however, where no clear political line could be drawn; allegiance varied from valley to valley, from castle to castle. Jasper set to work in these parts to win support for his brother, the King, persuading and conciliating where he could, striking ruthlessly where force was needed, creating with skill, firmness and patience a strong base in Wales on which the House of Lancaster could rely in danger. In particular he took care to fortify the castles of Tenby and Pembroke, foreseeing the value of the harbours which they dominated, an outlet to countries beyond the sea. He made Tenby his own headquarters, assigned Pembroke to his sister-in-law and her little son.

In all these measures he acted in concert with the Queen and her friends in England. He made up his quarrel with her, became henceforward her loyal supporter. His early sympathy for the Duke of York was destroyed when the King was attacked and wounded at St. Albans.

The precarious calm established in England after York's victory did not last long. For a short time he resumed his former office of Protector while the King suffered a relapse into insanity; but the King recovered and took the government back into his own hands. York still clung to power, he even succeeded in gaining the King's confidence; but the Queen was his indefatigable enemy, and the King was accustomed to be led by her. The rivalry between the parties grew more and more menacing, there were frequent brawls; everyone waited for the civil war to be renewed.

Early in 1458 the King put forward a plan after his own heart to settle the differences by peaceful arbitration. He summoned the leaders on both sides to meet him in London; but as he forgot to put a limit on their retinue they arrived attended by such hosts of armed men that the stage was set for a battle rather than a love-feast. Anxious citizens kept guard day and night and were greatly relieved when the conference broke up without agreement on any controversial issue, but at least without violence. The proceedings ended with a solemn ceremony at St. Paul's Cathedral, where the Duke of York walked arm in arm with the Queen. The King was overjoyed at the success of his peacemaking. A year later all those who took part were at war.

The Queen went to Cheshire and Shropshire to raise forces. She left the King behind; but she took with her the six-year-old Prince Edward, giving him as much prominence as she could to catch the eyes of the people. She supplied him with a lot of little badges in the form of a silver swan, the emblem of his celebrated ancestor and namesake, Edward III, and there was an emotional scene when he distributed them among her leading supporters. His birth indeed inspired her with new ideas and ambitions. She was the mother of the heir to the throne; she had no need any longer to put up with King Henry, his fits of madness, his impractical dreams, his unworldliness when he was sane. She hoped to persuade him to abdicate in favour of Prince Edward, who would wear the crown while she herself ruled on his behalf through a long minority.

The badges brought their wearers no luck. Most of them were killed in a skirmish trying vainly to prevent the Earl of Salisbury, Warwick's father, from reinforcing the Duke of York at Ludlow. The Queen, however, was undeterred, rallied her forces at Coventry, where many of the local nobility and gentry joined her, according to the chronicler, "for the love they bare to the King but more for the fear they had of the Queen," whose looks were "so terrible that to all men against whom she took a small displeasure her frowning was their undoing." Whether it was that the frowns of the Amazon goaded her supporters to desperate feats of courage, or that York was disheartened, weakened by the defection of many unwilling to fight against the King—the result was in any case that the Lancastrian army took Ludlow by storm. Perhaps the greatest source of weakness in York's position was the threat from a hostile Wales in his rear, where Jasper Tudor's work was already bearing fruit. York himself barely escaped Jasper's hot pursuit as he fled across the mountains to the sea and took ship for Ireland.

Jasper was made a Knight of the Garter in reward for his services. He attended the Parliament held at Coventry after the victory, and it is evidence of the new respect enjoyed by the Welsh through his efforts that a petition received attention complaining of the "unjust exactions and cruelties of English officials in Wales." No English King since Richard II had been accustomed to listen to complaints where the petitioner was a Welshman, the offender English. This Parliament, however, was mindful of the help given by the Welsh to King Henry's cause. The red rose triumphed, the Duke of York and his principal supporters were declared traitors by Act of Attainder.

Sudden oscillations of fortune were a feature of the Wars of the Roses. Within a year of the sack of Ludlow the Earl of Warwick, who had found refuge at Calais, was back in England raising an army again, and the King's forces meeting him at Northampton suffered crushing defeat, the King himself was taken prisoner. The Queen fled with Prince Edward into the west; but near Chester a servant whom she trusted robbed her of her money, and she barely saved her life by slipping away into the woods while he rifled her baggage. Her escort abandoned her, all but four men, with whom she travelled in secret across Wales, riding by night, spending the day in hiding. Her hopes were raised when a messenger came to her with a token that she recognised from the King, and she would have followed him if one of her own men had not warned her that it was a trap to lure her back into England. They killed the messenger and rode on, arriving without further misadventure at Harlech Castle.

There their troubles were over. David ap Eynon—a celebrated chieftain as tall as the giants of his native legends—who held the castle for Jasper Tudor entertained her hospitably, till Jasper himself was informed and came in person to conduct her to Pembroke to join his own sister-in-law and nephew. As soon as a ship could be found she sailed to Scotland.

Meanwhile the Duke of York returned from refuge in Ireland and advanced in triumphal progress to London. He had no part in the victory at Northampton, which was won by Warwick alone, and he was anxious not to let his too powerful supporter outshine him. Hitherto, even while he fought against the King, he had professed himself a loyal subject acting in the King's best interest; but now he gave orders for the Royal arms to be emblazoned on his standard, and when he entered the House of Lords at Westminster he strode to the empty throne and laid his hand on the cushion to sit down there. Angry glances and murmurs checked him, and the Archbishop of Canterbury reminded him that it was his duty on his arrival to go and see the King. He replied haughtily that it was not his duty to see anyone, it was the duty rather of others to come to the Duke of York. Nevertheless, he went across to the palace. Finding the door of the King's room shut, he broke it in. The King, luckily for himself, was not there.

This arrogance alienated the sympathy even of his closest supporters. Warwick in particular took offence, refused to allow his oath of allegiance to the King to be violated. King Henry himself showed unexpected firmness. When he was told that the Duke of York claimed the throne he replied:

"My father was King, his father was King before him. I have worn the crown forty years from my cradle. How can my right be disputed?"

York was impressed, he dared not persist with a claim that aroused so little support. He offered to pay homage to King Henry, acknowledge his right to reign as long as he lived, on condition that he himself was created Prince of Wales to succeed to the throne on the King's death. The proposal disinherited Prince Edward, but the King accepted it. He might have defended his son's rights more vigorously if, when the Queen urged him to abdicate in the boy's favour, she had not shown him how much more they mattered in her eyes than his own.

The agreement reached in London provoked her to fury. She was succeeding very well in winning support for her cause in Scotland. King James II was closely related to the House of Lancaster, son of James I, Queen Catherine's friend, by his marriage with Lady Jane Beaufort. He sent a Scottish army over the border to help the Lancastrian nobles in the north of England, and even when a cannon inspected too closely exploded in his face and killed him the campaign went on uninterrupted, the alliance was confirmed by the Queen Mother on behalf of her infant son, James III.

The combined host of Scots and Lancastrians swept down into England, and York and his friends taken by surprise made haste to compose their private quarrels, gathered what forces they could and advanced north to stem the invasion. The opposing armies met near Wakefield, and although York was advised to wait for reinforcements the presence of the Queen among the leaders on the other side put him on his mettle; he refused to retreat "for dread of a scolding woman, whose only weapons are her tongue and her nails." He gave the order to attack at once.

Another abrupt change of fortune was in store. He was beaten as soundly as the Lancastrians were by Warwick at Northampton. He himself was captured and beheaded, so too was the Earl of Salisbury, Warwick's father. Their severed heads were taken to York and stuck up over the south gate. The Duke's own was adorned with a paper crown to invite the mockery of everyone entering.

The Scots pressed on towards London, plundering indiscriminately on the way, and the Queen was neither able nor willing to restrain them. She shared their exultation, it was not in her nature to curb her feelings. The riotous behaviour of her allies, the suffering which the country endured, were long remembered against her. They cost King Henry the sympathy of public opinion.

For the moment, however, the prospect was bright for the red rose. Both the leaders on the other side, York and Salisbury, were dead, and although the latter's son, Warwick, was already a capable general, York's heir—Edward, Earl of March—was a young man of nineteen with little experience of command in the field. He was now in his hereditary domains in the eastern marches of Wales gathering support to avenge his father; but his position there had the same weakness as his father's two years earlier at Ludlow, that he was threatened by Jasper Tudor, who had most of Wales behind him.

Ever since the disaster at Northampton and the Queen's flight to Scotland, Jasper had been busy preparing to renew the war, to rescue his brother from captivity and restore him to power. For this purpose he could count on the loyalty of the Welsh, and he added considerable detachments of French and Irish, taking advantage of easy access to the sea to sail across and recruit them. His plan was to invade England from the west while the Queen led a Scottish invasion from the north. She played her part with success, its fruit was the victory at Wakefield; he himself made haste to follow this up by attacking Edward of York in the eastern marches, before he could reinforce the Earl of Warwick and other survivors of the defeated party.

Jasper's army moved east up the valley of the Towy and crossed the mountains by passes well known to him through Radnor forest. His father, Owen Tudor, accompanied him, an old man by this time of nearly sixty; but nothing would induce him to stay quietly in Denbighland engrossed in the management of farms and woods, while the crown worn by Catherine's son, his benefactor, was in danger. The victory won by their Scottish allies, the great army collected by Jasper, filled him with hope. He was determined to be in at the kill, the final overthrow of the rebels.

Edward of York was already setting forth for England, but when news of the approaching Welshmen reached him he turned to meet them at Mortimer's Cross near Leominster. Uncanny portents heralded the battle. The sun rose with the appearance of three suns which closed together again, and a shower of rain followed of the colour of blood. The Welsh were much alarmed; but Edward, less vulnerable to superstition, assured the English that this was a sign sent from heaven to encourage them, presage of victory. He was a true prophet, the Welsh were defeated, put to flight. Jasper himself escaped in disguise into Wales; but Owen, no longer as agile as in his youth, was surrounded and taken prisoner, fighting stoutly to the last.

The English carried him off with them to Hereford. Edward wanted a victim to pay in blood for his own father's execution; King Henry's stepfather suited the part. Owen, however, could not believe that he was to die, he had too much faith in his destiny. He was still expecting a reprieve as they led him through the streets to the market-place, and it was not till he saw the headsman waiting with his axe, and his cloak was taken from him, the collar of his red velvet doublet loosened, that he gave up hope. He laid his head on the block, a head accustomed, as he told them, to a softer pillow when it lay on Queen Catherine's lap.

The severed head was fixed high on the market cross, but a woman came from her house at night and climbed up to it, washed the face, combed the hair, and set candles round it in tiers, more than a hundred, which she lit. Some said that she was mad, others that she practised an ancient rite of which Owen was worthy, an honour paid long ago to the greatest heroes.

Edward's victorious army went on into England, but he made no great haste to join Warwick in the defence of London. If Warwick failed his own reputation would stand higher, his prowess shown at Mortimer's Cross, and his supporters would learn to regard him as the only trustworthy champion of their cause. He was still at Gloucester when the Scots and Lancastrians reached St. Albans, and Warwick trying to bar the way suffered heavy defeat there in battle, the second fought in that unhappy town during the war. The victors pursuing the remnants of Warwick's army across a common found King Henry sitting alone under an oak tree, smiling to himself as he watched the course of events. They did not recognise him at first, and he narrowly escaped harm, till a servant ran to the Queen and told her, and she came out in haste to look after him. There is much in this couple to recall the king and queen in a game of chess, the red queen darting from end to end of the board to free a king held and hemmed in by hostile knights, bishops and castles within a move of checkmate.

They spent the night at St. Albans at the abbey, and on the following day the King knighted his son, the eight-year-old Prince Edward. Two of Warwick's officers taken prisoner in the battle were brought into the room, and the Queen insisted that the little boy should be their judge and condemn them to death. One of them was a veteran of the French wars, distinguished for the courage with which he fought to retain Normandy for the English. As he was led away to execution. he pronounced a curse on the Queen for her ingratitude, and on the child whom she encouraged in cruelty. She was determined, however, to reassert her son's rights, intended the ceremony to wipe out the memory of the King's weakness in recognising another Edward as heir to the throne.

The news of that other Edward's victory at Mortimer's Cross, the disaster inflicted on her expected reinforcements from Wales, upset her calculations. Warwick rallied his scattered forces, joined up with Edward in the Cotswolds, and the two advanced together on London where the citizens were ready to greet them as saviours. They won favour, and the Queen suffered corresponding disadvantage, from the riotous behaviour of the Scots on their progress south, which made them feared and hated wherever they went. The gates of London closed to the red rose would open freely to the white.

It was a hard decision for the Queen when the capital lay within her grasp; but her Scottish allies, many of the English nobles too, grew uneasy so far from home. Caution prevailed, and the army retired northward. The King went with it, his rescue was the one achievement of the campaign.

Edward of York entered London unopposed. Opinion had swung so violently against the Lancastrians for bringing the Scots into England that people of every degree applauded now when he renewed his father's claim to the throne. Even Warwick refrained from protest, having lost too much prestige by his defeat at St. Albans. There was no desire shown any longer to postpone the new line of succession till the reigning King's death. Henry VI was deposed, and the whole House of Lancaster from Henry IV onwards held guilty of usurpation. On the 4th of March 1461, Edward of York was crowned King as Edward IV. He took as his personal badge the trinity of suns that rose on the dawn of his career, his victory over Jasper Tudor at Mortimer's Cross.

The Lancastrian army remained undefeated in the north, and the new King set off without delay to bring the war to a conclusion. The decisive battle was fought at Towton between Ferrybridge and York on Palm Sunday. The Lancastrians resisted stubbornly; but when a snowstorm came on, blinding their archers as it drove in their faces, the issue turned against them, and they fled with great slaughter. King Henry, his wife and son found sanctuary in Scotland, but they were made to pay for it by cession of the town of Berwick-on-Tweed. It was a bargain never forgiven them in England.

The white rose was triumphant, and most of the leaders on the other side transferred their allegiance to King Edward. In Wales, however, Jasper Tudor stood fast, indomitably loyal to King Henry, building up new forces of resistance. His character recalls the famous line of the Latin poet Lucan: *victrix causa deis placuit sed victa Catoni*, and his reward at first like Cato's was unbroken disappointment. As soon as possible after the victory at Towton, King Edward turned his attention to the west. He offered pardon to any who surrendered, Jasper himself was among the few excepted. Many laid down their arms in response to the overture, the defiant were overpowered. Castles believed to be impregnable fell one after the other to the English, Tenby and Pembroke in the south, Denbigh and Carnarvon in the north. Harlech alone held out, the giant David ap Eynon yielded neither to force nor bribes.

Jasper made a last stand with his army outside the walls of Carnarvon. He was defeated and fled to Ireland to try again.

The capture of Pembroke Castle put his sister-in-law, the Countess of Richmond, and her four-year-old son Henry into great danger. Since Edmund Tudor's death, which left her a widow at the age of fifteen, she had married again; but her second husband, Sir Henry Stafford, a younger son of the Duke of Buckingham, was fighting for the House of Lancaster in the civil war, and she stayed on at Pembroke under Jasper's protection. The tranquillity that she sought there was interrupted by the English invasion, and her alarm was increased when King Edward procured the attainder of her little son and the confiscation of his estates. It was the policy of the new government to conciliate former enemies; but Jasper Tudor was known to be irreconcilable, his nephew was worth no concession.

There was no threat however to the boy's life. He was left undisturbed with his mother at Pembroke Castle, no longer a guest but a prisoner, in charge of Sir William Herbert who was among King Edward's chief supporters in Wales, largely responsible for the victory of the white rose there. Long afterwards Henry Tudor—Henry VII, as he had then become—told the Flemish historian, Philip de Comines, that he spent most of his childhood in prison. The statement is true, but the imprisonment was not of a sort hard to endure. Herbert was an easy gaoler, and his wife took great liking for the boy, grave and reticent even at this age, but gentle in disposition and pleasant-spoken. He enjoyed the company and shared the studies of her own children, four sons and six daughters, of whom Maud, her father's favourite, was intended to be his bride. It was a proposal greeted with much approval in Wales, uniting two leading Welsh families, whose conflict in the Wars of the Roses, an issue mainly English in origin, was deplored by their fellow countrymen.

The Lancastrians, however, were not content to sit idle under defeat. From her refuge in Scotland the Queen directed raids into the north of England, where she could still rely on support from the nobility and gentry. Jasper Tudor was no less active in the west, slipping across the sea from Ireland again and again to hatch a plot in Wales or lead a rising there in the vain hope of restoring his brother to the throne. He visited Scotland, too, took part in more than one of the Queen's raids across the border, and was in the garrison of Alnwick Castle when it surrendered. Luckily for him, his enemies failed to recognise him. He shared the safe-conduct granted to the defenders to return home, unarmed, with white staves in their hands.

Wales, however, was his favourite scene of operations. He was on native ground there, among people whom he knew, and he retained the advantage of a foothold at Harlech where David ap Eynon still held out for the red rose. Even so, his repeated efforts were unsuccessful, thwarted by Herbert's vigilance. Like his father and grandfather, like his kinsman Owen Glendower, he lived as a hunted fugitive slipping from fastness to fastness in the hills, owing safety to his knowledge of the country and the loyalty of his followers.

Among his narrowest escapes was an occasion at a harbour on the coast of Flint, where a friendly ship was waiting to take him off. His enemies were close on his heels, suspecting his purpose, and he only avoided recognition by mixing with the men loading cargo on the wharf and boarding the ship in their company with a great bundle of pease straw on his back.

This is the period to which tradition ascribes the birth of his illegitimate daughter, Ellen, his only known child. She herself is no figment of legend; she grew up and married in due course, about 1490, a cloth merchant of Bury St. Edmunds, John Gardiner, and their son Stephen—of whom more will be heard later in this story—became a Bishop under Henry VIII, chancellor under Mary I. Ellen's mother is the only woman recorded on intimate terms with Jasper till he reached his fifties, when, early in Henry VII's reign, he married Catherine Woodville, sister of Edward IV's Queen and widow of the second Duke of Buckingham. She was at least forty at the time, the marriage was childless.

To these bare facts the bards, his friends, add details for which no firm evidence can be found, but which are not inconsistent with the events of his life, do much indeed to explain them. It is said that the girl who gave birth to Ellen, a shepherd's daughter, was his companion on his secret adventures, her father's cottage beneath Snowdon his headquarters in Wales. He did not marry her, the social barrier was too great, even greater than that which his own mother defied; but he remained true to her, refused to marry anyone else as long as she lived.

While he persisted in efforts to stir up insurrection in Wales, the Queen was busy with equal lack of success in Scotland. Her difficulties were aggravated by the knowledge that she and her family had outstayed their welcome, that the Scottish government was anxious to restore peace with England. She collected her forces for the last time, they pressed forward to the Tyne; but at Hexham they suffered irreparable defeat, most of the leaders were either killed in battle or captured and put to death. She herself fled with her son to the coast, and after many hardships and dangers they found a ship to carry them to Flanders and made their way safely to her father's court in Lorraine. She resigned herself at last to exile, the exclusion of her son from his heritage.

King Henry was left behind. He spent the battle of Hexham in a castle a few miles from the scene, and when the extent of the disaster became known his attendants hurried him off into hiding in the moors farther south, where he had many supporters ready to offer hospitality in their houses. He had enemies there too, however, and soon after midsummer a monk betrayed him to them. At Waddington Hall near Clitheroe they interrupted him at dinner. His faithful chamberlain, Sir Richard Tunstall, held them off for a time with his sword, then in the confusion, the clash of weapons, crash of falling dishes, he caught him by the hand and ran with him out of doors into a wood. But Henry was incapable of looking after himself, even to the extent of lying hidden among the trees. There was a hue and cry, and the hunters came on him without difficulty. Tunstall alone against so many fought in vain to save him, barely escaped himself with his life to wander across country into Wales and join the garrison at Harlech. Meanwhile, King Henry's captors rode south to hand him over to King Edward.

Warwick met them at Islington and insisted on further humiliation for the fallen King on his ride through London. His spurs were removed, his ankles tied to the stirrups, and a placard was fixed to his back proclaiming him a felon. He was led like this along Cheapside, exposed to the jeers of the crowd, then he disappeared for five years into the Tower. The squalor in which he was kept there resembled that of his grandfather, Charles VI of France. His only relief was the mental weakness inherited from him, affording bouts of merciful oblivion.

CHAPTER 5

In 1465 King Edward sat secure on his throne. The former King was deposed and safely shut up in prison, and his dominating wife driven from the country, no longer hovering on the frontier but resigned at last to defeat. The whole party of the red rose shared her discouragement; a few followed her into exile, most of those left at home made haste to submit, to accept the pardon readily offered by the new government. In Wales the influence prevailed of Sir William Herbert—"Black William," as he was known to the Welsh from his thick black hair and beard—and that of Jasper Tudor declined.

From the age of four to thirteen Henry Tudor lived with his mother at Pembroke Castle in Herbert's custody. His daily life was more the concern of the women, of his mother and Lady Herbert, than of his host whose attention was occupied by affairs of state in England. Nevertheless even the busiest find opportunities for familiar conversation, and Herbert was not the man to forget that the boy's father was once his friend. When Henry grew up there was much in his behaviour to recall Herbert's example, his cautious patience, his shrewdness, above all his humanity and lack of vindictiveness.

Black William owed his eminence to his own efforts. His ancestors made enemies in Wales by supporting the English against Glendower; they took the English surname of Herbert to disguise their origin, and went to live as merchants in England. He himself, in his first mention in a public record, is described as a "chapman" of London. He served in the war in France, and on his

return he attached himself to the Duke of York; but the Duke at
that time was still loyal to King Henry, and the Tudor brothers
themselves were among his supporters. Herbert became very
friendly with Edmund Tudor, and when the rival parties at last
took up arms he joined him in supporting the Lancastrians. In
the first few years of the struggle he was active in promoting the
cause of the red rose in Wales.

The battle of Northampton was the turning point of his career.
Warwick's victory, the capture of the King and the flight of the
Queen, followed by the Duke of York's triumphant return to
power, convinced Herbert that the white rose smelt sweeter than
the red. He changed sides, but unlike many others who did so he
remained faithful to his second choice, did not change again. He
was in Wales when York himself was defeated at Wakefield and
put to death. Undeterred by the disaster, he accompanied York's
son to London and saw him crowned as Edward IV.

Thenceforward he was among King Edward's most trusted
friends and associates, his principal adviser in the policy which
inspired the reign, to restore conditions in which trade could
flourish and the country recover from the disorder and impoverish-
ment created by civil war. His own mercantile experience fitted
him to win the confidence of the growing class of men who
owed their wealth to productive effort rather than inherited privilege. These were the people whom Duke Humphrey had once
protected; but Herbert, an obscure Welshman, was more effective
for the very reason that he was a new man like themselves, sharing
their interests. He was the forerunner of a succession of talented
ministers of humble birth who served the next dynasty, Wolsey,
Cromwell, Cecil, and like them he earned the jealousy and hatred
of the old nobility.

His most dangerous enemy was Warwick, the greatest noble in
the realm, who had contributed more than anyone by his support
to King Edward's victory. For a time an open breach was avoided;
but the rivalry between the two was apparent in the conflicting
advice which they gave on foreign affairs. Herbert was anxious
to promote an alliance with Burgundy because of the dependence
of English commodities, especially wool, on trade with the Flemish
ports. Warwick, on the other hand, insisted on the value of friendship with France. Burgundy and France were bitterly opposed;
it was not possible to be friends with both.

In France, Charles VII—Queen Catherine's brother, the Dauphin crowned by Joan of Arc at Rheims—was dead, and his son who succeeded as Louis XI had no fear of English reconquest; nothing was left of Henry V's dominions except the town of Calais. Louis could contemplate alliance with England on terms of mutual advantage and listened favourably when Warwick proposed a marriage between King Edward and his sister-in-law, Bona of Savoy. Much to Warwick's mortification the scheme was upset when King Edward revealed that he had a wife already, having secretly married a widow of no very exalted station whose former husband, John Grey, had served in the Lancastrian army. Her maiden name, Elizabeth Woodville, is remembered because of the part played by her kinsmen, the Woodvilles, in subsequent events.

Warwick laid the blame on Herbert, who stood most to gain from his discomfiture; but in fact the marriage owed less to policy than to King Edward's susceptibility to an attractive face and figure and the woman's refusal to gratify him without a wedding. Polydore Vergil, an Italian scholar who lived in England under the Tudor dynasty, describes Edward IV as a man *qui facile puellis oculos adiceret,* "with eyes that rested easily on girls."

Although Herbert did not make the match he gave Warwick ground for resentment by the assiduity with which he cultivated the friendship of the Queen's kinsmen, men of undistinguished birth like himself, owing promotion to the King's favour. He persisted the more vigorously in his efforts to improve relations between England and Burgundy, and was rewarded when the new Duke of Burgundy, grandson of John the Fearless, sought and won the hand in marriage of Margaret of York, King Edward's younger sister. English trade flourished in consequence, and the Duke himself, a widower in his thirties, had reason to be satisfied, acquiring a young bride who inherited the good looks of the Plantagenets. A less fortunate trait which she shared with her brother was a wayward taste in love. Scandalous stories preceded her when she went to be married at Bruges, and although the Duke tried to discourage them with an edict condemning scandalmongers to be ducked in the canal she herself remained an unfailing source of inspiration.

The Burgundian marriage was a rebuff to Warwick who was still anxious to negotiate a treaty with France. Unaware of the progress made with Burgundy, he even invited French ambassadors to England to meet King Edward and discuss terms. They arrived with rich presents of gold and jewellery; King Edward—usually lavish in his generosity—sent them home with a crate of old hunting horns and leather bottles. It was an insult well calculated to rankle with Louis XI, who himself was notorious for parsimony, unaccustomed to part with his money for anything less than a hundredfold return.

Warwick retired in disgust to his estates in Yorkshire. Herbert's spies intercepted a messenger carrying letters from him to the Lancastrian exiles; but although the dependents who acted as intermediaries were punished not even Herbert dared to touch Warwick himself. The effect was only to embitter Warwick the more against Herbert for spying on him, while his belief was strengthened in the inviolable privilege of his own position.

The Lancastrian leaders took comfort from the widening rift among their enemies. Jasper Tudor incorrigibly hopeful sailed across to Wales, landed with a small band of fifty or so men at Barmouth, where he received reinforcements from David ap Eynon, the still unsubdued custodian of Harlech. For a time he succeeded in rekindling old loyalties, travelled about the country raising support, even holding assizes in the name of his brother, King Henry; but his opponents were better organised than in the past, Herbert had spent the intervening years to good effect, giving people a taste for peace and order, encouraging them to resist the troublemaker. Even the bards were no longer unanimous in Jasper's cause; Black William, too, was a Welshman, and his achievements deserved the gratitude of Wales. When he advanced with a large army the insurgents scattered before him; many were caught, others melted away into the hills, Jasper among them, always elusive, protected by lucky stars and the devotion of faithful companions. From a friend's house by the sea he found a ship to carry him to Brittany to await the opportunity for another attempt.

Meanwhile Herbert besieged Harlech Castle, the only stronghold left in the kingdom to the red rose. David ap Eynon, having held out for years against assault and overtures alike, surrendered at last to overwhelming force. He himself was taken prisoner to London, and with him Sir Richard Tunstall, King Henry's faithful chamberlain who tried to save him at Waddington Hall. Both were shut up in the Tower, both pardoned and released. King Edward preferred clemency, it suited his inclination no less than his interest.

In reward for this victory in Wales, Herbert received the title stripped from Jasper Tudor of Earl of Pembroke. He was at the height of his career, able to impose his policy on the council, where he enjoyed the favour of the King and the support of the Queen's rising kinsmen. Warwick could endure the upstart's success no longer. He won over the King's brother, the Duke of Clarence, to his side, offering him his daughter Isabel in marriage, and while they were at Calais celebrating the wedding the men of the north, where his influence was paramount, rose at his instigation and marched south to seize the government. They claimed, like King Edward's own father at the outset of the Wars of the Roses, that they fought only to save the King from evil advisers.

As soon as it became clear that the rising was well supported Warwick himself crossed the sea to lead it. King Edward with few forces available advanced as far as Nottingham and sent an urgent message to Herbert who was in Wales to come and help him. Herbert responded quickly to the appeal, glad, in the words of the chronicler, "to deserve the King's liberality which of a mean gentleman had promoted him to the estate of an earl." He gathered a large army, the Welsh flocked to his standard, eager to follow him into England against Warwick, who typified their hereditary enemy, the Norman baron.

In the Cotswolds they were joined by reinforcements under the Earl of Devon, and the combined armies moved on together till they came in touch with Warwick's northerners at Edgecote near Banbury. It was late in the evening; battle was deferred to the next day, meanwhile the allies entered Banbury to find lodgings in the town. Devon arrived first and installed himself at an inn; Herbert, following, envied him his quarters, there was a pretty girl pouring wine who caught his eye. Argument arose, and when Devon spoke roughly to the girl Herbert for a fateful moment forgot his statesmanship. His hot Welsh temper flared up, quickened to fury when Devon taunted him with his obscure origin and boasted of the glorious pedigree of his own family, the Courtenays. Blows were narrowly averted, the Welsh outnumbered the English. Devon walked out in dudgeon, leaving Herbert in possession of the inn and the girl.

It was a costly victory. Devon collected his men, withdrew with them to a position twelve miles from the town. There they remained in the morning, refusing to move when the battle began. The Welsh left to fight alone against Warwick's army suffered crushing defeat.

Herbert himself was captured, and with him his younger brother.

He knew that there was no chance of saving his own life, he pleaded only that his brother might be spared. His words are recorded as he stood at the block:

"Let me die for I am old, but save my brother who is young, lusty and hardy."

Warwick paid no heed. Both were beheaded. There was great mourning in Wales when it became known that Black William was dead.

The victory at Edgecote left Warwick for a time irresistible. He even took King Edward himself prisoner, carried him off to Yorkshire and shut him up in Middleham Castle; but the warders were unable long to resist either the King's personal charm or his generous promises of reward, and as soon as he was free he put himself at the head of his supporters. He was popular in the country, and few were willing to endure a renewal of the civil war. Even those who regretted King Henry's deposition were in no mood to let his successor share his fate, to accept in his place a King at Warwick's bidding, least of all the Duke of Clarence, Edward's disloyal brother.

Warwick saw that he had overreached himself, and an uneasy peace was patched up. Nevertheless the jealousy rankled which he had nourished since the beginning of the reign when he himself, the veteran, was defeated at St. Albans and young Edward of York, victor at Mortimer's Cross, was crowned in triumph in London. For his own part Edward had not forgiven and was waiting for an opportunity to avenge Herbert's death. The outbreak of an insurrection in Lincolnshire provoked a final rupture between them. Edward accused Warwick of instigating it, and after a vain attempt to elicit support from other powerful nobles Warwick and Clarence fled together to Dartmouth and took ship there for France. Both were proclaimed traitors.

Herbert's death brought little interruption to the life led by Henry Tudor at Pembroke Castle. King Edward ordered that the widow should retain possession of his estates. Great changes, however, were in preparation, whose effect was destined soon to be felt in Wales. Warwick in France was bent on revenge, and his words fell on sympathetic ears when he inveighed against King Edward, whose alliance with Burgundy the French resented and feared. King Louis, who had not forgotten the crate of old horns and bottles, invited the exiled Queen to his court, brought her and Warwick together. The outcome astonished all Christendom, the news at first defied belief. Warwick and the Red Queen were reconciled. She forgave, or professed to forgive, the deposition and imprisonment of her husband, he the execution of his father whose severed head shared indignity with the Duke of York's after the battle of Wakefield. The two henceforward were allies to vent their common hatred on King Edward, restore Henry VI to the throne of England.

In pledge of friendship the Lancastrian heir, Prince Edward, was betrothed to Warwick's younger daughter, Anne. The boy was already seventeen, he did not take after his father. An observer who knew him records that he "talks of nothing but of cutting off heads or making war."

If Jasper Tudor disapproved of Warwick's treachery he was too shrewd not to profit from the opportunity. Nine years had gone by since his defeat at Mortimer's Cross, when his plan for a double invasion of England from west and north was frustrated. Since then disapppointment had followed disappointment; the adventures on which he embarked were on too small a scale, too ill-supported to deserve much hope of success. The prospect was very different now when he had Warwick on his side, King Edward's most powerful subject, the man responsible more than any other for putting him on the throne.

He made haste to join Warwick in France, and they prepared an expedition to invade England. When all was ready they embarked together, leaving the Queen to follow as soon as the issue was clear. They landed at Dartmouth and advanced eastwards, gathering strength on the way. The speed of their success exceeded their most sanguine expectations. Many who supported the white rose while it was the winning cause changed sides when a strong show of force recalled them to their old allegiance. King Henry's name still carried weight; Warwick was still greatly feared, few dared to oppose him. King Edward himself was taken by surprise, his army hastily mustered melted away. He fled to Lynn on the Wash, and escaped by sea to seek refuge with the Duke of Burgundy, his brother-in-law.

So rapid a victory needed consolidation. While Warwick went on to London to get King Henry out of the Tower and put him back on the throne, Jasper set off for Wales, his old stronghold, where he was surest of loyal support. The Welsh accepted him again as their leader, he had no rival any longer since Herbert was dead. He quickly recovered his estates including Pembroke

Castle, where he found his nephew Henry grown from a child of four to a boy approaching fourteen. During these years while he was held prisoner in the castle the boy had been treated as a member of the family; Lady Herbert engaged a capable tutor for his education, and even when her husband's defeat and execution destroyed hope of the marriage arranged for her daughter Maud the disappointment made no difference to the care and affection with which she fulfilled her charge.

The parts were reversed now with the triumphant return of Henry's uncle; but he rewarded her with the same forbearance as she herself had shown. He left her undisturbed at the castle, claiming back only the title of Earl of Pembroke, which was his own, given to Herbert by Edward IV as spoils of war. Nevertheless, on his departure from Wales to join Warwick in London he took the boy with him. They had been parted for too long; he was anxious to re-establish his influence, to remind him of the duty which they both owed to King Henry, to the ties of blood. In England he brought him to Eton to be educated at the school which King Henry himself had founded there.

Through this autumn of 1470 and the early months of 1471 England was ruled once more in the name of Henry VI; but it is doubtful whether he was fit to rule or indeed the effective ruler. He is described as a "man amazed and utterly dulled with troubles and adversity"; the shadow of long imprisonment .clung indelibly to his mind. His friends, however, dressed him up in Royal robes and made him ride in procession through the city, where he was cheered by enthusiastic crowds. If his appearance lacked majesty it inspired affection and pity; the warmhearted rejoiced that his undeserved suffering was over. Many revered him for his goodness, many as a symbol of stability. He had been King for forty-eight years, his restoration seemed to promise the peace and order for which the nation longed.

At his own wish he paid a visit to the school at Eton whose foundation was among the achievements that afforded his greatest satisfaction. The story is that Jasper accompanied him and introduced him to the boy Henry, who was nephew to them both. Shakespeare describing the scene tells how the King laid his hand on the boy's head, with the prophetic words:

> Make much of him, my lords; for this is he
> Must help you more than you are hurt by me.

It is usual to dismiss this incident as a legend to flatter Henry VII after he came to the throne. Henry VI at the time had a son of his own, Prince Edward, still alive to succeed him, and by the terms of the alliance concluded in France before the invasion it was agreed that if Prince Edward left no heir the succession should devolve on the issue of the Duke of Clarence and Warwick's elder daughter, Isabel. Legend is more apt, however, to distort and exaggerate fact than to invent pure fiction. It is very probable that King Henry showed interest in Henry Tudor. He was much attached to his brothers, stood by them and his stepfather in the old days, and he knew how loyally they supported him in return. Jasper, the only survivor of the three, was among the few leaders in the Wars of the Roses on whose name no suspicion of treachery could fall. No misfortune dismayed him, he never gave up hope, was always ready to suffer danger and hardship in desperate enterprise. Two brothers could scarcely be more unlike, the one scholarly, unworldly, self-effacing, the other a man of action as much at home in the wilds as in a city, adept in adventure and intrigue. There was great sympathy, nevertheless, between them, and King Henry was aware of the affection felt by Jasper for his nephew, the sense of duty urging him to fill a father's place. Was Shakespeare wrong in believing that these were circumstances that favoured a flash of precognition?

Early in the new year the Queen set out with Prince Edward to join her husband in his restored kingdom; but adverse winds hindered her, on three occasions she sailed from Harfleur and was driven back with heavy damage to her ship on to the French coast. She was still in France when King Edward, having begged a small force from the Duke of Burgundy, returned to England to recover his crown. He tried to land in Norfolk, but his reception was so hostile that he put to sea again and sailed north to the Humber. A violent storm scattered his ships, only a few including his own made harbour. Soon afterwards, however, his youngest brother, Richard, Duke of Gloucester, arrived with reinforcements, which he had brought to land farther up the coast.

Even so he had scanty forces to support an invasion, particularly when he found how reluctant public opinion was to depose King Henry again and renew the civil war. He was held up at York, where the garrison threatened to attack unless he retreated; he replied that he came as a loyal subject of King Henry, that his only purpose was to reclaim the title and estates due to him as Duke of York. The citizens believed the lie and opened their gates to him. It was not till he advanced farther into England and proclaimed himself King that they learnt how easily he had deceived them; they were bitterly ashamed of themselves for their credulity.

At Banbury good news awaited him, a cruel blow for the Lancastrians. His middle brother, George, Duke of Clarence (his father had three sons, Edward, George and Richard, in that order), who had been Warwick's fellow exile in France, his ally in restoring Henry VI, changed sides, and he and King Edward were reconciled. Clarence, married to Warwick's elder daughter, had been won over to his father-in-law's plans by the promise that on King Henry's death he himself would succeed to the throne, that Prince Edward would be set aside. He was much displeased, therefore, when Warwick allowed his younger daughter to be betrothed to Prince Edward, and the young couple and any children born to them received a place in the succession superior to his own. The crown was as little likely now to revert to him as when King Edward and his line intervened. Faced with a choice of evils Clarence sought forgiveness from his brother, left his father-in-law in the lurch.

King Edward advanced towards London with Clarence's men as well as his own to support him. Warwick's army was not strong enough to block the way. Jasper hurried to Wales to gather help, and the remaining leaders fled. King Henry was left alone in London, and there King Edward found him—in Polydore Vergil's words—"as a victim ready for sacrifice," lingering in the Bishop's deserted palace beside St. Paul's, not knowing where to go. He was shut up once more in the Tower.

Warwick could put the issue off no longer. He led his army on London for a decisive battle, and King Edward came out to meet him. The adversaries met near Barnet where they fought in a mist so thick that no details of arms or banners could be distinguished; men were lost in the gloom, friends mistaken for enemies, attacked and killed in the confusion. Whether he owed it to better tactics or blind chance, the outcome was complete victory for King Edward. Warwick himself fled, was overtaken in a wood and died fighting.

Meanwhile the weather at sea had improved enough for the Queen to cross, and she and her son landed with their army at

Weymouth. They knew nothing yet of the disaster at Barnet. When the news reached them the Queen herself was anxious to turn back, unwilling to persist without Warwick any longer to defend her. She took her son to Beaulieu Abbey and sought sanctuary there, fearing less for her own life than his. He, however, was no longer a child, he was a young man nearly eighteen, full of martial ardour. Supported by others of like mind among the leaders he persuaded her that it was too early yet to give up hope. She agreed at last to his proposal to press on to the Severn to join the forces which Jasper Tudor was bringing from Wales.

The nearest bridge over the Severn was at Gloucester; but the citizens wore the white rose, they refused to admit the Red Queen and her men and forced them to go on upstream to Tewkesbury. The diversion gave King Edward time to catch them up. He defeated and destroyed them at Tewkesbury, while Jasper was still at Chepstow too far away to save them.

Prince Edward was among those taken prisoner after the battle. He was brought to King Edward who asked him how he dared to enter the realm so presumptuously, and when the Prince retorted that he came to recover his father's inheritance the King struck him in the face with his gauntlet and ordered the men-at-arms to lead him away and put him to death. King Edward was by nature a merciful man; on this occasion he lost his temper, provoked by a defiant answer, an insolent tone. In any case, if the battle of Tewkesbury was to be the last of the civil war, he could not prudently leave the prince alive, heir to the House of Lancaster, to encourage a fresh outbreak. From what is known of the Prince he himself would have acted no less harshly if he had been in King Edward's place.

The Queen, watching the battle from the roof of a house near the town, fled for refuge to a neighbouring nunnery when the issue became clear. She was found there and carried off to London, imprisoned like her husband in the Tower; but the two were kept apart, it is doubtful if he knew of her fate. After a month or two she was allowed greater liberty, sent to live at Wallingford Castle under the care of an old friend, Alice de la Pole, widow of the Earl of Suffolk who promoted her marriage, who was her admirer, her devoted servant in her youth till his murder by mutinous sailors. It is a rebuttal of the scandal spread about him and her that she retained his widow's friendship, chose her at this time of trouble and sorrow to be her companion. Lady Suffolk was a daughter of the poet, Chaucer.

The Queen stayed at Wallingford for four years, then her father raised the money for her ransom and she went home to France. She was a broken woman, without ambition or the energy to pursue it. Her son was the source of all her interests, his death left her life a void. No trace of her beauty remained, an unsightly disease of the skin disfigured her face. She died in 1482, eleven years after the battle of Tewkesbury.

King Henry survived the battle, the final ruin of his cause, by little more than a fortnight. Late in the evening following his enemy's triumphal return to London he was found dead in the Tower on the floor of the chapel. The evidence showed that he had been stabbed with a dagger, taken by surprise apparently when he was saying his prayers. A tradition has grown up accusing the King's brother, the Duke of Gloucester, of the murder, fostered by his enemies when he himself came to the throne as Richard III. It is known indeed that he was in the Tower in the course of the night; so too were many others capable of the crime. Horace Walpole, writing long afterwards in the calm of the eighteenth century, asks appropriately: "Was Edward's court so virtuous or so humane that it could furnish no assassin but a prince of the blood?"

No matter whose hand held the dagger, it was Edward IV who gained the advantage, and he took care that the death should be established beyond dispute by giving the body a public funeral. The crime served the same purpose for the House of York as the murder of Richard II for the House of Lancaster seventy years earlier. The wrong committed by his grandfather in usurping the throne lay heavily on Henry VI's conscience, he believed that the troubles of his own reign were a punishment. There was a Latin saying current at the time: *De male acquisitis non gaudet tertius heres*, "Ill-gotten gains breed trouble in the third generation." Richard II, strangled at Pontefract Castle, was avenged by a dagger in the chapel of the Tower of London.

CHAPTER 6

Henry Tudor was no longer at Eton when King Edward sent his soldiers to look for him. His uncle Jasper removed him as soon as news arrived of the invasion from the Humber; he took him to Wales and left him there with his mother while he himself gathered forces to support Warwick and the Queen. He was at Chepstow on his way back to England when he heard of the successive disasters to his cause, the defeat and death of Warwick at Barnet, and the destruction of the only remaining Lancastrian army at Tewkesbury, the Queen captured, Prince Edward killed. While he waited, uncertain whether to go on, his hopes received a final blow. King Henry, his brother, was dead too, found murdered in the Tower. There was no one left for whom to fight.

Already his enemies were active, and only a timely warning from the Bishop of Llandaff saved him from an ambush prepared in the town. The ringleader he caught and beheaded; but his debt to the Bishop had to wait till happier times, when he presented a peal of bells to Llandaff Cathedral. He retreated west into country where his influence was stronger. Even there he was not out of trouble; he was besieged in Pembroke Castle till a dispute arose between the commanders of the besieging force, two brothers, one of whom reproached the other for the persecution of a true Welshman. Jasper's friend collected a mob armed with forks and billhooks, under whose protection he travelled safely with his party, including his nephew, to Tenby and took ship to cross to France. It was the French King who encouraged the attempt to restore Henry VI in England, and the survivors of its failure had a right to expect refuge from him. In addition—although this argument was more likely to appeal to a Tudor than to Louis XI—he was a kinsman, Queen Catherine's nephew, Jasper's first cousin.

French hospitality was not put to the test. A storm drove the ship off course on to the coast of Brittany, forced it into St. Malo for shelter. Duke Francis II of Brittany, in whose territory the party landed, was on bad terms with France. King Louis coveted the duchy and was for ever stirring up trouble there. It was important, therefore, for the Duke to maintain friendship with England. Nevertheless he received the castaways with kindness. King Edward was not yet so firmly back on the throne that his rivals could safely be rejected.

There was perturbation at King Edward's court when it became known that the Tudors, uncle and nephew, had escaped abroad. Of all the enemies of the white rose Jasper was the most irreconcilable, the most resourceful, never likely as long as he lived to give up hope of avenging his brother's murder. His nephew, Henry, was also a source of danger, acquiring new importance since the death of Prince Edward at Tewkesbury. Slender as were his claims to the throne—a paternal grandmother who was consort to Henry V, a maternal grandfather begotten out of wedlock by John of Gaunt—his name already aroused interest among the disaffected remnant of Lancastrians; there was a shortage of male heirs in the House of Lancaster, and the civil war had removed even the few available. It was recalled that his mother's family, the Beauforts, were released from the stigma of bastardy by Act of Parliament, except for the purpose of succession to the throne. An amendment to the Act could annul the exception too.

King Edward was sufficiently alarmed to send envoys to Brittany offering an alliance against France and a generous payment in money in return for the surrender of Henry Tudor. The Duke, however, put him off, professing reluctance to violate hospitality, aware too that he could derive more advantage by keeping the boy in his hands. The most that he conceded was a promise not to allow his guests to endanger King Edward's security, and in proof of his words he parted them, confining Henry at Vannes, Jasper in a remote fortress in Finistère. Their English servants were taken from them, replaced with Bretons. The separation had a wholesome effect on Henry's character; it was a testing experience for a boy of fourteen to stand on his own among foreigners in a strange land. Luckily for him, the language spoken by his Breton guards was near enough to Welsh to be intelligible.

His mother rejoined her husband, Sir Henry Stafford, in England. Although he fought for the red rose in the civil war, and his father was killed commanding the Lancastrian army at the battle of Northampton, he was by nature a man of peace with no taste for public affairs, and he was glad to take advantage of the pardon offered by King Edward to former opponents who submitted. His wife was of the same opinion; having seen her son safely out of the country in his uncle's charge, she could do no more to help him. She and her husband retired to live on what was left of their estates, spending much of their time at Collyweston near Peterborough. Both were interested in learning, she also in practical schemes for the welfare of the surrounding labourers and her dependents. The piety which had evoked visions of St. Nicholas in her youth was maturing into a character remarkable among the women of her time, devout and charitable, enriched with a cultivated mind. Among the work that occupied her at Collyweston was a translation from Thomas à Kempis, *De imitatione Christi*, which she rendered into English from a French version.

As the danger receded of a renewal of the civil war King Edward was able to resume his plans for restoring commercial prosperity. He no longer had Herbert to help him; but he was an apt pupil, and the policy worked out between them in the previous decade began now to bear fruit, encouraging trade to flow, wealth to accumulate. Few Kings have combined qualities usually so incompatible, an exuberant enjoyment of the pleasures of life, a shrewd head for money. He loved to wear splendid clothes, to eat and drink to excess, and no pretty girl remained a virgin long in his company. At the same time by skilful management without oppressive taxation he replenished the treasury, fostered such a revival of confidence that foreign merchants sought an emporium in London. Winning a kingdom devastated by anarchy he left it solvent, even prosperous at his death.

During the civil war he proved himself an able commander, especially in his victory over Warwick at Barnet; but he had no craving for military glory, he drew greater satisfaction from his conduct of a war with France, from which he earned much profit without the loss of a man. He owed King Louis a grudge

74

for encouragement of the Lancastrian exiles, and when his brother-in-law and ally, the Duke of Burgundy, invited him to cooperate in the invasion of France he raised an army for the purpose, brought it across to Calais and advanced on to French soil. He found no allies there to support him. The Duke was pursuing his own campaign in Switzerland, and it became clear that he intended the English to fight for him in France alone.

Meanwhile King Louis sent envoys offering a large sum of money and an annual pension if the English army went home. News of the negotiations reached the Duke in Switzerland, and he hurried back in indignation, arrived storming and blustering in the English camp. King Edward had a hot temper, too, it was never policy to threaten him. The outcome of his interview with the Duke was a treaty of peace concluded with France. He led his army back to England with his arrows unspent, his men unscathed, more richly rewarded than if thousands had died in battle, great cities had been laid waste and plundered.

Under the terms of the treaty England renounced interest in the fate of Burgundy; but when the French asked whether they were free also to press their claims against the Duke of Brittany they were told that he remained under English protection, that any threat to the integrity of his territory would be resisted. It suited King Edward to keep Brittany as a source of annoyance to the French; it suited him too that he placed Duke Francis under a debt of gratitude, gave him the right to renew his request for the surrender of Henry Tudor. He was careful in doing so not to offend the Duke's susceptibilities. He assured him that he meant the boy no harm, that his purpose was to marry him to one of his own daughters.

Duke Francis was in failing health, enfeebled in mind; he allowed himself to be governed in most matters by his chief minister, Pierre Landois, a former tailor raised to power, an ardent champion of Breton independence. Landois set great store by the English alliance, and he persuaded the Duke to agree to King Edward's proposal. A mission led by the Bishop of Bath and Wells sailed accordingly from England to collect the fugitive, who was taken from Vannes and brought to St. Malo to meet them.

It was an alarming prospect for Henry Tudor. He put no trust in King Edward's promise, foresaw that he was destined in England not for a wedding but the headsman's block, and his distress so preyed on his mind that little deception was needed when he reached St. Malo to produce all the symptoms of a fever. His illness delayed the departure of the envoys escorting him, and in the meantime many friends whom the quiet charm of his manners had won for him while he was at Vannes were active on his behalf at the Duke's court. The most influential, Admiral de Quelenac, was absent on his estates; but as soon as he heard what was happening he hurried back, strode with accustomed informality into the Duke's presence and reproached him for his breach of faith, telling him that he was sending Henry to certain death.

The Duke who had a warm heart was put to shame. He ordered Landois to go to St. Malo and recover the boy before it was too late. Landois himself seems to have had second thoughts, doubtful of the expediency of parting with so valuable a hostage. He carried out his errand with speed and efficiency, visited the English envoys in their lodgings, held them in conversation on the pretext of some trifling business, while his servants looked for Henry in his room, overcame the guards, and helped him to escape across the town into sanctuary in the abbey church. He was so ill by this time that he barely survived the journey; but the relief of finding himself in safety was a tonic. His spirits rose, his temperature went down.

The pious Bishop of Bath and Wells was in a quandary. His calling obliged him to respect the inviolable sanctity of the church, the Breton clergy refused to waive its rights. Landois to whom he complained laid the blame on the English themselves for their failure to guard the boy more carefully. Meanwhile a favourable wind blew, the captain was impatient to sail. With vain protests the envoys departed, leaving Henry Tudor behind and much gold paid in advance for his surrender. All that it bought for King Edward was custody of the prisoner for three days and the Duke's assurance that he would be held under restraint as before at Vannes.

Henry's forebodings of what awaited him in England received support not long afterwards from the example of the Duke of Clarence. Edward IV was no bloodthirsty tyrant, he preferred to let live rather than to kill; but few whose survival was inconvenient escaped the fate of Henry VI in the Tower. He had good reason to distrust his brother Clarence, who had conspired against him with Warwick and the Lancastrians, joined them in restoring Henry VI for a brief interlude to the throne. The reconciliation that followed between the brothers before the battle of Barnet, Clarence's help in Warwick's defeat, checked the harm done but could not blot out the memory. It was hard to forgive and forget that when the red rose blossomed Clarence obtained a place for himself in the succession, ousting his elder brother— especially hard when he behaved as if he still were heir presumptive, arrogantly defying the council and the King himself.

When his wife, Warwick's elder daughter, died he was anxious to marry Mary of Burgundy, his sister Margaret's stepdaughter, the Duke's only child and heir, and he was bitterly resentful when King Edward foreseeing danger from the match withheld his consent. It is not known how far Clarence's resentment prompted him to treason. The charges brought against him ranged from preparation of insurrection to the employment of sorcerers to threaten the King's life. He was arraigned before Parliament to answer to a bill of attainder, found guilty, imprisoned in the Tower under sentence of death. The King however was reluctant to order his brother's execution. While he hesitated he heard that he was dead.

Shakespeare lays the blame for Clarence's murder, like that of Henry VI, on the youngest of the three brothers, the future Richard III. It was politically expedient in Shakespeare's day to blacken Richard's character. Clarence earned many enemies by his arrogant behaviour; but his brother Richard was not among them, he even pleaded for him to save him from disgrace. An odd story has persisted that the murderer, whoever he was, plunged his victim head foremost into a butt of Malmsey, the sweet wine imported from Crete. Malmsey was a wine to which Clarence was much addicted.

The retired life led by Henry Tudor's mother, the former Margaret Beaufort, suffered abrupt change in 1481 when the death of her husband, Henry Stafford, left her a widow for the second time. She was forty years old; but in the following year she married again, and as her third husband, Lord Stanley, was steward of the King's household she had to go to live in London. Stanley himself was a widower, and having a large family already he accepted her condition that the marriage should not be consummated. Her purpose in marrying him was in fact to get him to exert his powerful influence in her son's favour. He had been a consistent supporter of the white rose in the civil war and stood high in King Edward's favour. She for her part was content to forgo her Lancastrian sympathies, devote her time to learning and religion.

They had been married little more than a year when King Edward died. His death was sudden, unexpected; he was still in the prime of life, and in spite of putting on weight he enjoyed vigorous health. The symptoms attending his short illness suggest inflammation of the appendix leading to peritonitis. The event took everyone by surprise. Few arrangements had been made to govern the realm during the minority of his son and heir, a boy of twelve, who was proclaimed King as Edward V. It was the dying King's wish that his brother Richard, Duke of Gloucester, should take charge, but the Queen and her kinsmen were resolutely opposed, jealous of Richard's power and afraid (so little ground had subsequent calumny) that he would punish them for Clarence's murder. At a meeting held in his absence a council of regency was appointed, offering him the title of Protector but without supreme authority.

The young King was at Ludlow, established there since he became Prince of Wales in furtherance of his father's policy to unify Welsh administration. The House of York inherited the huge estates of the Mortimers in the Welsh marches; its victory in the civil war added those of adherents of the House of Lancaster. The whole principality was becoming a Royal appanage, and it was Edward IV's intention to replace the marcher lords, tyrants hated by the Welsh for centuries, with a single authority on the English model over which the Prince of Wales at Ludlow would preside. Till the boy came of age his maternal uncle, Lord Rivers, acted on his behalf.

The death of Edward IV and accession of Edward V upset these plans. Lord Rivers set off at once with the young King to take him to London to be crowned.

Richard Duke of Gloucester had reason to be anxious. During his brother's reign he had been on bad terms with the Queen, an ambitious woman jealous of the affection binding the two brothers, the gratitude felt by the elder for the younger's loyalty. Richard stood by his brother when Clarence betrayed him; he shared his exile, came back with him to fight to restore him to the throne. He played little part, however, in life at court, occupied for most of his time with local government in the north. He was at Middleham Castle in Yorkshire when the news reached him of Edward's death, and it filled him with dismay. He was a stranger in London, had few friends there on whom he could rely.

In contrast the Queen and her kinsmen, her brothers and her two sons by her former marriage, were well organised to promote their own interests, as was shown by their success in limiting the powers given to the Protector. As soon as they had the young King in their hands they would become invincible. He had been brought up among them, accustomed to submit to their influence. For the third time in England in a century the cat was a kitten, and on this occasion the danger was aggravated by a mother-cat with rapacious claws.

Richard took steps to prevent the King from joining her. He hurried south, intercepted Lord Rivers at Northampton and held him there under arrest. On the following day he took charge of the boy-King and travelled with him to London. In the meantime he had gained an important ally, who came to meet him at Northampton, Henry Stafford, Duke of Buckingham, nephew of the Henry Stafford who was stepfather to Henry Tudor. Although he played little part in public affairs in the previous reign Buckingham was a man of restless ambition, proud of his Royal descent which he traced from Edward III's sixth and youngest son, Thomas of Woodstock. He was no friend of the House of York; both his father and his grandfather died fighting for the red rose. It suited him, however, to support Richard against the Queen's faction; any dispute touching the succession to the throne afforded a chance for him to press his own claim.

Richard's arrival in London accompanied by the King and reinforced by Buckingham provoked consternation among the Woodvilles, the Queen's kinsmen. She herself fled to sanctuary at Westminster, where her elder son by her former marriage, Lord Dorset, joined her. Meanwhile preparations went on for Edward V's coronation, with the only difference that the part of guardian was transferred from his maternal to his paternal uncle. The young King was established in residence at the Tower, which was a Royal palace in those days, not just a prison, and his mother was persuaded to send his ten-year-old brother Richard to keep him company there.

At this stage Robert Stillington, Bishop of Bath and Wells, intervened, the same who travelled to Brittany on a fruitless errand for Edward IV to obtain the surrender of Henry Tudor. He told Richard that when Edward IV married the Queen he was already contracted to Lady Eleanor Talbot, daughter of the Earl of Shrewsbury, that the unfulfilled contract invalidated the subsequent marriage. Lady Eleanor herself later married someone else and by this time was dead, but the Bishop insisted that the legal effect remained unchanged. Richard did not dispute it, the argument suited his interest too well. He knew that his victory over the Woodvilles was only temporary, their hold on the boy-King's favour secure.

A sermon preached at Paul's Cross revealed the news to the nation that Edward V was illegitimate, unable to reign. A coronation ceremony followed soon afterwards, but the King crowned was Richard III.

Less than three months had passed since Edward IV's sudden death. The succession of events bears the mark of improvisation, as if force of circumstance alone drove Richard from decision to decision, till the loyal brother usurped his nephew's title. The fate of the two boys, the "Princes in the Tower," is among the unsolved mysteries of history. When the Tudor dynasty came to power, and it was expedient to blacken Richard's memory, he was by common consent condemned as the murderer; but the official account of the crime—not put out till more than fifteen years after the event—contains, as can be shown, so much inconsistency and error that it carries no weight. Even Sir Thomas More, writing under the Tudors and repeating the story of the wicked uncle, the murdered nephews, has to admit that "some remain yet in doubt whether they were in his days destroyed or no." The very uncertainty that prevailed about them argues against King Richard's guilt. The crime could afford no security for his title without incontrovertible proof that the boys were dead, a public funeral such as his brother provided for Henry VI. Mystery (as the succession of pretenders in the following reign confirmed) was more dangerous than the boys themselves alive under his care.

Soon after his coronation he travelled in state to the north and called a Parliament to meet at York, where his record of able government assured him a cordial welcome. It seems indeed that the country as a whole viewed his accession with relief, glad to be spared the dangers of a long minority. He had powerful enemies, however, many anxious to win profit for themselves from the weakness of the Royal title, a few inspired by loyalty to Edward IV and provoked to resentment by his son's exclusion from the throne. The most important of the latter was John Morton, Bishop of Ely. In his earlier years he was an ardent Lancastrian, faithful to the red rose and suffering exile on its behalf as long as hope remained; but after the final disaster at Tewkesbury, the death of Henry VI and his son, he made his peace like many others with King Edward, who recognised his ability and employed him in high office.

King Edward's death and his son's bastardy freed him from obligation to the House of York, and he returned to his old allegiance. No direct heir was left to the House of Lancaster, and even the illegitimate line of the Beauforts was so thinned by war and execution that it had no stronger claimant to offer than Margaret, Henry Tudor's mother, now Lady Stanley. She had no desire to sit on the throne herself; all her ambition was centred on her son, and she was glad to waive her own claim on his behalf. His title, too shadowy to be a serious menace while Edward IV lived, acquired weight from the eagerness of Richard's enemies to set up a plausible rival. In Brittany the Duke appreciated the change produced by events in England on his hostage's prospects. He released the exiles from custody, Henry and his uncle Jasper were allowed to meet again.

Richard hoped at first to win Morton to his side, tried to establish friendly relations with him. Shakespeare has preserved the story of the strawberries in the Bishop's garden at Holborn, how Richard praised them and Morton sent him a basketful. These overtures came to nothing; Morton had already made up his mind, and although the Stanleys played a prominent part in the coronation—Margaret even held the new Queen's train—they were all involved together in plotting revolution. Richard forestalled them by arresting both Stanley and Morton. The former was soon released, for fear of offending his powerful connections; but Morton was sent prisoner into Wales to be confined by the Duke of Buckingham in his castle at Brecon.

Buckingham was in high favour. Richard relied so heavily on his support and was so anxious to retain it that he undid his brother Edward's reforms in Wales, the unification of the country under Royal authority, to re-establish Buckingham there as a marcher lord with greater powers than ever. When he himself departed for the north he left Buckingham in London, who remained there for a short time before returning to Brecon. He had the opportunity during that interval to do what he would to the Princes in the Tower, knowing that his orders would be obeyed, that no one dared oppose him. Unlike Richard, he had no need to prove that the boys were dead. It was enough for him that, when the time came to press his own claim to the throne, no one should be able to produce them (their disappearance could be laid on Richard) to split his followers.

At Brecon where Morton was his prisoner the two were soon on familiar terms. Sir Thomas More—in his unfinished history of the reign of Richard III, for which he owed information to Morton—describes Buckingham as "a proud-minded man" who "evilly could bear the glory of another," and he records a conversation in which Morton urges and the Duke listens eagerly to arguments for treason. Morton veils his meaning in caution. Professing unwillingness to dispute Richard's title "since he is now King in possession" he adds:

"But for the weal of this realm I could wish that, to those good abilities whereof he has already right many little needing my praise, it might yet have pleased God for the better store to have given him some of such other excellent virtues meet for the rule of a realm as our Lord has planted in the person of your Grace."

With those words the history breaks off. More lays down his pen, feeling perhaps that he shows Morton, his friend and patron, in too unfavourable a light. Morton was devoted to Henry Tudor's interest; but it is clear that to win Buckingham's help, to persuade him to betray the King, he appeals in More's account to his ambition, tempts him with the crown.

As the conspiracy spread it gathered many whose purposes were incompatible; they were united only in enmity to King Richard. A Welsh doctor who attended Lady Stanley visited the Queen Mother (the mother, that is, of Edward V) in sanctuary at Westminster, acted as go-between to obtain her support on the understanding that Henry would marry her eldest daughter Elizabeth. Meanwhile messengers travelled in secret to Brittany to warn Henry Tudor himself of what was happening. He was twenty-seven years old by now, winning many friends by his unassuming manners. The education which he owed to his mother's efforts and to those of the Herbert family earned him remark in a country where few could read, few even sign their names. Duke Francis himself was favourably impressed, and when King Richard's envoy came to protest at the freedom given to the exiles he put him off with empty excuses. He was already supplying Henry with money and equipment for an expedition to invade England. It was even said that he was ready to offer him the hand in marriage of his daughter and heiress, Anne.

The insurrection, however, was abortive which Morton and Buckingham planned. King Richard's suspicions were aroused, the conspirators had to take action before they were ready. Buckingham raised an army in Wales, risings broke out in Yorkshire and Devonshire; but the King, ignoring the lesser dangers, advanced at once against Buckingham, his most formidable opponent. The Severn was in flood, the rebels were unable to cross, and while they waited for an opportunity discontent provoked mutiny among the Welshmen, most of whom had been forced into service, lacking any enthusiasm for the cause of a marcher lord. The army melted away without fighting a battle, and Buckingham deserted fled into hiding on a farm near Shrewsbury. The farmer gave him up to King Richard, and he was beheaded.

Buckingham's death took the heart out of the rebellion. The leaders of the Woodville clan, brother and son of the Queen Mother, fled to Brittany. Morton escaped from Brecon, reached his diocese of Ely and embarked for Flanders. Lady Stanley was deprived of titles and property and committed to custody; but the custodian appointed was her husband, and she suffered little hardship. King Richard still feared to break with the Stanleys, hoped to be reconciled.

Before these events were known in Brittany, Henry Tudor had set sail for England. The storm which filled the Severn so that Buckingham was unable to cross scattered Henry's ships. Many returned to port; his own became separated from the rest during the night and was alone when dawn revealed the English coast. He was lying off Poole harbour near enough to see that the shore was beset with soldiers; but he was uncertain whether these were Buckingham's men waiting to reinforce him or King Richard's to oppose his landing.

A boat was sent to find out, and as it approached land the crew shouted across the water and received the reply that King Richard was in flight, that these were Buckingham's soldiers ready to escort Earl Henry to his camp. Henry remained unconvinced, he refused to put into harbour till the other ships of his fleet joined him. While he waited he grew more and more uneasy; no boat put out from the shore bringing the commander of the troops to greet him. Suspecting a trap he gave orders to hoist sail and make for France. His caution saved his life. Buckingham was dead, the soldiers were Richard's.

The wind carried him to Normandy. Important changes were taking place in France. Little more than a month earlier King Louis XI had died, and his son who succeeded him as Charles VIII was a boy of thirteen, weak in mind and deformed in body. The government of the kingdom was taken over by his elder sister Anne, wife of the Lord of Beaujeu, a woman of resolute character. Her father, no feminist, described her as *la moins folle femme du monde*. Her first concern on achieving power was to remove her father's dependents and replace them with her own, a task made urgent by fear of her cousin, the Duke of Orleans (son of the poet Charles d'Orléans taken prisoner at Agincourt), who would inherit the throne if her brother had no son. He was already building up a party of supporters among the nobility.

Anne de Beaujeu was too preoccupied with these cares to wish to meddle in English politics, and when Henry Tudor asked for safe-conduct to travel across France to Brittany she granted his request without delay so as to be rid of him. He returned to Vannes to find the town full of English refugees, who told him of the disastrous outcome of Buckingham's rebellion. His only comfort was that most of the leaders had escaped with their lives to join him there. The year 1483 ended with a solemn ceremony held on Christmas Day in the church at Rennes, where all paid homage to him as King of England, and he for his part, to placate the Woodvilles present, swore that his Queen would be Elizabeth, heiress of the House of York. His confidence owed not a little to the letters, even funds, which his mother contrived to send him from England with her husband's connivance, if not with his active support. She assured him of her continued efforts on his behalf.

His hopes received a blow when he applied for renewed help to Duke Francis. The vow sworn at Rennes to marry Elizabeth of York was a rebuff to the Duke's plans for his own daughter; but in any case the failure of the recent expedition made him less favourable to Henry's claims, he was unwilling to waste more money on an adventure in whose chance of success he was losing trust. He had fresh reason, moreover, as the months went by to deter him from interference in England. The Duke of Orleans seeking allies to promote his interests in France made overtures to Brittany, offering to protect Duke Francis from French encroachment in return for his help in removing Anne de Beaujeu and her friends from power. Pierre Landois, the former tailor who was the Duke's chief minister and an ardent champion of Breton independence, advised his master to accept the alliance, even at the risk of offending wealthy nobles who feared for their estates in France. He warned him, however, that Brittany could only support the Duke of Orleans and defy the French government with impunity if he took care not to quarrel with England, where King Richard was securely established.

In consequence when King Richard sent envoys demanding Henry Tudor's surrender, or at least his incarceration, they received a more attentive hearing than the earlier mission. The Duke's growing infirmity made their task easier as it left Landois free to negotiate much as he chose. News of these developments reached Morton in Flanders; he employed many spies who had access to official sources of information, and he sent Henry an urgent message to leave Brittany surreptitiously as soon as he could. Henry showed it to his uncle Jasper, and they made their plans accordingly. Duke Francis was in retirement for his health's sake in a castle near the French border, and Jasper, gathering the leaders of the English refugees, gave out that the Duke wished them to visit him there. He revealed nothing more for fear of betrayal; but on the way he took a wrong turning on purpose, and they wandered lost in country known to him alone till they reached a village across the frontier, safe in France in Anjou.

Henry himself was not with them; it seemed better that he and his uncle should travel separately so that both should not be taken together. He stayed on a day or two at Vannes, then set off with five servants to visit a friend who lived outside in the country. There were so many English in the town, so many comings and goings, that no one suspected his true purpose. After some five miles, however, he turned aside into a wood, where he changed clothes with one of the servants, and the two of them rode on with roles reversed, servant as master, master as servant, never stopping except to bait their horses till they were in France. He escaped just in time. Landois having reached agreement with the English envoys sent horsemen to arrest him, and when they found him gone they galloped in pursuit. He crossed the French border only an hour before them.

The support given in Brittany to the Duke of Orleans predisposed Anne de Beaujeu in Henry's favour, if only to thwart the Bretons. She shrank no longer from provoking conflict with England when she saw how Brittany sought friendship with King Richard, relied on him for help against France. The colony of English exiles transferred itself to French soil, and Henry Tudor held court there. He received great encouragement when the Earl of Oxford, a veteran of the Lancastrian cause in the Wars of the Roses, escaped from the fortress near Calais where Edward IV had imprisoned him, and came to join the exiled court at Paris, bringing the governor of the fortress too. Oxford's was a famous name among Lancastrian leaders, he had a record of faithful service to the red rose. Henry much preferred him to Buckingham's cronies and the Woodvilles.

He had the more reason to distrust the latter when he heard that King Richard and his sister-in-law were reconciled, that she and her daughters had left sanctuary in Westminster and resumed their place at court. She even persuaded the Marquess of Dorset, her son by her first marriage, to desert Henry's cause and return to make his peace in England. Dorset himself might be no loss; but the example was dangerous as month followed month and the exiles sat idle, lacking sufficient money and influence. Henry sent an officer after him, who caught him up at Compiègne and brought him back under arrest.

Henry did not share the idleness to which his supporters were condemned. Welsh bards record that he paid several visits in secret to Wales at this time, renewing acquaintance with old friends of his uncle Jasper and rekindling the traditional loyalty felt for his family. He was determined not to repeat the disappointment suffered at Poole. The next fleet that he led across the sea would make for the Welsh coast, where he could count on a friendly population. King Richard foresaw this; he gave orders for a close watch to be kept there, for lamps fastened on frames of timber to be set up on coastal hills, ready to be lit to give warning of invasion. The vigilance of English soldiers increased the danger of Henry's journeys. He was sitting down to dinner one evening with his host at Tremostyn on the estuary of the Dee when his enemies broke in. An open window behind him saved him, he fell backwards through it and escaped. Ever afterwards it was known as "the King's hole."

On his return to France disturbing news awaited him. King Richard's wife was dead, and there were rumours that he intended to apply for a Papal dispensation to marry his niece Elizabeth, the bride destined for Henry to unite the red and white rose.

Richard issued a public denial later; but a letter written by the girl herself shows her much attracted to her uncle, eager to become his wife. The rumours at any rate served Richard's cause to good effect, confusing the plans of his opponents. Henry took them sufficiently seriously to propose alliance by marriage with the Herberts, the playmates of his childhood at Pembroke Castle. His old love, Maud, was already married to the Earl of Northumberland, but her younger sister Cicely was still available.

It is typical of his attitude to the English Crown that the chance to strengthen his claim by intermarriage with the House of York meant so little to him. If he could not have Elizabeth of York he would be content with the daughter of a leading family of Wales. Her name would attract Welsh sympathy, help him to sustain the part of a Welsh conqueror.

At last the fleet which he was equipping at Harfleur was ready. It was no formidable armada. French encouragement was more lavish in promises than in money. His total force when he sailed out of the Seine on the 1st of August 1485 amounted to no more than two thousand men, described by an onlooker as "the worst rabble that one could find." Reports of its weakness reached King Richard, who awaited its arrival without alarm. He had confidence in the strength of his defences, the loyalty and ability of the commanders who guarded the coast.

The commanders, however, were Welshmen, as also were most of their soldiers. When Henry's army landed at Dale on the shore of Milford Haven his secret visits paid earlier to Wales bore fruit not only in the numbers of recruits who flocked to his standard, the red dragon of legendary Cadwallader, but also in the unwillingness shown by his opponents to give battle. The story is told of Rhys ap Thomas, a local chieftain, that having sworn to King Richard that an invader would have to enter "over my belly" he lay on the ground at Henry's feet and invited him to step on him to satisfy his oath. The governor of Pembroke Castle alone remained loyal to Richard; but he was helpless to check disaffection among a garrison devoted to Jasper Tudor, men who remembered Henry himself as a boy.

The invaders advanced up the coast, provoking little or no resistance. They were no less immune when they struck across the hills and came down the Severn into England. They were at Shrewsbury before King Richard at Nottingham heard how lamentably his precautions had failed. Taken by surprise he sum-

moned the principal nobles of the realm, including the Earl of
Northumberland and Lord Stanley, to join him. Northumberland
obeyed, but Stanley put him off with excuses. Richard suspecting
treachery kept his son, Lord Strange, Henry's stepbrother, as a
hostage.

Henry himself was equally distrustful of his stepfather. He
knew that he had his mother's full support, she had assured him
of it in her letters to France; but Lord Stanley refused to commit
himself, he could still withdraw his sympathy, still fight for
Richard if fortune favoured the cause. His behaviour was less
foreseeable than ever now that his son was a hostage in Richard's
camp. The anxiety that Henry felt on this account seems to lie
at the root of an incident recorded by most of the chroniclers.
As his army advancing east approached Tamworth he hung back
with a small escort of twenty men. The rest of the force entered
the town to lodge there for the night, and when darkness fell
and he was still missing there was consternation. Not even his
uncle Jasper or Lord Oxford, whom he had appointed commander-
in-chief, knew whether he was absent on purpose or by mis-
chance. King Richard's forces were dangerously near. At dawn
a party was setting out to look for him when a horseman appeared through the hazy twilight. It was Henry riding alone.

He replied curtly to questions that he had been in conference
with secret allies, who brought good news.

Polydore Vergil adds details of the night's adventures, probably
told him by Henry himself: that he became parted from his escort
in the darkness, lost his way and wandered into a village some
three miles off, where he dared not ask to be directed or reveal
who he was in case he was in hostile territory. He spent the night
there in a shepherd's hut in great distress of mind, fearing not
only immediate danger but also that the accident was a presage
of calamity. The battle of Bosworth which changed the course
of English history lay little more than a day ahead. Both pro-
tagonists approached it with foreboding. Richard's nightmares are
on record and have often been described.

It is still unexplained how Henry's escort came to lose touch
with him. Had he a secret assignation with undeclared allies at
which he desired no witness? Was it a trap to lure him away
alone into the night? He was a man who kept his thoughts and
doings to himself. It is evidence of the gravity of the danger from

which he extricated himself that he confessed to Vergil how badly he was frightened.

Safe back in the camp he recovered his resolution quickly. In the course of the day he visited Lord Stanley at Atherstone, and this time he had no need to feign satisfaction; events proved his success.

Bosworth lies about midway between Atherstone and Leicester. Richard's army was nearly twice as large as Henry's, and it had the advantage of rising ground. Henry however could not avoid combat; the choice lay between battle or retreat, irrevocable failure. Although the odds seemed to be against him there were circumstances to encourage hope. At a short distance from the battlefield Stanley's forces stood waiting, uncommitted and unpredictable, but powerful enough to determine the issue on whichever side they intervened. Henry knew, in addition, that the Earl of Northumberland, who commanded Richard's rearguard, was wavering in his allegiance. Northumberland's wife was a Welshwoman, Herbert's daughter Maud; he was jealous too of the influence that Richard enjoyed in the north.

The Earl of Oxford led the main body uphill to the attack, Henry himself commanded the reserves on a small knoll to the west. The opposing armies met, remained for a time locked in combat, then Oxford drew his men back a short way to close ranks, consolidate their position. The battle had barely begun, the advantage if any was Richard's; but Stanley's intervention or Northumberland's treachery could turn the scales against him at any moment. It was this danger apparently that persuaded him to withdraw with his bodyguard from the fighting front, gallop off suddenly to attack the enemy's reserves. He could see Henry Tudor among them; his purpose was to seek and kill him before either Stanley or Northumberland had a chance to defect. The death of the leader would put an end at once to the invasion. All would make haste to pay homage to King Richard III.

The attempt all but succeeded. Henry's small force was overwhelmed, he himself hemmed in by Richard and his knights, saved only by his esquire, William Brandon, bearer of his dragon standard, who interposed himself and paid for his devotion with his life. The Stanleys watched his predicament; the nearest—Lord Stanley's brother, Sir William—made up his mind at last, charged to the rescue, so that the attackers had to turn to defend themselves. The diversion had decisive effect; Stanley's men outnumbered their opponents, killed them off one by one. Richard himself fell mortally wounded, died fighting fiercely to the last, the only King of England to die on the battlefield.

He wore a circlet of gold round his helmet, emblem of royalty. It was detached by his fall, rolled away under a hawthorn bush. When the battle was over, the victory won, Lord Stanley found it there. He set it on the victor's head, crowned him King Henry VII.

PART II

The Dynasty

CHAPTER 7

Comparisons are odious. It is generally agreed today from examination of the evidence that the portrait drawn of Richard III by Shakespeare, and by Tudor chroniclers before him, is a calumny inspired by political motives. One can do justice, however, to the last of the Plantagenets without unjustly condemning the first of the Tudors. It does not follow that Henry was a monster because Richard was not. The two men were enemies, rival claimants to the throne. If Richard had not been defeated at Bosworth he might have made an excellent King. Henry won the battle, reigned in fact, and much of value came from his achievement.

The charge most often brought against him is that of coldness of heart. Few deny him clarity of mind, strength of will, practical ability; but these qualities are adduced as evidence of his inhumanity, interests limited to the acquisition of wealth and devoid of feeling. There is support for this view in the ruthless purpose with which he pursued his chosen policy. He kept strict account of money, cared little for the protests of those from whom he exacted it to fill his treasury. There was a hardness to his character against which it was dangerous to butt.

This was the aspect shown in public, but even here there are details inconsistent with the type. Few contemporary kings were so reluctant to pronounce sentence of death. He killed only in the last resort, preferred to let live. All who knew him as a boy were impressed by the gentleness of his manners, and although he used force on many occasions when he grew up, fought courageously himself in battle, violence was distasteful to his na-

93

ture, his favourite weapons were diplomacy and intrigue. Except for a few insignificant engagements his reign was free from foreign wars. The caution with which he avoided them owed as much to the peaceful bent of his temperament as to his fear of the expense, his dislike of wasting money on military adventures. There is no hypocrisy in his insistence on recording in the preface to a treaty that "when Christ came into the world peace was sung."

Qualification is needed too to the indictment which accuses him of avarice. The assiduity with which he accumulated money, the harsh measures by which he exacted it, served the purpose of building up funds for the administration and defence of the state. The weakness of Royal authority, the poverty of its resources, its dependence on too powerful nobles, were the principal causes of the Wars of the Roses, condemning the country to more than a decade of anarchy. Edward IV was aware of this and took action to divert wealth into the treasury from trade and industry. Henry VII followed his example, and with more time at his disposal he carried it out to greater effect. The rich suffered from his exactions, and their complaints have echoed down the corridors of history. The poor escaped, having nothing that the King could take. He was no Robin Hood plundering the rich to give to the poor; but all classes benefited from the order which he acquired the means to enforce.

If he was careful of public money he was far from niggardly in his personal habits. His court was as magnificent as any in an age that loved gorgeous display, and although the motive owed much to shrewd policy, using pageantry to enhance Royal prestige, it is clear that his own tastes played a part, that he enjoyed dressing up in smart clothes. He was a patron of learning and the arts, and especially of music to which he was devoted. Italian scholars like Polydore Vergil were taken into his service to propagate the ideas and values of the Renaissance flourishing in their own country. Nor was native talent neglected; he employed the poet, John Skelton, as tutor to his son. His accounts show, moreover, that he was generous in presents to his family and others around him; entries range from costly jewellery for the Queen to gratuities for the girl who brought almond butter or the woman who quenched his thirst with two glasses of water as he rode past her cottage.

Few Kings have kept their thoughts more to themselves. He

was reticent from childhood, and the adventures of his early life confirmed him in secretive habits, encouraged him to cherish his privacy. His enemies attributed his reserve to lack of human feeling; but the rare glimpses afforded of his private behaviour give a very different impression, that of a man dependent on the affection of those dear to him to make up for his fear and suspicion of the world. Stern and formidable to the arrogant, he was gracious and kindly to his intimates, to anyone indeed who came to him without pretensions. The charm of manner which won friends for the exile in Brittany and France did not desert him when he became King of England. Polydore Vergil, of course, was biassed in his favour; but he wrote as an eyewitness when he described how the King's face lit up as he talked, how his grey eyes twinkled.

Most of the portraits that survive show him in his last years, many indeed are painted not from life but from his death mask. A very different impression is given by contemporaries who knew him in his youth, as in the following description:

"He was a man of body but lean and spare, albeit mighty and strong therewith, of personage and stature somewhat higher than the mean sort of men be, of a wonderful beauty and fair complexion, of countenance merry and smiling, especially in his communication."

Another observer records that the surest way to provoke his displeasure was to bring an accusation against anyone without the support of exact evidence; for "he would take it to be said of envy, ill-will and malice."

Soon after his victory at Bosworth he announced his intention to marry Elizabeth of York, but he put off the wedding till he himself had been crowned. He wished to make plain that he claimed the throne by right of conquest, not through his wife's descent from the House of York. Her name was useful to reconcile former opponents, sentiment was nourished on the theme of the union of the red and white rose; but in his first speech to Parliament he insisted firmly that he owed his title to "the true judgment of God as shown by the sword on the field of battle." The challenge to English tradition was applauded by the Welsh, who wielded the sword. It strengthened their belief that his accession avenged the Saxon invasion, reconquered Britain for its ancient inhabitants.

Although he refused to let his title depend on his wife's, political motives were responsible for the marriage. If the course of events had been different Anne of Brittany or Cicely Herbert could have been his choice. It does not follow, however, that relations between a married couple are unhappy because their union suits political expediency. Elizabeth of York fared no worse than other princesses of the time, whose hand in marriage was treated as a bargaining counter in politics. She herself could contemplate without reluctance the prospect of marrying her uncle Richard. She was of a sweet-tempered, unassuming nature, no more anxious to interfere in affairs of state than Henry was to permit it. There is no reason to suppose that she resented the place allotted her, the firmness with which he insisted that he was King, she no more than his consort.

She was also, as witnesses aver, remarkably good-looking, with long yellow hair flowing down her back. Henry was susceptible to feminine beauty, his taste was fastidious. If he craved for a hidden refuge where he was free to put off his public mask he could not have chosen a wife better fitted to share it. They were constantly together, their letters are affectionate, no disharmony arose between them even when her mother was suspected of treason and a pretender who claimed to be her brother stirred up rebellion. Erasmus pays tribute to her intelligence, the sincere piety of her religion; her only habit that conflicts with her husband's was that of running up debts, due to her irrepressible generosity to her friends and kindred. Henry, the strictest of accountants where his own expenditure was concerned, satisfied her creditors without demur.

It is evidence of the felicity of the marriage that, in an age when few kings or noblemen lacked a mistress, Henry remained faithful to his wife. Elizabeth had no rival.

A bond that drew husband and wife still closer was the affection felt by them both for Henry's mother. It was among his first actions after his victory at Bosworth to annul the attainder pronounced by King Richard, restore her honours and estates. She resumed and was commonly known thenceforward by the title of Countess of Richmond, which recalled her first husband, Edmund Tudor, Henry's father. Her daughter-in-law was no stranger to her. At the time of the struggle between Richard, still Protector, and the Woodvilles, when the Royal Family fled into sanctuary at Westminster, Elizabeth being the eldest, old enough to know her own mind, preferred the hospitality offered by Lord Stanley, and she stayed in his house under his wife's care till her mother became reconciled with King Richard and returned to court. The friendship begun then between the young girl and her hostess persisted as long as they lived.

The Countess of Richmond has been ill served by encomiasts anxious to preserve the fame of her piety and learning, the strictness of her moral principles. The impression left is that of an almost inhuman austerity, and it is reinforced by portraits which show her dressed as a nun. A much warmer, gentler character is revealed when one reads her letters, a woman whose ability to inspire love needs no effort of imagination. She was devout but she was not sanctimonious, her dignity was tempered with humour; her charity is no cold fulfilment of religious duty, it is nearer the virtue defined by St. Paul which "suffers long and is kind." Forms of address were more florid in her day than in ours; but there is more than polite convention, there is a ring of feeling from the depths of her heart when she begins a letter to her son: "My own sweet and most dear King, and all my worldly joy."

Her third husband, Lord Stanley, having made up his mind just in time to be on the winning side at Bosworth, was rewarded with the title of Earl of Derby and continued to enjoy high office till his death in 1504. There is no reason to suppose that they lived on other than cordial terms, in spite of the peculiar condition which she imposed on marrying him and her later request to which he agreed towards the end of the century for a formal separation. It was a marriage of convenience contracted when both parties were in middle age; his motive was to insure himself by acquiring a wife of the Royal blood of Lancaster, in case the white rose were again ousted by the red; hers was to use his powerful influence on behalf of her son exiled in Brittany. Little as his vacillation can have pleased her when the beloved invader landed in Wales, she had great patience and could make allowances for his anxiety for his own son, who was a hostage in King Richard's hands. For years afterwards she presided over his household, entertained his friends with quiet dignity, and when at last they separated it was without disagreement to enable her to devote herself more fully to religion.

There was no one to whom Henry owed more than his uncle, who had been a father to him when he was a boy, his counsellor and supporter in exile, singleminded in devotion and never disheartened, sharing the burden of the adventure which ended victoriously at Bosworth. For thirty years, except for the short inter-lude of the restoration of Henry VI in 1470, Jasper Tudor had lived as an outlaw hunted and imprisoned, more at home in the pathless woods of the Welsh mountains than among the amenities of a court. He was now in his middle fifties; the last decade of his life was full of honours. Henry was prompt to create him Duke of Bedford, employed him continually in high office, in-cluding that of high steward of Oxford University. A more ap-propriate position which he occupied was that of Chief Justice for South Wales.

Something has been said already of his secret love for a girl in Wales, who became his mistress, and of the birth of his daughter, Ellen, who married a cloth merchant at Bury St. Edmunds, John Gardiner. Ellen's mother seems to have died before 1485. In the autumn of that year Jasper, hitherto unmarried, took for wife the widow of the Duke of Buckingham. She was twenty-eight at the time, born Catherine Woodville, youngest sister of Edward IV's Queen and aunt to Henry VII's Queen, Elizabeth of York. It is unlikely that he knew her while she was Duchess of Bucking-ham as he was in exile during Edward IV's reign, and Buckingham himself was an opponent till his abortive rebellion against Rich-ard III. The marriage was childless.

In spite of increasing age Jasper refused (like his father before him) to remain inactive when his military services were needed. He took the field and was present at the decisive battle to crush a revolt which broke out early in the reign, and in 1492 when he had turned sixty he commanded the army raised to invade France. It was his last campaign; he died three years later, in December 1495. His life spans the rise of the family from ob-scurity to supreme power. He was the child of an irregular union, of a French princess of the House of Valois and a despised and impoverished Welsh soldier, with whom till he was five years old he lived hidden from the world, undisturbed in Eden, and from whom for reasons past his understanding he was suddenly and cruelly parted. The course of his life thereafter, the fluctuation of his fortunes, has been traced in the preceding chapters. His death received a public funeral attended by the greatest in the realm, where the chief mourner was his nephew, the King of England.

Ingratitude was never among Henry's faults. Few, if any, who helped to raise him to the throne went unrewarded. The Bishop of Ely, John Morton, who plotted assiduously on his behalf against King Richard and sent timely warning to save him from the emissaries of the Duke of Brittany, became at once his chief minister, was promoted, in due course, Archbishop of Canterbury and obtained through Henry's influence with the Pope a Cardinal's hat. Less exalted supporters had advancement suited to their rank; Henry had an excellent memory for faces, and no knight or priest who befriended him in adversity, not even his old Welsh nurse, was too humble for his recognition. The best-known example is perhaps William Brandon, his standard-bearer at Bosworth, who saved his life at the expense of his own. Brandon was a man of no means, a mere esquire not even knighted, and his death left his widow and baby son, Charles, all but destitute. King Henry not only provided for their support, but when his own children were old enough he took Charles Brandon to be brought up with them at Windsor as their playmate. The friendship begun in childhood led the boy when he grew to be a man to heights which the noblest born might envy. Plain Will Brandon's son became Duke of Suffolk.

Henry's first child was born in September 1486, and there were great rejoicings when it was announced that it was a boy. Wales rejoiced especially on hearing that the name given him was Arthur. There was policy in the choice of the name; Henry reinforced his claim to rule by right of conquest by representing himself as heir of the ancient princes of Britain, and he had scholars at work tracing his line back far beyond old Sir Tudor at the court of Edward III, working out a pedigree which equipped him with ancestors at Camelot. He himself seems to have put faith in their researches; he combined shrewdness in practical affairs and in his judgment of men with a taste for romantic pageantry. He was proud of his Welsh origin, cherished his memories of the country and people, and added the red dragon of Wales to the Royal arms where it remained till the accession of the Stuarts.

The Welsh conquest of England left relations between conqueror and conquered in many respects little changed. The English retaining wealth and power were still the rulers, the Welsh the ruled. That is not to say that the Welsh King was careless of the interests of his flesh and blood. One of the first acts of Henry VII when he began to reign was to revoke the penal laws imposed on the Welsh by Henry IV to punish them for Glendower's rebellion. When his throne became more firmly established he turned his attention to restrain the marcher lords, the petty tyrants in their Norman castles, who had oppressed Wales for centuries by their arrogance, greed and internecine feuds. It was a problem which Edward IV tried to solve when, taking advantage of the extension by heredity of his own family estates, he sent his son and heir to Ludlow to govern them, to be Prince of Wales in fact as well as in name. The prince's youth and his father's sudden death cut short the attempt before it could bear fruit. Henry Tudor carried it further when his own son Arthur was old enough to hold court at Ludlow, served by a council whose jurisdiction extended over the whole principality of Wales and the marches; but Arthur died young, the King had other cares to distract him, the council at Ludlow exerted no more than a shadowy authority during his reign. He bequeathed a solemn charge to his heir, Henry VIII, to complete his work to relieve the condition of Wales.

Towards the end of Henry VIII's reign the charge at last was fulfilled. An Act of Parliament reorganised the administration of Wales, assimilating it to that of England. English law replaced Welsh, the Welsh language was banished from official use; nevertheless the statutory union of England and Wales was greeted almost everywhere with satisfaction. It abolished the privileges of the marcher lords, enforced orderly government; above all, it allowed no discrimination between English and Welsh, the Welshman suffered no disability to exclude him from responsible office. The Welsh had their reward for placing a Tudor King on the throne.

Henry VII relied on their support as much to retain the Crown as to win it. As the shock of defeat at Bosworth and King Richard's death wore off the party of the white rose recovered energy in England, unwilling to recognise a King who reigned by right of conquest. Within six months of his coronation an insurrection broke out in the north, led by Lord Lovell who had been King Richard's chamberlain and escaped from Bosworth into sanctuary. Henry was at a disadvantage; most of the army which accompanied him from Wales had gone home, and he was not sure yet how far he could count on sympathy in England. He hurriedly collected some three thousand men, ill-armed and ill-equipped, and sent them north under the command of his uncle Jasper, now Duke of Bedford. Their success against the rebels owed less to military force than to Jasper's good judgment. He ordered heralds to ride ahead to the opposing camp to offer amnesty to any who laid down their arms. Numbers of the rebels already regretting their boldness took advantage of the opportunity, and as Lovell's army melted he himself slipped away under cover of night, fled to the coast and embarked for Flanders.

The danger to the throne was averted for the time, but not for long. The dowager Duchess of Burgundy, born Margaret of York, was a sister of Edward IV; she was devoted to the cause of the white rose, an irreconcilable enemy of the Tudor supplanter. Much had changed in Burgundy since her brother sent her to Bruges to become the Duke's bride, and gossips too free with stories of the escapades of the English Venus were ducked in the canal. Her husband was dead, killed in battle; so too was his heir, her stepdaughter Mary, from a fatal fall from a horse. The present Duke of Burgundy was Mary's eldest son Philip, still a boy under the guardianship of his father, Maximilian King of the Romans (a title borne by the Habsburgs as rulers in Germany). Margaret, however, retained estates in Flanders as her jointure, and she kept open house there for conspirators ready to unseat King Henry.

The House of York had two male heirs available. The stronger claim was that of the young Earl of Warwick, son of Edward IV's brother, the Duke of Clarence who died drowned in Malmsey wine; but he was only twelve years old at this time and weak if not deranged in mind. He had lived secluded even in his uncle Richard's reign, Henry kept him in custody in the Tower. The other claimant was a man in his early twenties, John, Earl of Lincoln, son of Edward IV's younger sister Elizabeth. His father was a son of the Earl of Suffolk, Owen Tudor's lax gaoler at Wallingford, who became the trusted minister of Henry VI. When Richard III was left childless by the death of his only son he chose Lincoln rather than Warwick to be his heir.

After Henry's victory at Bosworth Lincoln swore allegiance to him and accepted a seat on the council. He stood aloof from Lovell's abortive rising in 1486, but in the following year when he received news of a more serious revolt planned in Ireland he left the court to join Lovell and Duchess Margaret in Flanders. He himself, however, was not the claimant in whose name supporters of the white rose were urged to rise against King Henry. The conspirators professed to have the Earl of Warwick with them in Ireland. Their story was that he had escaped from the

Tower, and a boy of the right age was shown whom they treated with the respect due to royalty.

It was an odd story; the boy's identity has since been established. His name was Lambert Simnel, and he was the son of a tradesman in Oxford, sent for schooling to a priest, Richard Symons, who was much impressed by his intelligence and manners. The idea came to Symons to put young Simnel's talents to useful account by passing him off as the heir to some great family. At first, it seems, he intended him to impersonate the younger of Edward IV's sons, one of the "Princes in the Tower," whose fate was unknown; then rumours reached him of Warwick's escape from custody, and he changed his plans to grasp the opportunity. The rumours were without foundation; but when Symons learnt this it was too late to change again, Simnel was already acclaimed in Ireland as Edward VI. Warwick's name was Edward, the young prince's Richard.

Lincoln raised troops in Flanders and brought them to join the Irish levies collected to invade England. He knew the true Earl of Warwick well by sight, had shared lodgings with him in King Richard's reign; it is probable too, that as a member of the council, he had good information that the boy was still in the Tower. Nevertheless he accepted the impostor's title without dispute, paid homage to him with seeming conviction. He had no alternative; to object at this stage would have brought irretrievable discredit on the cause. In the event of victory he could no doubt have found means to eliminate Simnel, substitute himself.

King Henry gave orders for the true Earl of Warwick to be produced from the Tower and paraded through the streets of London; but if any report of these proceedings reached Ireland it had little effect. The invaders persisted in their purpose, landed on the coast of Furness and advanced east into Yorkshire, gathering support. Henry was in much the same plight as Richard before the battle of Bosworth, threatened by an enemy who could count on local sympathy. King Richard's memory inspired affection in the north of England as potent as that enjoyed by the Tudors in Wales. The Irish, however, were unpopular, and this time the Stanleys were firm in their allegiance. When the Royal army mustered in the midlands the rebels turned south to confront it, instead of pressing on to York where friends awaited them. Lincoln was impatient of delay, eager to bring the struggle to an issue.

He met the vanguard of the Royal army on the Trent near

Newark and attacked at once, relying on superior numbers; but many of his Irishmen were armed only with clubs and scythes, and his German mercenaries from Flanders, better equipped, were too few to stiffen them. The King's soldiers stood their ground, fighting stubbornly, and when the main body arrived to reinforce them the battle was won. Lincoln himself was killed, his followers fled.

Lovell, his principal confederate, escaped with his life, putting his horse to swim the Trent and riding on uncaptured across country to his estates at Minster Lovell in Oxfordshire. He had a hiding-place in the manor-house known to no one else except a trusted retainer, who brought him food and drink and looked after him. Some mishap occurred, the visits ceased, the secret door could only be opened from outside. More than two centuries later, when repairs were being carried out to a chimney, a vault was found containing the skeleton of a man seated at a table with book, paper and pen, grim evidence that Lord Lovell, King Richard's friend and chamberlain, died there of starvation.

The defeat of the rebellion put an end to the schemes of Richard Symons and Lambert Simnel. Both were arrested, and the former was thrown into prison where he stayed till his death. Simnel received more merciful treatment, having the excuse of extreme youth, led astray by the teacher responsible for his education. King Henry pardoned him and sent him to work in his kitchen, from which he was promoted later to take charge of the Royal falcons. The forbearance shown him was good policy, the sight of the pretender carrying dishes of meat and pouring out wine brought ridicule on the white rose. He lived to a ripe age, married and had children.

Clemency was extended too to his supporters in Ireland. Their leaders, including the Earl of Kildare, who as Lord Deputy held chief authority in the realm, were brought under guard to London; but instead of the executioner's axe they had to suffer only Henry's irony:

"My masters of Ireland," he told them, "you'll be crowning apes next."

Afterwards he invited them to a banquet where their glasses were filled by a waiter to whom they had recently paid homage as "Edward VI." Mortification yielded to relief when Henry took courteous leave of them, and they were sent back to Ireland alive and restored to their former positions in the administration and judiciary. Even Kildare was allowed to resume office as Lord Deputy. There was good sense as well as clemency in Henry's policy. It would have been difficult to punish the Irish rebels without stripping the country of everyone capable of governing it, so many of the leading men were implicated.

A mysterious incident arising out of the rebellion is the disgrace that befell Edward IV's widow, the Queen's mother. On Henry's accession he gave her high position at court and restored part at least of the jointure confiscated by Richard III; but now her revenues were taken away again, and she herself was dismissed to live on a small pension at the abbey at Bermondsey, the same to which Henry's own grandmother, Queen Catherine, was relegated some fifty years before. The cause of her downfall was kept secret; but it is hard to believe that her punishment was unconnected with the revolt, with which it synchronised so closely.

Although her eldest daughter was Queen and she herself treated with respect she was a disappointed woman. Henry insisted on reigning in his own right and acknowledged no debt to his wife's kinsmen. Even if some of them received offices of profit, the rewards fell far short of the glorious prospect open to the Wood-villes when King Edward died, leaving the young King Edward V a docile tool in the hands of his mother's family. It is certain that the dowager resented the frustration of her ambition, and there is probability in the suggestion that has been put forward that her offence now was to coach Simnel in details of the life of the Royal Family, to enable him to play the part of the Earl of Warwick with verisimilitude.

Her banishment was not for long. Three years later her annuity was increased, and she began to appear at court again. A marriage was even proposed for her with the King of Scotland, James III, but it fell through when the intended bridegroom was murdered by his nobles. She played little further part on occasions of state. When she died in 1492 an observer recorded with displeasure that no member of the family attended her funeral at Windsor except a bastard daughter of Edward IV. Her own daughters made amends a day or two afterwards when they came to pay their respects and join in singing a dirge, all except the Queen who was confined to bed by the birth of a daughter, Princess Margaret. She had delicate health, there was good reason for her absence; but she and her mother were not in sympathy, any more than were Henry and his mother-in-law.

CHAPTER 8

In spite of civil war and a change of dynasty the aims pursued by Henry VII were very close to those of Edward IV, especially in the encouragement of manufacture and trade. Ideas picked up from "Black William," King Edward's wise counsellor, bore fruit in the mind of the boy who was both his prisoner and his pupil at Pembroke Castle; but unlike Herbert cut off prematurely by his enemies Henry lived to establish his work on a firm foundation. The pressure that he applied to the rich to fill the Royal treasury had the effect also of curbing the unruly power of the nobles. Cardinal Morton has earned fame, or infamy, in history from the device known as "Morton's Fork," but it bears the mark of Henry's own mind. The principle on which it worked was that those who spent lavishly had the money to contribute a portion to the King, those who spent little could afford to do so from what they saved.

Fiscal measures of this sort inflicted irreparable loss on the nobles, unable any longer to recoup themselves by lawless violence; but the merchants took little harm, they paid out of mounting profits. The King fostered their interests, providing favourable conditions for trade so that his golden geese might continue to lay him eggs. Much of the wealth that he took from them went to enforce law and order, on which their prosperity depended.

There is a story about him in Kipling's *Rewards and Fairies* describing his treatment of the shipwrights caught pilfering in his dockyard. He spies on them, punishes sternly, ends up by sparing their lives. It is fiction, but it rings true of his character:

"Nay, never lift up thy hands to me. There's no clean hands
    in the trade.
But steal in measure," said Harry our King. "There's measure
    in all things made."

King Henry expected little of human nature; he was accustomed
to compromise, preferred half a loaf to no bread. He was also
very proud of his ships, did much to ensure that goods entering
and leaving English ports were carried in English bottoms.

Another purpose in which Edward IV and Henry VII were at
one was the avoidance of foreign war. It claimed Henry's attention at an early stage in his reign as the French persisted in their
designs against the duchy of Brittany. He himself was in close
relations with both parties, having been the guest and at times
the prisoner of the Duke during his years of exile and owing
gratitude to France for his final escape and the facilities put at
his disposal for the invasion of England. The issue however tran-
scended any personal obligations. Ever since the reverses suffered
in Henry VI's reign, which put an end to the English occupation
of France, it had been English policy to support the Dukes of
Burgundy and Brittany, who ruled nominally as feudatories of the
French Crown, but in fact as independent sovereigns. The two
great duchies bordering France on either side helped to check
the reviving power of the French monarchy. Brittany was especially important, commanding the southern entrance to the narrow seas.

When Henry fled from Brittany to France, on his way to victory at Bosworth, the aged Duke's minister, Pierre Landois, was
still in control of affairs, seeking help from the England of Richard III against French aggression. The course of events in England, the defeat and death of King Richard, were a grave setback
to this policy, and the nobles who hated Landois, the enemy of
their privileges, took advantage of his discredit to seize and murder
him. They were supported by French troops, and the Duke was
unable to resist.

Brittany found a champion, however, in the French heir presumptive, the Duke of Orleans, who escaped from prison in France
to lead the movement for Breton independence. His courage and
ideals inspired fresh hope, and the old Duke and his daughter
were warmly attached to him. As the war developed both sides
appealed to England for help, and King Henry wishing neither

to quarrel with France nor to allow Brittany to be overwhelmed offered to mediate. His purpose was frustrated by the ardent sympathy felt in England for the Breton cause. An armed expedition sailed in defiance of his orders from the Isle of Wight to cross the sea and repel the French invaders. This escapade deprived him of any chance of success as a mediator; it served only to bring disaster to Brittany. The French army won a decisive victory at St. Aubin, thousands of Bretons were killed, and Orleans himself was taken prisoner, shut up securely again in France in a fortress. The news broke the old Duke's heart. He died nine days later.

His heir was his daughter Anne, once intended as a bride for Henry Tudor. She was now twelve years old, and the fate of Brittany turned on the struggle between rival suitors for her hand in marriage. Henry himself was no longer among them; but there was no lack of princes in Europe eager to grasp the opportunity. They included Maximilian King of the Romans, soon to become Holy Roman Emperor, and Don Juan, son of the King of Spain; but the guardians of the young Duchess favoured Alan d'Albret, whose domains stretching from Bordeaux to the Pyrenees ensured protection close at hand, prompt and effective. D'Albret, however, was old enough to be Anne's father, he had a family already of twelve children of his own. She objected with outspoken disgust to the match, to his age and pimpled face.

Bitter dispute followed. His partisans gathered a faction and took up arms against her, now in conflict, now in alliance with the French. There was such confusion that the sincerest well-wisher might hesitate, uncertain where or on what side to intervene. King Henry lent her troops, and they occupied a number of castles on her behalf; but he refused to declare war on France, the truce concluded on his accession remained in force. Some hope of understanding emerged when the Breton leaders opposed to the Duchess sought a reconciliation; they agreed not to impose d'Albret on her, if she would accept Maximilian in his place. A wedding was celebrated at Rennes at which Maximilian was married by proxy to his thirteen-year-old bride, and to add solemnity to the occasion a ceremony followed in which Anne climbed naked into bed in the presence of many distinguished witnesses, and Maximilian's envoy bared his leg to the knee and thrust it in beside her under the bedclothes. The purpose, says Polydore

Vergil, was to let her know that the marriage was as good as consummated.

The symbol was without effect. The French attacked the more vigorously, dismayed that Brittany should fall into the hands of the House of Habsburg, and Maximilian was too busy elsewhere, too short of money to defend the interests of his putative wife. The wedding, moreover, made an enemy of d'Albret, insulting proof that his suit was rejected, whether or not Anne's comments on his appearance had come to his ears. He was in command of the garrison at Nantes and he surrendered it to the French; they swept on into Brittany, captured Redon from the Spaniards, Concarneau from the English, besieged Anne herself in Rennes.

She made a fateful decision. If the war went on there would soon be no Brittany left. The country was devastated, overrun by foreign soldiers; allies or enemies, all behaved alike, plundering and killing. King Henry offered her a ship to escape and continue the struggle from abroad; but outside the walls of Rennes the French tempted her with peace if she married their King. Charles VIII might be personally unattractive, but he could hardly be uglier than d'Albret, and at least he was young, not yet twenty-two. They were married in Touraine in December 1491, and this time she shared her bed with more than a man's foot and shinbone.

The marriage was the fulfilment of a purpose, the union of France and Brittany, on which the regent, Anne de Beaujeu, had set her heart. She felt now that her work was done. Her brother was old enough to manage his own affairs. Gradually by easy stages she resigned her authority, then retired into the country to spend the remaining thirty years of her life there in domestic peace, giving up power without regret. Even her father had once conceded that she was *la moins folle femme du monde*. In France she bore the name of *Madame la Grande*.

There was indignation in Europe over the marriage of Anne of Brittany to the King of France. Both Maximilian and the King of Spain vowed vengeance, but neither was in a position to carry out the threat. The former was busy fighting for the crown of Hungary, the latter approaching the climax of his long struggle to expel the Moors. England alone was free to take action; public opinion raged fiercely against France, the traditional enemy, and King Henry himself was in no mood to refrain. This was his first experience of foreign policy as a reigning monarch. He had tried the methods congenial to his nature, relying on negotiation, cautious manipulation of the balance of forces, and the result was humiliating failure; French violence, the sheer weight of arms had prevailed. It added bitterness to his regret that the victim was Brittany, the ancient settlement established overseas by Britons flying from the Saxon invasion. He prided himself on the lineage which traced his descent from King Arthur.

In a letter written to Pope Innocent VIII he spoke of war as a hateful necessity, insisted with feeling on his reluctance to shed blood, but added that the French left him no choice, no neighbour was safe from their aggression. It is a familiar plea; but King Henry has at least the distinction that, professing himself a reluctant warrior, he maintained consistency by winning a bloodless victory.

He spent many months collecting forces of ships and men, raising money for the purpose without difficulty, the war was popular in England, the tax paid with few complaints. When all was ready, however, he still delayed, waiting through the spring and summer of 1492 in the hope that his allies, Maximilian or the Spaniards, would move to support him. Neither responded, and at last in the autumn the English fleet sailed to invade France alone. Henry's uncle Jasper, Duke of Bedford, held the command in spite of his advanced age; but the King himself accompanied the expedition, ready to take control when any issue of policy arose.

The army disembarked at Calais, still English soil, the only foothold remaining from the old domains of Henry V, and envoys were sent to Maximilian in a last effort to appeal to his sense of shame, his honour outraged by the theft of a bride symbolically wedded and bedded. They returned unsuccessful. Maximilian did not lack the will, but he was without the means at present to avenge the insult. Flanders, the nearest source of manpower, was part of the inheritance of his former wife, Mary of Burgundy, and on her death the title passed to their son, the Archduke Philip. The Flemings were jealous of their rights, none too docile under the government even of the lawful heir; they would take no orders from his father.

King Henry could wait no longer. He advanced into France and laid siege to Boulogne. The town was strongly fortified, capable of holding out for months. The operation begun so late in the year was likely to last into the winter, bringing difficulties and privations on the besieging forces. Henry, however, knew what he was doing, the seemingly fruitless siege had a purpose. As long as his army sat before Boulogne he could avoid battle; its mere presence in the country was a threat to French security without the need of further acts of warfare. He had information from Paris that the young King Charles, free from his sister's supervision, cherished glorious dreams of conquest beyond the Alps, that he planned to subjugate Italy like a second Charlemagne, even to drive the infidel from the Holy Sepulchre. His impatience would have little time to spare for an English army in the north, would want to be rid of the nuisance as quickly as possible.

Henry was right. No French army opposed him, an envoy came instead to offer peace on favourable terms. The fate of Brittany was past mending, Charles and Anne were married and must remain so; but the French were willing to compensate the English for all the expense to which they had been put, and to renew the pension promised by Louis XI to Edward IV. Like King Edward seventeen years earlier King Henry led his army back unscathed, wealthier by a sum equivalent today to many millions of pounds.

There was disappointment in England over the tame ending, and some discontent from those taxed for a war that was not fought; but the money saved was spent at home to productive purpose, and Henry's invasion, bloodless but lucrative, taught Europe that England under its new dynasty had strength to command fear and respect.

Maximilian, however, was indignant; he complained that he was about to raise forces if he had been given the time, and he never forgave Henry for abandoning the campaign. He could rely on sympathy for his grievance in Flanders from the dowager Duchess, Margaret of Burgundy, his former wife's stepmother, indefatigable champion of the white rose. Her court was a haven for conspirators, a sounding board for rumours hostile to Henry Tudor. She had given active support to the rebellion organised five years before on behalf of the pretender Lambert Simnel, and now she had a fresh scheme in mind in which she hoped to interest Maximilian. Having failed with Simnel she was ready to try again with Perkin Warbeck.

This young man claimed to be Richard Duke of York, the younger of the "Princes in the Tower." It was an easier part to sustain than that chosen by his predecessor; even the most credulous lost faith in Simnel impersonating the Earl of Warwick when the true Earl was brought from the Tower and exhibited in public. Warbeck ran no such risk; the true Duke of York could not be produced in the flesh, no one knew where he was, whether indeed he were alive or dead. King Henry was at the same disadvantage as King Richard. The fate of the boys was a mystery, he could not lay the ghost by indicating the grave.

Perkin Warbeck was born in Flanders at Tournay, where his father owned boats on the Schelde. He himself took service with traders, both on the river and at sea, and in the course of his travels he became proficient in many languages. He was peculiarly gifted, learnt to speak English without a trace of a foreign accent. In the autumn of 1491 he was employed by a Breton merchant trading to Ireland with a cargo of silks and similar wares, and when the ship put in at Cork he dressed up in some of the finery to go on shore. The Irish were greatly impressed by the figure that he cut, his good looks, the air of distinction with which he bore himself. With Lambert Simnel fresh in their minds they insisted that he was the Earl of Warwick, the true Earl at last, no impostor.

Warbeck made haste to deny it; he knew what happened to Simnel, how easily he was exposed. The crowds on the waterfront at Cork were undeterred. They were sure that the distinguished stranger was a prince of the white rose; if not the Earl of Warwick, some other even more exalted. The rumour spread, fanned by English exiles who seized the opportunity with avidity, that this was Richard Duke of York saved from death by a miracle. Perkin Warbeck no longer disclaimed the honour.

The rulers of Ireland were in a quandary. Most of them had been involved in the late rebellion, had been pardoned by King Henry and renewed their oath of allegiance in return for reinstatement in office. They incurred grave risk by repeating the offence; they knew that they would not escape so lightly again if they failed. On the other hand, they were unable and unwilling to resist the pressure of popular opinion enthusiastic in the pretender's cause. Warbeck was accorded Royal entertainment like Simnel before him, and even Kildare, the Lord Deputy, encouraged him with hope of support; but no one was in a hurry to translate promises into action, there were even signs as the months went by that the Irish were tiring of their guest.

His fortune was revived by the outbreak of war between England and France. A message came from Charles VIII inviting him to the French court, and he accepted with delight, flattered by the prospect of living on familiar terms with a King. He did not enjoy the experience for long; King Charles and King Henry made peace, and the pretender to the English throne was no longer welcome on French soil. He moved on quickly to find safer refuge in Flanders as the guest of the dowager Duchess.

She had little knowledge of her nephew, Richard Duke of York. She was already in Burgundy married to the Duke when he was born; her only chance of seeing him was on a visit paid to England when he was eight years old. It is possible that she persuaded herself that she recognised the grown man of twenty, who came now to greet her as his aunt; if she had doubts she did not reveal them, it suited the cause too well that her nephew should rise from the dead. The story is that while Perkin Warbeck was at her court she took him in hand to educate him, to tell him as much as she knew about the boy whose identity he claimed, and to inculcate manners appropriate to a prince of Royal blood. It was a task similar to that undertaken by her sister-in-law for Lambert Simnel.

The appearance of the new pretender poisoned the fruits of King Henry's victory in the war with France, marred the image which he was building up of a dynasty securely established, a prosperous and contented realm. As long as the nuisance was confined to Ireland he had means at his disposal to deal with it; but the threat became formidable when Warbeck could defy him from Flanders, safely outside his jurisdiction, seeking and obtaining recognition from the rulers of sovereign states. He knew that it was useless to expostulate with the dowager Duchess; but he sent an embassy to Maximilian to beg him to use his influence with her to get rid of her guest. Maximilian was in no mood to oblige; he replied that authority in Flanders rested with his son Philip, who was not yet of age, and that in any case the Duchess had the right to entertain whom she would on her own lands. Henry tried to apply pressure by cutting off commercial intercourse with Flanders; but the Flemish market was of vital importance to English graziers, and the embargo served less to impress Maximilian—who cared little for the Flemings—than to frustrate Henry's own policy of fostering English trade.

The maintenance of his dynasty on the throne, however, took precedence even over the interests of the merchants and producers. It was the prerequisite on which all his plans depended, and his vulnerability, the weakness of his own title, made him the more resentful of Warbeck's pretensions. He was anxious that his family should be accepted on equal terms by other crowned heads, and was trying to arrange the betrothal of his son, Prince Arthur, to the youngest daughter of the King of Spain. Many difficulties hindered the negotiations, they were aggravated to exasperation by an impostor attacking the credit of the Tudors.

Spain was a newcomer to the comity of Europe, having just emerged from centuries of disunity, during which not only was the country split between Christians and Moors, but the Christians themselves were an agglomeration of quarrelling states. Two of these, Aragon and Castile, grew in time to dominate the rest, and when Ferdinand II became King of Aragon and his wife Isabella inherited the throne of Castile they ruled the combined kingdoms between them. Spain began to take shape as a nation, and Ferdinand applied himself to the expulsion of the Moors who, in spite of territorial losses in the past, still held most of the southwest, the emirate of Granada. His preoccupation left him little attention to spare for events elsewhere, and few Spanish troops responded to the appeal for the defence of Brittany; but King Henry set store by the alliance, and he ordered a thanksgiving service in St. Paul's Cathedral when news arrived in January 1492 of Ferdinand's capture of Granada, the end of the power and civilisation of the Moors in Europe.

Another event occurred shortly afterwards which was destined to exalt Spain among the nations. A Genoese seaman, Christopher Columbus, managed to interest Queen Isabella in his plans for a voyage of discovery across the western ocean. She persuaded King Ferdinand to equip a fleet of three ships for the purpose, and Columbus sailed with them into the sunset. When at last he returned he brought news of unknown lands; he described how he went ashore and planted the Spanish flag in the soil, and he had presents for the King and Queen, gold, parrots, captive natives. In these first landings he touched points on the coast of Cuba and San Domingo; but in the course of later voyages he visited other Caribbean islands and the South American mainland. All this territory he claimed for the Spanish Crown, and Pope Alexander VI —a Spaniard himself, the celebrated father of Cesare and Lucrezia Borgia—issued a bull giving Spain sole dominion in the Western Hemisphere.

It was a prize grudged by the English, especially by the merchants of Bristol, who had long been attracted by fables of Hy Brasil, the golden island in the west, and sent ships in quest of it year after year. In spite of the leadership of John Cabot, a Genoese like Columbus and no less adventurous a seaman, who had settled in England, they had no success. There was an occasion early in 1490 when King Henry might even have enlisted Columbus in his service. King Ferdinand was still engrossed in war with the Moors, and no other nation on the continent of Europe showed interest in the proposed voyage. Columbus sent his brother Bartholomew to seek a patron in England. King Henry, however, was still insecure on his throne, had not yet built up the funds that he needed to restore the prosperity of the country. He was unwilling to risk money on distant adventure. Bartholomew Columbus left his court disappointed, England lost the opportunity to discover America.

In later years when he saw what wealth accrued to Spain he regretted his lack of boldness, and he sent Cabot to follow the example set by Columbus; but Cabot was mainly interested in trade with Japan, in the discovery of a northwest passage that would shorten distance. He sailed therefore in a northerly direction, finding icebound seas, frozen cliffs. Still he believed that this was the coast of Asia, and as the climate improved he landed on Cape Breton Island, hoisted the English flag and took possession of the country in the name of King Henry VII. On his return to England his account of his voyage encouraged great hopes; King Henry himself was persuaded that a new trading route could be opened for the spices and silks of the East. He advanced money to Cabot for a second expedition; but again the course was set to the north, the ships were carried by wind and current to Greenland, then to Baffin Land, and although they extricated themselves from the ice and struck south, still looking vainly for Japan, their provisions gave out and they had to turn and go home. Cabot died soon afterwards a disappointed man, and King Henry lost interest in western exploration, which had gold for the Spaniards, only icebergs for himself.

Cabot's voyages have carried the story on too far. It is necessary to go back to Perkin Warbeck waiting for his opportunity to invade England, while he enjoyed the hospitality and tuition of the dowager Duchess in Flanders. He waited two-and-a-half years. In spite of a bold bearing he was of timid nature, reluctant to exchange the comfort and safety of Duchess Margaret's court for dangerous adventures across the sea. Meanwhile his friends were busy in England collecting and organising support. An invasion that relied only on foreign allies had little chance of success; they were anxious to give it an English complexion, to ensure that it would enjoy active sympathy from the remnant of the party of the white rose.

King Henry was aware of their activities, but he was without detailed information to enable him to arrest and convict them. His uneasiness was aggravated when suspicion fell even on Sir William Stanley, his stepfather's brother. It was Sir William whose belated intervention at the battle of Bosworth saved Henry from King Richard's onslaught; he was rewarded after the victory with the office of lord chamberlain. The conduct of the Stanleys during the reign of Richard III was not of a sort to inspire confidence in their loyalty; it was too evident that they waited to commit themselves till they were sure of choosing the winning side. The elder brother, promoted Earl of Derby, was unlikely to deviate again, being married to Henry's own mother who had great influence on him, but Sir William had no such motive to deter him if he was dissatisfied with his reward, or believed that public opinion was turning against Henry Tudor in favour of the resuscitated Richard Duke of York. He was a man of great wealth, who could afford to insure himself by generous subscription to the funds of the conspirators.

Suspicion became certainty when King Henry's spies in Flanders succeeded in bribing one of the English exiles, Sir Robert Clifford, to betray his accomplices. Clifford was among the most vehement of those who professed to recognise Perkin Warbeck as the son of Edward IV; but on receipt of £500 and a free pardon he provided evidence that exposed his friends in England to conviction and death. Stanley did not escape, he was tried before the court of King's Bench and found guilty. King Henry delayed the execution for six weeks, but neither his mother nor anyone else interceded on Stanley's behalf. He was beheaded on Tower Hill, the only member of the King's council to suffer disgrace in the course of the reign.

His brother, Lord Derby, retired to his seat in Lancashire, Lathom Hall, taking his wife, King Henry's mother, with him. If he feared for his prospects he was quickly reassured. King Henry and Queen Elizabeth came to pay him a visit of state; elaborate preparations were made to receive them, and they stayed there for more than a month enjoying his hospitality. It was important to make sure that treason among the Stanleys was confined to Sir William, but other motives for the visit could be combined. Most of those who knew King Henry describe him as a merciful man; it was in his character to do his best to comfort his mother and stepfather.

The execution of the leaders of the plot was a grave blow to Perkin Warbeck's plans, depriving him not only of support on which he relied in England but also of much goodwill among foreign princes who began to lose faith in his cause. Any sympathy that he retained he owed mainly to the series of victories won by the King of France, Charles VIII, in his invasion of Italy, which aroused such alarm in Europe that Pope and secular rulers combined in a "Holy League" to check French ambitions. King Henry having made peace with the French and accepted a pension from them was regarded as their ally, and anything that could annoy him deserved the League's encouragement. Perkin Warbeck's managers decided to take advantage of this favourable state of opinion, to invade England without further delay.

The expedition sailed at the end of June 1495, made for the coast of Kent and anchored off Deal. The men of Kent bore a reputation for turbulence. Less than fifty years before this, under the leadership of Jack Cade, they had risen against the government of Henry VI, stormed and entered London. They fought however for the redress of grievances, men of sense and substance, who deplored a weak King's inability to maintain order. A new King sat on the throne now, strong enough to impose respect for the law, and they throve under his firm and capable administration. They were in no mood to welcome an impostor arriving to disturb the peace. When Warbeck's men landed from the ships to proclaim him they were greeted with incredulous jeers, bidding them take him back to his father's boat-yard at Tournay. The Mayor of Sandwich armed the townsmen, the farmers grasped pitchforks and scythes, and by the time that soldiers came to reinforce them the battle was over. A few of the rebels escaped to the ships, the rest were taken prisoner; most of them, foreign and English alike, were hanged.

Warbeck saved his skin, watching the battle from the ship's deck. When he saw his followers repelled he gave orders to hoist sail and put back to sea. Abandoning the attempt to invade England he sailed away down the Channel and crossed to Ireland.

His reception there was less cordial than on the earlier occasion. There were many changes in the government, the chief offices were held by men chosen and appointed by King Henry, loyal to his interest. Kildare himself, the former Lord Deputy, was deposed, summoned to London to answer charges of violence, treason and sacrilege.

Kildare was head of the Fitzgeralds, the most powerful family in Ireland. He was a man of great physical strength, headstrong and hot-tempered, but quickly appeased by friendly words and warmhearted. When he appeared for trial before King Henry his most vehement accuser was the Bishop of Meath, whom he had chased with drawn sword into a church and dragged by main force from the altar. He did not deny the incident, but pleaded that he had forgotten it, and he sought diversion by telling a racy story creditable neither to the Bishop's morals nor his dignity. The King was amused, could not help laughing, and Kildare took advantage of his good humour to declare that the Bishop had learning, he himself had none and was unable to argue against such an opponent on a point of law. The King in reply told him to choose and instruct a learned advocate, and Kildare stared round at everyone in the room. Then he turned to King Henry:

"Well, I can see no better man than you, and by St. Bride I'll choose none other."

The King laughed: "A wiser man might have chosen worse."

The Bishop tried to recover lost ground by a fierce attack on Kildare, with a long list of his misdoings, leading to the conclusion that "all Ireland cannot rule him." King Henry nodded:

"If so, he's the man to rule all Ireland."

Kildare's attainder was annulled, his titles and possessions were restored, and in the following year he went back to Ireland to resume office as Lord Deputy. King Henry never had occasion to regret his indulgence, the tact and good humour with which he treated his prisoner. The effect was to make him his friend; the two men took a liking to each other, the strongest bond to ensure Kildare's loyalty. For the rest of his life he used his powerful influence in Ireland steadfastly in support of the Tudor King.

Although he was still in London when Perkin Warbeck came to Ireland reports of the favour shown him by King Henry, and a wholesome fear of alienating it, deterred any of his faction from joining the rebel cause. Warbeck led his fleet to Waterford, and when the town refused to surrender he laid siege; but the citizens resisted with spirit, and the government sent troops to reinforce them, so that after a week or so he gave up the attempt and sailed away, pursued in his turn by ships from Waterford till he found safety at Cork. Even here disappointment awaited him; the greeting had none of the ardour expressed when his adventure began four years before. He lost hope of Irish support, was unwilling to stay longer; but he was ashamed to go back to Flanders to tell the Duchess Margaret and Maximilian how little he had accomplished with the fleet equipped for him at such expense.

A last resort was left him; he sailed for Scotland. The Scots had no reason to be attached to the white rose, to a claimant who held himself out as heir to the House of York. When they intervened in the Wars of the Roses it was on behalf of the House of Lancaster. Their traditional enmity, however, disposed them to favour anyone who made trouble for their southern neighbour. If Perkin Warbeck gained the throne of England his seat would be so insecure that he would have to rely on Scottish support to retain it.

Misfortune pursued the fleet on its voyage to Scotland. Many ships were wrecked in a storm, others were scattered and sailed home. Warbeck himself was cast ashore when his ship sank on a reef off the Irish coast; he crossed the mountains in disguise, found his way to a small port, where a Scottish ship picked him up.

He was received with great honour in Scotland. King James IV had a chivalrous temperament susceptible to a pitiful story, the wrongs inflicted on a helpless child; but even if he was not fully convinced the pretender's claims were too useful to Scottish policy to be rejected. He provided the "Duke of York" with sumptuous clothes, paid him a generous allowance, even found him a bride from the best blood in Scotland, Lady Catherine Gordon, a kinswoman of his own and daughter of the Earl of Huntley, his chancellor. She accepted so handsome, lively and intelligent a suitor with no reluctance. As long as the marriage endured she remained devoted to him.

Nearly a year went by before preparations were complete for the invasion of England. King James extracted a promise from his protégé that when he sat on the English throne he would restore the town of Berwick-on-Tweed, recaptured from the Scots in Edward IV's reign by Richard, then Duke of Gloucester. News of this compact reaching England provoked indignation, deprived

Warbeck of any chance of the support that he expected from former adherents of the white rose. The Scottish army crossed the border, but no one heeded its appeal to the people to rise against the "usurper," Henry Tudor. The Scots consoled themselves by plundering and devastating. Their behaviour was so outrageous that Warbeck himself expostulated with King James, fearing the damage done to his cause. King James took offence; he was in no mood to be rebuked by Warbeck, who had misled him with exuberant forecasts of English rebels flocking to his standard. Within three days the invaders were back in Scotland.

Even so, King James could not bring himself to deny hospitality to his guest. Many tempting offers were made for his surrender, not only by King Henry but also by France and Spain, where the pretender could be used as a lever to apply pressure on England. The Scots refused to give him up. Nevertheless he had outstayed his welcome, and it was a relief to King James when an honourable opportunity arose to get rid of him. A revolt had broken out in Cornwall provoked by taxation, and although King Henry put it down with little bloodshed, sparing everyone but the leaders, the discontent remained unallayed. The plan was made therefore that Warbeck should land in Cornwall to incite the rebels to fresh effort, while the Scots distracted King Henry by invasion in the north.

Warbeck and his Scottish wife, with the child already born to them, sailed from Ayr in a ship provided by King James; but instead of following the course planned he changed his mind, decided to try his luck again in Ireland. It was a disastrous decision; Kildare was back as Lord Deputy, eager to prove his loyalty. When he heard that the pretender had landed he spared no effort to catch him, and his influence carried such weight among the Irish that Warbeck was safe nowhere; even Cork turned against him, and he barely escaped with his life to Kinsale. A message reached him there from Cornwall, urging him to come and lead the rebels, as had been promised. Reverting belatedly to the original plan, he embarked with his party in four fishing boats and crossed the sea to Whitesand Bay near Lands End.

The timing however was upset by the excursion to Ireland. In the north of England the Scots had already made their agreed raid and been repulsed. King Henry could give his attention undistracted to the rising in Cornwall, where some three thousand men rallied to Warbeck when he raised his standard at Bodmin.

They were not an impressive force, lacking armour or suitable weapons, and when they tried to storm Exeter they were beaten off with heavy losses. Abandoning the siege, they went on towards Taunton.

Most of the west country was aroused by now to resist them. Local magnates mustered their retainers, and King Henry himself was approaching with a considerable army. Warbeck's nerve failed. He was an odd mixture of timidity and exuberant impulse, bolder at the beginning of an adventure than at the end. With three companions he stole away under cover of night, fled to sanctuary at Beaulieu Abbey. The Cornish rebels, deserted by their leader, lost heart and submitted to the King.

Warbeck was persuaded to leave sanctuary and give himself up on the promise that his life would be spared. He was brought to King Henry at Exeter, where he made full confession of his imposture, describing his early life in detail, his travels in the service of various merchants till the fateful occasion at Cork when he was induced to impersonate the second son of King Edward IV. A letter survives which he wrote to his mother at Tournay to tell her what had happened to him and asked her to send him money, *afin que mes gardes me soient plus amiables en leur donnant quelque chose.*

His wife and child were at St. Michael's Mount, waiting to hear the issue of the campaign. King Henry sent horses and an escort to bring them to Exeter, and on her arrival he treated her with great kindness, all the honour due to her rank in Scotland. Warbeck was made to repeat his confession in her presence; but after that they were kept apart, not allowed to sleep together. She accompanied the King on his return to London and was given a place as lady-in-waiting in the Queen's household, where—not to recall her husband's claims, but because the name matched her beauty—she was known as the "white rose." After Warbeck's death she twice married again, lived on till she was over sixty.

Precautions were needed to convey the pretender out of the west country to protect him from his own followers, who bitterly resented not only his flight to Beaulieu but also the imposture which he admitted. He had no escape from publicity, however, on reaching London, where he was paraded on horseback through the streets, exposed to the jeers and curses of the mob. An Italian observer, an envoy from the Duke of Milan, records that he bore himself bravely.

Afterwards he was given a lodging in the Royal palace at Westminster, even allowed a measure of liberty. There was much comment on the leniency with which he was treated; the same Italian wrote to the Duke of Milan that "the King here is most clement and pardons everybody, even the common people of Cornwall." Few suffered for the rebellion with their lives. King Henry had no desire for revenge; but he took care that the offenders paid dearly from their purses, that the treasury throve on the fines.

Safe in his lodging at Westminster, Perkin Warbeck had reason to be thankful for his luck; but feckless impulse rooted in daydream was again his undoing. On a fine night in June, about six months after his capture, he eluded his sleeping guards and crept out of the window. There was a great hue and cry when he was missed, armed parties searched the country around. He had no plan, no accomplices, no hope of escape; he fled for refuge to the Carthusian monastery at Sheen, where he begged the prior to intercede for him. King Henry kept the promise given at Beaulieu, the prisoner's life was spared; but the escapade deprived him of his comfortable quarters in the palace, his recreation in the park. He was taken to the Tower, exposed on a scaffold of barrels to public mockery, then confined in a windowless cell, and nothing more was heard of him for two years.

CHAPTER 9

Ferdinand of Spain denied that he ever was taken in by the "Flemish boy," ever regarded the affair as anything but a jest. All the same, with Perkin Warbeck out of the way, negotiations proceeded more smoothly for Prince Arthur's marriage to the Spanish princess. The Tudor dynasty seemed to be established; even Duchess Margaret sent apologies for her support of the pretender, and King James of Scotland was ready for reconciliation, likely to accept the offer of King Henry's elder daughter as bride.

For a time, in April 1498, there was danger of a renewal of the old quarrel with France over Brittany. King Charles VIII, having survived all the alarums and excursions of his invasion of Italy, was killed in his country house at Amboise by stumbling and striking his head against the lintel of a door. His widow, Anne of Brittany, withdrew to her own duchy, claiming that the union with France lasted only while her husband was alive, that his death restored Breton independence. She was twenty-one years old, left childless, eminently nubile; the courts of Europe buzzed with the expectations of diplomatic matchmakers. Their eagerness bred second thoughts in her, reminding her of the misery inflicted on her people by foreign invasion, marauding soldiers in her father's lifetime. The new King of France on the other hand, Louis XII, was the former Duke of Orleans, her father's old friend and her own. He was still in the prime of life, debonair, gay and adventurous, a poet's son with a cultivated mind and a kind heart that earned him later in his reign the name of Louis the Good. His wife Jeanne was the daughter of Louis XI, who forced him when he was little more than a boy to marry her on pain of death. She was, as her father himself told her, deplorably ill-favoured, short, swarthy and bent, and although she deserved pity for her disadvantages, and respect for the patience with which she bore them, her husband neither was nor ever had been in love with her. Even at the time of his marriage his heart was set on Anne.

It needed little persuasion therefore for Anne to agree to his proposal. A French title bestowed on the Pope's son, Cesare Borgia, assured a sympathetic hearing at the Vatican. The marriage of Louis and Jeanne was annulled, and for the second time Anne became Queen of France. The union of France and Brittany was resumed.

Although it suited English policy to encourage Breton independence Henry was unwilling to quarrel with the new King of France, who paid without demur the pension agreed by his predecessor. In any case all his attention was demanded in the following year by renewed troubles at home. The hopes aroused by the capture of Perkin Warbeck were found to be premature; still another pretender arose to impersonate the imprisoned Earl of Warwick. The plot was quickly suppressed and the impostor hanged; but Henry's confidence was shaken, there were accomplices of higher standing who escaped undetected. Some suspicion fell on the Earl of Suffolk, nephew of Richard III and brother of the Earl of Lincoln killed fighting for Lambert Simnel. Hitherto, unlike his brother, he had remained loyal to King Henry whose favour he enjoyed. He was involved neither in Simnel's nor in Warbeck's rebellion; but as an indubitable heir of the House of York he could be a dangerous rival if he chose.

He was an arrogant young man with an awkward temper, and it happened this summer that he killed an opponent in a drunken brawl. When he was indicted for the offence he expressed resentment, insisting that Royal blood put him above the law, and at last he left the country and fled to Flanders. King Henry suspecting that wounded dignity was not the only reason for his flight, and fearing the outcome if he stayed long at the court of the Duchess Margaret, sent a conciliatory message inviting him home. Suffolk's ruffled feelings were soothed, he was persuaded to return and restored to honour; but he was no longer trusted, a watchful eye was kept on him.

Many who saw King Henry at this time reported a great change in his appearance; he began suddenly to look like an old man. It was never his habit to divulge his thoughts; but his anxiety was evident, and rumour was busy with stories of secret plots. It was said that a priest claiming supernatural power foretold an attempt on his life. Henry was not free from superstition; but he was too shrewd to believe that the man depended on clairvoyance alone to support his prediction. He increased his vigilance, and when the storm broke he was ready, acting so promptly, revealing so little that it is uncertain to this day how gravely the throne was endangered.

The victims who suffered were Perkin Warbeck and the Earl of Warwick. They occupied cells in the Tower one above the other, and they were accused of holding treasonable conversation through a hole in the floor. It is likely enough that Warbeck indulged in dreams of restored freedom and greatness, even that he found a credulous listener in Warwick, simple-minded and ignorant, whose whole life since childhood had been spent hidden behind prison walls; but they were without means to translate words into action, more formidable conspirators were needed to afford cause for the alarm felt by the King's government.

Warbeck was hanged, Warwick beheaded. There were grounds for the King's impatience with the former, who had twice been shown mercy already. For Warwick's death no such excuse can be found. His only offence was to be Edward IV's nephew, a son of the Duke of Clarence. He was punished for the impostors who assumed his name. Their boldness, the seemingly endless succession broke even King Henry's nerve. Panic drove him to kill an unoffending simpleton.

He had reason to fear too that as long as Warwick was alive the marriage would be thwarted which he desired for Prince Arthur with the Spanish King's daughter, Catherine. Her father was unwilling to send her to a country where a rival claimant survived to contest the throne. She herself declared long afterwards that the unhappiness which closed her married life was divine punishment for the crime on which it was founded.

Now at last the difficulties impeding the marriage were removed, the protracted negotiations concluded. King Henry even dropped his objection to the number of Spanish ladies-in-waiting whom she would bring with her; he gave way on condition that their faces and figures were agreeable to his taste. In October 1501 after a stormy voyage she landed at Plymouth, and was married to Prince Arthur on the 14th of November in London. Both were fifteen years old, she the elder by a few months.

After the wedding the couple went to live at Ludlow Castle. King Henry's purpose followed the example set by Edward IV, to unify Welsh administration under the control of the Prince of Wales. His own son was older than King Edward's when he made the experiment. At Ludlow, Prince Arthur was able to take part in practical affairs, begin his apprenticeship to government. Catherine attended by her bevy of approved beauties settled down to married life in Wales.

For nearly five months they lived together as man and wife. In years to come great issues hung on the question whether the marriage was consummated; but even at the time King Ferdinand insisted on information, and the evidence sent to Spain was explicit enough to satisfy him that his son-in-law was capable of begetting an heir. Catherine, however, was not pregnant when the plague came to Ludlow in the spring. She escaped infection herself; but Arthur caught it and died, leaving her at sixteen a childless widow.

King Henry was at Greenwich, unaware even that his son was ill. A friar, his confessor, who was deputed to break the news, asked everyone else to leave the room, and the expression of his face and the text that he quoted from the Bible were a warning of pain in store. Even so, the shock was too sudden, the King was overcome; he asked for the Queen to be fetched so that they might share their sorrow between them. When she arrived she kept firm control of herself, reminded him that he still had a son left, Prince Henry, to succeed him, and two daughters as well, and that he and she were young enough if they wished to add more to the family. Her voice comforted him, he was calm enough to thank her when she left.

On her return to her room it was seen how much the effort had cost her. She could restrain her own feelings no longer, was in such despair that her women became alarmed and sent to the King, begging him to come to her. The parts were exchanged as he soothed her, reminded her of the wise counsel that she herself had given him. The story from a contemporary source affords one of the few glimpses available of their private life.

When she spoke of bearing further children he took her at her word. She became pregnant, the birth was due early in the following year. She was in the state rooms at the Tower when her pangs came on prematurely; but she was safely delivered of a daughter and seemed to make a good recovery. Then a week later symptoms of fever appeared; messengers galloped through the night to fetch her doctor from Gravesend, but before he arrived she was dead. She died on her own birthday, thirty-eight years old, and her child survived her only a few days.

The King sent two of his officers to make what arrangements were needed, then he went away by himself, would have no one come near him in his sorrow.

Death was busy around him at this time. Less than two years earlier he lost his trusted minister, Cardinal Morton, the friend of his youth who conspired on his behalf against King Richard, and to whose timely warning he owed his escape from Brittany. Although Morton played a leading part in the fiscal policy of the reign he was no advocate of rapacious extortion, he even restrained the King himself from measures provocative of hardship. Sir Thomas More, educated in his household, spoke highly of his wisdom, principles and humanity. His death compelled the King to rely on cruder instruments, the lawyers Empson and Dudley, who were less concerned to fill the treasury than their own pockets.

If Morton had lived his knowledge would have saved King Henry from foisting a clumsy myth on the world. The circumstances in which it arose are as follows. The Earl of Suffolk, pardoned for his flight to Flanders and allowed to resume his place at court, chafed nevertheless under the suspicion which his conduct earned him. He was a man of violent moods full of his own importance, and since the execution of the Earl of Warwick he regarded himself as head of the House of York, a worthier occupant of the throne than any Tudor. For a second time he fled abroad, crossing to Calais, whence, with the connivance of Sir James Tyrell, governor of the outlying fortress of Guisnes, he escaped into Austria to the court of Maximilian. Any English rebel could count on a cordial welcome there.

He himself was out of King Henry's reach, but strict inquiry was made on English territory to find his accomplices. Tyrell's part came to light, and when he refused to give himself up the army from Calais laid siege to Guisnes. After a stubborn defence he surrendered and was taken prisoner. He had been a prominent supporter of the House of York in the old days, knighted after the battle of Tewkesbury, promoted by Richard III to be his master of horse; but after Bosworth he submitted to Henry VII, served him with distinction, and there had been no reason to doubt his loyalty.

Ample evidence was available now to convict him of complicity in Suffolk's escapade; but King Henry's advisers were unwilling to leave it at that, they saw their opportunity to use him to better purpose, to put a story into his mouth that would solve the mystery of the "Princes in the Tower," cut short at last the succession of troublesome impostors. His earlier career, the favour that he enjoyed under Richard III lent credibility when it was announced that he had signed a confession describing how he murdered the boys on King Richard's orders. Although the details were made known no document was shown to confirm them, nor was anything heard from Tyrell himself. He was hastily beheaded in prison.

The story of the murder of the two boys and of Tyrell's part in it has attained literary immortality through Shakespeare's genius; but scholars from Horace Walpole onwards have drawn attention to the inaccuracies and improbabilities with which it is riddled, many so egregious that one can only be amazed at the shortness of public memory, or the faith inspired by an official pronouncement, which enabled them to pass muster barely twenty years after the event. King Henry himself was in exile in Brittany at the relevant date, he knew too little to be able to correct the blunders in the compilation; but Morton who lived at King Richard's court, and was on familiar terms with those who frequented it, would have been aware of them at once. If a fictitious solution of the mystery had to be put out he would have taken care to make it more convincing.

The Queen's death clouded an event that took place at this time and which was in fact as great a triumph for English policy as Prince Arthur's marriage to Catherine of Spain. Peace was at last concluded with Scotland when James IV agreed to take the elder of King Henry's daughters, Princess Margaret, as his wife. Her mother lived to attend the ceremony of betrothal in the palace at Sheen (renamed Richmond shortly before, to commemorate the title borne by the King and his father); but she died in the following month, and the King alone saw his daughter off on her journey to Scotland to her wedding at Holyrood. He rode with her as far as Collyweston, his mother's house in Northamptonshire, there they parted.

Margaret was fourteen, her husband thirty. He had been married in all but name to a Scotswoman, Lady Margaret Drummond, to whom he was devoted, and who died mysteriously poisoned by his enemies. These were unpropitious circumstances for a second marriage with a bride so much younger than himself, and Margaret Tudor was not easy to live with; she was full of complaints of her accommodation, her entertainment, her company. It was a relief to King James when she turned her discontent on the Earl of Surrey, for whom her father was responsible, having appointed him to take charge of her and act on his behalf at her wedding.

Thomas Howard, Earl of Surrey, was among those who fought for Richard III at the battle of Bosworth and suffered disgrace for it, but rose later into favour with Henry VII. At the time of the rebellion of Lambert Simnel he was imprisoned on suspicion in the Tower, and when a false report came of the King's defeat the governor offered him the keys to let him escape. He refused them, declaring that he would accept freedom from no one but the King himself. Henry rewarded him by restoring his title and estates and gave him command of his forces in the north, where he carried on vigorous war against the Scots. When he met King James at the celebrations at Holyrood the two old adversaries found much in common, former campaigns to refight, and Margaret left out of the conversation was jealous.

King James learnt in time to bear with the tantrums of his English wife. Two sons were born who died in infancy; but a third survived with important consequences for England and Scotland alike, when Margaret's great-grandson inherited the crown of both kingdoms. Henry's council warned him when he was negotiating the Scottish marriage that it could have this effect, that a King of Scotland might sit on the English throne. He replied with a foresight confirmed by events that the great would draw the less, that there was less danger for England in union with Scotland than in bygone dreams of the conquest of France.

He had reason to be satisfied with the success of his Scottish policy; but Prince Arthur's death upset his plans for closer relations with Spain. The Spanish princess was left in England a widow, and her father demanded that she be sent back to him, demanded too the repayment of her dowry, a portion of which King Henry had already received. While the two Kings haggled over this her mother, Queen Isabella, proposed that she marry the new heir apparent, Arthur's younger brother, Henry. Catherine did not take kindly to the idea of marrying a boy nearly six years younger than herself, but she wrote to her father agreeing to do as he wished. She was not unhappy in England, lived on affectionate terms with her mother-in-law, with her father-in-law too as is shown by a report sent to Queen Isabella describing a hunting expedition on which he took her in Windsor Park, accompanied by his younger daughter, seven-year-old Princess Mary.

Meanwhile application was made to the Vatican to enable her to marry her brother-in-law, Prince Henry; but the closeness of the relationship caused misgivings even to Pope Alexander, and he died before he could comply. Her position was made more difficult by her mother-in-law's death, and the demand was renewed for her return to Spain, where the rumour provoked alarm that King Henry himself intended to marry her. It is possible that he entertained the idea, as did Richard III of marrying his niece, Elizabeth of York. The difference in age was little greater than that between Richard II and his child wife, Isabel de Valois, King Henry's great-aunt. Royal marriages were an instrument of diplomacy adjusting conflicting interests without recourse to war. Personal feelings were irrelevant to the issues at stake. The sorrow felt by King Henry at the loss of his wife was no reason in his eyes to neglect political advantages open to him as a widower.

In view of the opposition expressed by the Spanish King and Queen nothing more was heard of the proposal, and soon after-wards the new Pope, Julius II, gave consent to Catherine's betrothal to Henry Prince of Wales. He announced his decision at once in a letter to Queen Isabella of Spain to comfort her as she was dangerously ill; but she was uneasy in her mind as if she had a presage of difficulties to come, and she asked for a copy of the formal bull of dispensation. Before it arrived she was dead.

Her death was a threat to the recent unification of Spain, which depended on the marriage of the crowns of Aragon and Castile. Her husband claimed that her will appointed him governor of her kingdom, but the Castilian nobles were unwilling to recognise any authority other than that of her heir. This (as her only son predeceased her) was her eldest daughter, Joanna, who was married to Maximilian's son and heir, the Archduke Philip.

King Ferdinand's value was diminished as an ally. King Henry made no haste to take advantage of the Papal dispensation; he even turned to France to look for a wife for his son. It was no longer England but Spain that needed to strengthen its international standing. Catherine's plight was humiliating as she waited to know whether she was to remain a widow or become a bride, and her father made it worse by leaving her without money. It was his revenge to punish King Henry for his procrastination. She suffered no great want in consequence, King Henry supplied her needs; but he let her know his displeasure, the unwillingness with which he bore the burden imposed on him.

Harshness was alien to his habit, but his irritation was aggravated by her management of her household, the injudicious partiality shown for her confessor, a Spanish friar. Even her father's ambassador wrote home to complain of her infatuation, declaring that no one could stop her from selling a piece of plate every day to satisfy the follies of this charlatan, and he proposed that the Franciscan order in Spain should send a man of years and discretion to replace so "young, light, haughty and scandalous" a favourite. His opposition made her more stubborn than ever, more convinced of the friar's sanctity. King Henry himself remonstrated, succeeded only in provoking recriminations and tears.

His own matrimonial prospects occupied him rather than his son's. He was in the middle forties, still able to beget a new family. Of the three surviving children of his first marriage two were girls. It worried him that the male line of the dynasty hung on a single life. If Prince Henry shared the fate of his brother Arthur there would be no Tudor left to succeed.

So eligible a widower had abundant choice when it became known that he wished to marry again. Spanish influence was exerted on behalf of King Ferdinand's twenty-seven-year-old niece, Joanna of Naples, who lived with her mother at Valencia in Spain, and envoys travelled from England to visit her to report on her appearance and circumstances. They carried a list of questions given them by King Henry, which bear witness to his fastidious taste. Those relating to her person demanded a precision of detail that embarrassed them. Their answers were explicit enough about "the colour of her hair" and "her eyes, brows, teeth and lips," they did their best even "to mark her breasts and paps, whether they be big or small"; but when he asked if she had any "deformity or blemish in her body" they could only reply that she wore voluminous clothes, and refer him to a favourable opinion obtained from her physician.

From a portrait that survives, painted by Raphael, it is clear that little fault could be found with Joanna's beauty; but the report which the envoys brought back of her prospects, the political advantages of the match, was less encouraging. She was the daughter and heiress of the last King of Naples; but as his realm had suffered partition between France and Spain the title that she bore of Queen had no more than honorary value. A Spanish viceroy reigned in Naples, while she herself and her mother lived as pensioners of her uncle, King Ferdinand. He was fond of her, anxious to promote her interests, to marry her off to the King of England, but he had no intention of restoring as a wedding present her hereditary domains in Italy.

King Henry preferred to look elsewhere for a bride. He needed a connection powerful enough to hold a balance between France and Spain, and his thoughts turned to the House of Habsburg. Maximilian, its head, had recently been elected Holy Roman Emperor. As he was chronically short of money he was ready to forget his past quarrel with England when Henry, who had plenty to lend, asked for the hand in marriage of his daughter Margaret. She herself, however, was firmly opposed to the match. At the age of twenty-five she was already thrice married; first in infancy to Charles VIII of France, secondly (on his repudiation of the contract) to the only son of Ferdinand of Spain, who died a few months later, finally to the Duke of Savoy whom she loved dearly, but who died within three years. She was among the most gifted and spirited of the princesses of Europe. The lines are often quoted which she composed for her epitaph when she was seventeen and in great danger of shipwreck on her voyage to Spain; they may be rendered in English—

Here pretty Margaret in her grave is laid.
She married twice and yet has died a maid.

She survived the storm, reached Spain safely and was no longer a maid when she returned, but her child born there was dead. Her third marriage followed, the hardest disappointment of all because of the happiness so soon cut short that she found in it. Her misfortunes failed to break her spirit, but they left her determined not to take a fourth husband, either King Henry of England or anyone else.

He persisted, however, and an accident favoured his purpose. Her brother Philip and his wife Joanna, King Ferdinand's eldest daughter, were travelling from Flanders to Spain when gales scattered the fleet in the English Channel; the ship carrying the Royal couple lost its mainsail and was only saved from capsizing by the courage of a sailor who leapt overboard to cut away the shrouds. Philip himself was struck by a wave, hurled below deck with such force that everyone thought him killed. He sat awaiting death with Queen Joanna, who remained imperturbable, while the captain brought the crippled ship safely into harbour near Weymouth.

When news of these events reached King Henry he sent an escort to convey the Royal castaways to his court, where he received and entertained them with honour. It was a heaven-sent opportunity to discuss his proposal not only of marriage with Philip's sister but also of a political and commercial alliance with the dominions of the Habsburgs. His success in the former purpose was limited, Philip could only promise to do his best to overcome his sister's reluctance; but the political and economic discussions bore fruit in a treaty so favourable to English trade that the Flemish merchants complained bitterly of Philip's betrayal of their interests. A clause in the treaty bound both parties not to harbour rebels against the other. Among the victims was the Earl of Suffolk, still plotting in exile against King Henry. He was brought back to England under arrest, on the condition that his life would be spared. He spent the rest of the reign as a prisoner in the Tower.

While Henry and Philip conferred Queen Joanna renewed acquaintance with her sister Catherine, whom she had not seen for nearly ten years, since she herself left Spain to be married. Her behaviour deserves remark; it is among the cherished myths of history that she was insane, she has been labelled *Juana la Loca*, ("Mad Joan"). Yet the calmness with which she endured the threat of shipwreck is hardly compatible with a disordered mind, and nothing abnormal is recorded of her during this visit to England. The letters which Catherine wrote to her after her departure are full of affection and respect.

It is true that her married life with Philip was far from peaceful. His own nickname was "Philip the Handsome," and he lived up to it in a way that provoked her passionate jealousy, so that he referred to her behind her back as "the Terror." She was wilful like her sister, unwise in the violence with which she responded to his infidelity. She had the faults of a much provoked wife, but these are no evidence of madness.

The calumny had its origin in Spanish politics. On her mother's death she became Queen of Castile, and her father and her husband were rivals claiming the right to govern on her behalf. The Castilian nobles favoured neither; they resented Ferdinand's encroachment which imposed the domination of Aragon, and Philip was unpopular because he was a foreigner, a Habsburg. They insisted that they owed allegiance only to their Queen. To deter them, the report was put about that she was unfit to bear responsibility, mentally deranged. Both her father and her husband made use of it, but as they themselves were at odds each accused the other of maligning her.

Philip and Joanna left England to resume their journey to Spain. On their arrival the dynastic quarrel became fiercer; Castile was on the verge of civil war, till at Burgos the climate intervened, Philip caught typhoid fever and died. In spite of disagreement while he lived his death left Joanna overwhelmed with grief; but she was a widow whose hand in marriage might be coveted, still young and good-looking, Queen of Castile in her own right. To King Henry this was an opportunity not to be missed.

He allowed a year to pass, then proposed himself as her suitor. He had no need on this occasion to rely on an envoy's report, he retained a favourable impression from her recent visit. Her sister Catherine wrote to her as his advocate, giving him a glowing testimonial. She was anxious to promote the match, which would bring Joanna to keep her company in England.

Even King Ferdinand at first expressed approval, promising that if Queen Joanna wished to marry again it should be to no other person than the King of England; but he added a warning that their plans should be kept secret, for if she heard anything about them "she would most probably do something quite to the contrary." It is certain that she was a woman with a strong will of her own, but at this stage he implied nothing else to her detriment.

Shortly afterwards his attitude changed. He began to see the disadvantages of having Henry VII for his son-in-law. The danger of secession in Castile would be greater than ever if Joanna had the King of England as husband to support her. He was already suspicious of English encroachment on his influence, protested that even Cabot's voyages in the far north infringed the exclusive rights granted him by Papal Bull beyond the western ocean. All his work in expelling the Moors and uniting the country would be fruitless if he let Henry acquire a kingdom in Spain, in its very heart.

A discouraging note appeared in his replies about Joanna's marriage. He spoke of a *dolencia* (a malady) with which she was afflicted. The Spanish word is used of bodily complaints; Henry's first concern was to find out whether the trouble was of a sort to prevent her from bearing children, as the reinforcement of the dynasty was his chief purpose. Having assured himself that there was no such danger, he pressed his suit undeterred. He knew from his own observation that she was intelligent and active, no invalid.

Ferdinand could no longer avoid plain statement. He declared that his daughter was mad, published a story that she refused to be parted from her husband's dead body, carried it about with her wherever she went. No evidence was offered, no one was quoted who had seen her travelling with this unusual luggage. In any case her travels thenceforward were confined. Her father shut her up in a convent, where she suffered treatment which no reason was likely to survive, the revenge inflicted by the Church on a passionate opponent of the Inquisition.

Whether or not King Henry believed the story of the travelling corpse, he understood that he was wasting his time, that consent would never be given to the marriage. He abandoned the courtship, reverted to his former choice, Maximilian's daughter, Margaret of Savoy. She remained unwilling, however, and he made no great effort to win her. He was ageing fast, both looked and felt older than his years, and he may have doubted whether even if he found a wife to his liking he could play his own part to reinforce the line of the Tudors. A scheme in which he took more interest and which offered no less useful a prospect of alliance with the Habsburgs was the betrothal of his younger daughter Mary to Maximilian's grandson Charles, son of Philip and Joanna. It would serve as a rebuff to King Ferdinand, prepare the ground for a renewal of English influence on Castile.

Among the emissaries employed in the negotiations was a young chaplain called Thomas Wolsey, a butcher's son, whose diligence attracted favourable attention. The King rewarded him with promotion to the deanery of Lincoln, the first step in a career destined to the highest eminence in the following reign.

In December 1508 the eight-year-old Charles Habsburg was betrothed with solemn ceremony at the new Richmond to Mary

Tudor, a girl of twelve. Charles was heir to the greater part of the known world—to his grandfather's realm in Germany, his father's in Burgundy and the Netherlands, his mother's in Castile, his maternal grandfather's in Aragon and the Americas, all the gold of El Dorado. King Henry surveying the inheritance into which his daughter was marrying had reason to be satisfied with his work. He himself sat secure at last on his throne, having overcome his enemies at home with little bloodshed, established his power in Europe without fighting anything that deserved the name of war. Under his government law and order were firmly upheld, commerce throve, the treasury was full of money. Learning and the arts reborn in Italy were beginning already to find fertile soil, a hospitable welcome in England. The exiled fugitive in Brittany had become the founder of a dynasty of whose reputation and influence not even his legendary ancestor, King Arthur, need be ashamed.

He had four months more to live. A quinsy which attacked him earlier and from which he seemed to recover left a fatal weakness in his lungs; tuberculosis set in, and he died after a lingering illness on the 21st of April 1509, aged fifty-two. His mother died in the following June; she was sixty-six, she could not bear to survive him.

CHAPTER 10

Catherine found herself in a more embarrassing position than ever on her father-in-law's death, left in England under the protection of a youth of eighteen, her brother-in-law, and not knowing whether she was betrothed to him or not. The Papal dispensation was granted, there had even been a ceremony of betrothal; but as her father and father-in-law haggled over the terms the prospect of marriage receded, and the young Henry at his father's instigation even made a public declaration repudiating the contract.

Her anxiety was soon set at rest. The motive deterring Henry VII from a Spanish alliance was his hope, either by his own marriage with Queen Joanna or by his daughter's with her nephew Charles, of gaining advantage for England at King Ferdinand's expense; but as he lay dying, knowing that he would not live to carry out his plans and that his son lacked the necessary skill and experience, he advised him to marry Catherine without further delay. Many churchmen and lawyers expressed doubt of the validity of the dispensation in view of the closeness of the relationship; but the young King Henry VIII was attracted by the proposed bride, at ease with her after their long acquaintance, and he refused to listen to objections. He married her within two months of his father's death.

At eighteen he was young for his age. Everyone admired his good looks, his auburn hair, fresh complexion, muscular strength, his prowess with the bow and in the tennis court and the tiltyard. His mind too was well cultivated; he spoke French, Italian and Spanish, and was proficient in Latin, and like his father he was passionately fond of music. In character, however, he was still a boy, good-humoured, full of generous impulses, but unwilling to apply himself to the business of government, yielding without effort to the influence of anyone who relieved him of the burden. This pliability lay at the root of one of the first actions of his reign, the arrest and execution of his father's unpopular ministers, Empson and Dudley. It is true that they were guilty of embezzlement; but the outcry against them arose from dislike of taxation and would have been equally vehement if they had paid every penny extorted into the exchequer. The King yielded to their enemies who clamoured for their death. He was never bloodthirsty, even when he matured; but he had none of his father's reluctance to shed blood.

He gave Empson's house in Fleet Street to the former chaplain, Thomas Wolsey, who had served his father so diligently on embassy to the Emperor Maximilian, and whom he now promoted to his council. The secret of the influence that Wolsey attained was the care that he took to save the King trouble. While other councillors brought irksome problems for Henry's attention, recalling him to public business, Wolsey encouraged him to amuse himself, to leave the decision in his own capable hands. It was advice that suited the tastes of a young man who preferred the open air to the council chamber. So useful a servant earned rapid reward, became Bishop of Lincoln and in the same year Archbishop of York, when Cardinal Bainbridge, his predecessor, died poisoned at Rome.

An influence that carried even greater weight with Henry was that of the Queen; but Wolsey was too shrewd to treat her as a rival, he adapted himself to her will, made her his ally. The masterfulness of her character, evident in the management of her household even when she was only the widowed Princess of Wales, could assert itself now with ample scope in the security of her marriage to a King who was truly attached to her, glad to follow her guidance. She took advantage of his complaisance to promote the interests of Spain. Having got rid of the former envoy whose dislike of her ingratiating friar she neither forgot nor forgave, she offered to act herself as her father's ambassador in England. He could hardly have found a more capable and effective advocate. Far from bearing a grudge for past neglect she served him with filial devotion, so wholeheartedly that she could describe England in writing to him as "these kingdoms of your Highness." Ferdinand had reason to be pleased with so dutiful a daughter, so accommodating a son-in-law.

At first it suited Spanish policy to keep England quiescent while Ferdinand pursued his ambitions in Italy; but in 1512 his European allies fell out, he was at war with France and turned to his son-in-law to make common cause against the enemy. He kindled Henry's enthusiasm with dreams of the reconquest of the crown of France worn by Henry VI, and appealed to his piety by persuading him that his intervention was needed to save the Pope from French godlessness. The fire-eating pontiff, Julius II, a consistent devotee of the god of war, was indeed besieged by the French in Bologna.

Urged by his wife and his father-in-law, Henry responded as they intended. He collected ships and men and sent them to the Bay of Biscay with orders to land at San Sebastian to await Spanish reinforcement for the invasion of France. Guyenne, the last province of the Plantagenet domains to be lost, would be the first reconquered.

The English reached Spain, but no Spaniards came to join them. It was a wet June, the weather was atrocious, and the soldiers ill prepared for a long encampment suffered equally from drenching rain and the intervening spells of burning heat. They consoled themselves with Spanish wine, to which they were unaccustomed, and the effect on their temper and discipline was disastrous. Months went by, and still King Ferdinand delayed to send the promised help. At last in October the commanders, unable otherwise to avert a mutiny, led the men back to their ships and sailed home to England in defiance of orders.

So humiliating an outcome made the English the laughing stock of Europe, invited the taunt that they had abstained so long from war that they had forgotten how to fight. It was especially galling to the young King Henry, an inglorious prelude to his reign; but he was persuaded to restrain his indignation, took no vengeance on the erring commanders, wasted no time on recrimination against Ferdinand. He chose rather to refute the taunts by deeds which would restore his military reputation. A much stronger expedition was prepared, and in the following year he accompanied it himself to Calais to enter France by the front door, the traditional path of English invaders. During his absence he left Queen Catherine as regent, entrusting her with both civil and military authority. She had need soon to exercise the latter on the Scottish border.

Although James IV was married to Henry's sister Margaret there was ancient friendship between the Scots and the French binding each to intervene on behalf of the other if England attacked either of them. The Queen of France, Anne of Brittany, wrote to King James imploring him to keep faith and fulfil his obligation, and she enclosed her ring in token of her esteem. She had no motive other than concern for the safety of France; she herself was desperately ill at the time, in great pain from gallstones from which she died in the following winter. Nevertheless the gift of the ring provoked Queen Margaret's frantic jealousy, and having been hitherto on bad terms with her brother she now became his shrill partisan to avenge herself on her French rival.

Nothing that she said, however, could deter her husband from his purpose of invading England while King Henry was occupied abroad. He led his army across the Tweed and captured a number of castles. The English were ill prepared; but the Earl of Surrey (Margaret's uncongenial escort at her wedding) collected what forces he could, pursued the Scots and caught them up near Coldstream. They occupied a strong position on Flodden Edge, but were imprudent enough in answer to his challenge to come down on to low ground to give battle. They were terribly punished for their mistake, suffered overwhelming disaster, and King James himself was killed, leaving his son, a child of a year old, to succeed him as James V. In reward for this victory Surrey was restored to his hereditary title of Duke of Norfolk, which he forfeited when he fought on the losing side at Bosworth.

Meanwhile, King Henry was making progress in France. He laid siege to Thérouanne, where he was joined by the Emperor Maximilian. The histrionic gesture was typical of Maximilian that he left his army behind and arrived alone, dressed as a common soldier, to offer his services. His purpose was to impress the English with his poverty, his need of money; but his military knowledge helped the inexperienced Henry to defeat the French in the "Battle of the Spurs," an engagement that earned its name from the speed with which the French knights retreated. Thérouanne fell, and the English advanced against the rich city of Tournay—Perkin Warbeck's birthplace, if Henry had time to remember.

The most important of the prisoners taken at the "Battle of the Spurs" was the Duke of Longueville, closely related in an illegitimate line to the King of France. Henry sent him to England as a glorious trophy of his victory, asking Catherine to entertain him till his own return. She was in the middle of her preparations to repel the Scottish invasion, and the inopportune request annoyed her; she shut the distinguished Frenchman up in the Tower. Soon afterwards came the victory won by her own commander at Flodden, and when she wrote to Henry to announce it she assured him that it was worth "more than should you win all the crown of France." In return for the French Duke she sent him a "King's coat," the bloodstained plaid taken from James IV's dead body. Her exultation displeased him; he was glad of the Scottish defeat, sorry that James had to pay for it with his life.

The surrender of Tournay restored his pride in his own exploits. Maximilian came to visit him there, no longer in humble disguise but resplendent as Holy Roman Emperor and accompanied by his daughter, Margaret of Savoy. The girl of seventeen who composed her epitaph on the pitching ship, the young widow courted in vain by Henry VII, had grown into a mature woman of thirty-three content to exchange the cares of marriage for those of statecraft. Her father had such respect for her ability and wisdom that he left her in charge of the government of the Netherlands, where she was regent for his grandson, the Archduke Charles.

This boy was now thirteen, and much of the conversation at Tournay was concerned with the terms of his marriage to Henry's sister, Mary, to whom he was betrothed before the death of Henry VII. Maximilian, whose moods hung on the impulse of the moment, was well disposed. The success of the recent campaign wiped out the memory of the English disgrace in the Bay of Biscay, restored his confidence in the value of England as an ally, and Margaret supported him wholeheartedly in his opinion. She was favourably impressed by King Henry's good looks, even more by his charm of manner, frankness and easy good-nature.

His companion too earned her approval, a less cultivated but almost as charming edition of himself. This was Charles Brandon, son of the standard-bearer who saved Henry Tudor's life at Bosworth at the cost of his own. The victor showed his gratitude by inviting the orphaned boy to Windsor to be brought up with his own children in spite of his humble birth, and the friendship founded in childhood persisted when they grew up, strengthened by common tastes. Brandon shared Henry's love of outdoor sports, fell little short of him in athletic prowess. In intellect he was much the inferior, had no bent for study, but he made up for the lack by his cheerful and engaging temper.

At the age of thirty he was already a widower, after a number of matrimonial vicissitudes. As a young man he promised to marry Anne Browne, one of Queen Catherine's maids-of-honour, and on the strength of his word she bore him a daughter; but then he sought a dispensation to upset the contract and married a rich widow, Lady Mortimer, instead. Later he regretted his act and used his influence again with the ecclesiastical court, which annulled his marriage to Lady Mortimer on rather dubious grounds of consanguinity. So Anne Browne became his wife after all. By the time, however, that he accompanied the King to France she was dead, he himself ready to marry again.

Recent promotion encouraged his ambition and self-confidence. The Earl of Suffolk, held prisoner in the Tower since his unsuccessful revolt against Henry VII, had a brother in France who supported the French cause. Letters between the two were intercepted, and whether or not their contents were treasonable the opportunity was taken while the country was at war to put Suffolk to death, to deprive the remnant of the party of the white rose of a possible leader. King Henry conferred the forfeited title on Brandon, elevating it to a dukedom, so that he became Duke of Suffolk. He was in high favour; the envoy was.guilty of little exaggeration who described him to Margaret of Savoy as a "second king" with power to "make and unmake."

Margaret's friendly manner at Tournay convinced him that as Duke of Suffolk he was a fit husband for the daughter of a Holy Roman Emperor. The match had the added attraction for him that she was a woman on whom eyes rested with pleasure; her beauty owed less to her features than to the sweet and open expression of her face, her clear complexion, fair hair, and the natural gaiety which no misfortunes could suppress. She herself was willing enough to relieve the solemn business of state by flirting with the handsome Englishman, with whom she was soon on excellent terms in spite of his inadequate command of any language but his own. There was an occasion after dinner when he removed a ring from her finger to tease her; she called him *larron*, tried *dieffe* in Flemish without effect, she had to appeal to King Henry to interpret and explain that the word meant "thief." Even so, the Duke refused to give the ring up, and she let him keep it. The incident provoked gossip; the ring was easily recognised, taken for a love token. Her kindness too was misrepresented when she invited his motherless daughter, the child of his marriage to Anne Browne, to be brought up at her court.

The story ran through Europe that the Emperor's daughter, regent of the Netherlands, was about to become Duchess of Suffolk, wife of the King of England's upstart favourite, Charles Brandon. Maximilian himself was indignant and, acting as usual on impulse, veered suddenly to follow the advice of those in his council opposed to the English alliance. His change of policy received encouragement from Spain, where Ferdinand was jealous of the success achieved in France by King Henry, his son-in-law, and afraid of his growing power if his sister Mary married the Archduke Charles, to whom she was already betrothed.

Margaret was appalled by the result of her indiscretion. She was in disgrace with her father, and the friendly relations with England to which she was attached were in danger. It had never occurred to her to regard her flirtation with the Duke of Suffolk as anything more serious than a social pastime. She wrote to him in England, imploring him to put an end to speculation by marrying his ward, a child of nine. It was a custom prevalent at the time for the guardian of an infant heiress to go through a form of marriage with her so as to give him a title to her estates; but on reaching the age of consent the girl had the right to repudiate the contract. Suffolk refused to oblige, to tie himself to a child bride who could leave him stranded when she grew up. If he could not marry a Habsburg he had another woman in mind scarcely less exalted to make his wife.

This was Henry's sister Mary, betrothed but not yet married to Margaret's nephew, the young Archduke. The date agreed for the wedding was approaching; but the proposed husband showed no eagerness for the match with a bride older than himself. He complained that at the age of fifteen he wanted a wife and not a mother. Meanwhile, Suffolk back in England was much in her company, reviving a friendship that began when she was a child in the nursery at Windsor, he her brother's playmate, a boy old enough to inspire her with hero-worship. He was ready to be consoled for his failure to win Maximilian's daughter, she in no mood to force herself on Maximilian's reluctant grandson.

King Ferdinand dealt the final blow to English plans in Europe. Negotiating in secret he concluded a truce for twelve months between France and Spain. The news provoked resentment and consternation in England. The French war was of Ferdinand's own making. He had urged Henry into it, lured him on with promises; now when an English army was in France winning victories he withdrew his forces, made terms with the enemy behind his ally's back. Maximilian followed his example, accepted the truce without demur; then leaving his daughter to act on his behalf, to appease King Henry as best she could, he retired from public life for a course of spiritual meditation to fit him, as he told her, for canonisation after his death.

She had as little chance of success in the task assigned her as he in his. Unwilling as Henry might be to trouble himself with affairs of state, this was not an issue that he could delegate carelessly to Wolsey. He was personally involved, having led the invasion of France in person. His father-in-law's behaviour was a personal slight.

The most vulnerable target for his anger was his wife. Catherine was her father's ambassador, untiring in her efforts to adapt English policy to his interests. She could not escape blame for the war and its outcome. In the heat of the quarrel Henry reminded her of the flaws in their contract of marriage, even threatened her with annulment. He carried the threat no further, and nothing more was heard of it for many years; but it was at this time that Bessie Blount became his mistress, the mother of his only known illegitimate child, the Duke of Richmond.

The death of the Queen of France, Anne of Brittany, earlier in the year had an important bearing on the course of events. Her husband, Louis XII, was overwhelmed with grief; he was in poor health himself, and many doubted whether he would long survive the bereavement. The surprise was all the greater therefore when it became known that he intended to marry again. Yet he had good reasons—his own lack of a direct heir; the dislike and suspicion that he felt for his heir presumptive, Francis of Angoulême, a distant cousin; finally, his concern for the fate of his fifteen-year-old daughter Claude, whom Francis had married. If a new wife gave him a son Francis would be cut out of the succession, and the Pope could be persuaded to release Claude from her bond.

The revulsion of feeling aroused against Ferdinand and Maximilian in England suited his purpose, and he had a useful intermediary at the English court in the Duke of Longueville, the French prisoner taken at the "Battle of the Spurs," with whom

King Henry was on the friendliest terms. Careful overtures were made, leading to the proposal of a treaty of peace to be confirmed by the marriage of the King of France to an English princess. Henry was in a mood to agree to the plan, it appealed to him as an opportunity to repay his father-in-law in his own coin. He offered King Louis the hand of his elder sister Margaret, the widowed Queen of Scotland.

This offer evoked no enthusiasm. Too much was known of her in France, of her efforts to detach the Scots from the French alliance. Longueville, moreover, sent reports of her private life, her peevish discontent with her husband, her acrimonious bickering with her brother, the unseemly passion revealed as soon as she was widowed for a Scottish lord much younger than herself, the Earl of Angus. King Louis replied that if he married a sister of the King of England his choice was Mary, the younger. It was no disadvantage in his eyes that to accept him she would have to break faith with the Archduke Charles.

Her brother Henry was willing enough himself to rebuff the Habsburgs. If he hesitated to send Mary to France it was on personal rather than political grounds. She was his favourite sister, whose company soothed as much as Margaret's irritated him. Her gaiety and beauty were the delight of his court; an Italian observer described her as "a nymph from heaven." She was only eighteen, Louis was fifty-two, prematurely aged. She protested with tears when Henry urged her to consent to the match. It was not so much the discrepancy in age to which she objected, still less the rejection of the Archduke Charles to whom she was not attracted at all. The true cause of her distress was her unwillingness to marry anyone but Charles Brandon, Duke of Suffolk.

King Henry however persisted. He appealed to her loyalty, her duty to put the interests of England and the Tudor dynasty before her own. He reminded her too that her prospective husband was in no state of health to keep her tied to him for long. His arguments prevailed, and she yielded; but she made him promise that if she married this time for his pleasure he would leave her free next time to marry whom she wished. The compact with the Archduke Charles was formally renounced, a treaty of peace concluded with France, and Longueville stood proxy for King Louis at the wedding celebrated at Greenwich. The event created a great sensation in Europe, turned the tables on Maximilian and Ferdinand.

A month later Mary was escorted in state to Dover to sail to France. Henry accompanied her, his intention was to travel some way with her out to sea where a ship would take him off and bring him back to England; but the weather was so bad that the plan was abandoned, and he said goodbye to her on the waterfront. As he kissed her she recalled his promise, and he confirmed it.

Among the ladies-in-waiting who left England with the new Queen of France was a granddaughter of the Duke of Norfolk, Mary Boleyn, whose father, Sir Thomas Boleyn, had served prominently on diplomatic missions abroad. She took with her her little sister Anne aged seven; their mother was dead, and this was an opportunity to acquire fashionable manners from education at the French court. Soon after their arrival a dispute arose over the party; the French complained of the excessive number of English attendants and especially of the behaviour of their duenna, Lady Guildford, formerly the Queen's governess, who insisted on asserting her authority. The Queen wrote to her brother to ask him to use his influence on Lady Guildford's behalf; but King Louis disliked the woman, and she had to go. Most of the others were sent home at the same time, but not the Boleyn sisters. Their grandfather, the Duke of Norfolk, was in Paris and arranged for them to stay.

The Queen, having done her best for her governess, accepted her departure without heartburning. She wrote in her next letter that, much as she esteemed Lady Guildford, she was doing very well without her. The marriage on which she entered so reluctantly was not in fact proving unhappy. The lively society of the French court left her little time to lament her disappointment in love. Entertainments held in her honour, magnificent banquets and dances filled the days and much of the nights. In spite of his broken health, his liability to crippling attacks of gout, her husband made a gallant effort to rejuvenate himself, to resuscitate after thirty years the young Duke of Orleans, the gay adventurer in Brittany who won the heart of the Duchess Anne.

The strain of prolonged festivity was too much for him. Accustomed to keep early hours he was seldom in bed till after midnight and shared it when at last he retired with an amorous nymph. Little more than a month was needed to produce the inevitable result. He lay in his room dying, while Mary sat at his bedside soothing his pain, singing and playing the lute. Only a day or two before his death he wrote to her brother in England; the letter was full of her praises, declared that he loved and honoured her "more and more every day."

When she heard that he was dead she fainted. The marriage to please her brother was over, much more quickly than either expected, and she was free to marry again; but there was no exultation in her first response to the news, nothing but sorrow, she was of too affectionate a nature not to have grown fond of King Louis. She had ground for anxiety too when she considered her own position, left a widow in a foreign country, uncertain of her prospects. She disliked and distrusted the new King Francis, she said that he looked like the Devil.

He owed it to her that he was able to call himself King without delay; she made it known that she was not pregnant, that no posthumous child would upset his title. Nothing had come of Louis XII's hopes of an heir. Nevertheless as *reine blanche* —the name given in France to the King's widow—she had to submit to the custom which confined her indoors for six weeks, secluded from everyone but her women. The only intruder admitted was King Francis, who claimed the privilege to visit his wife's youthful stepmother to suggest eligible princes in Europe to whom she might ally herself. He did not neglect the opportunity while they were alone to make less seemly suggestions on his own account.

She wrote to her brother imploring him to arrange her return home, and reminding him of his promise on the quay at Dover. It is clear that he had not forgotten it, that he meant indeed to keep his word. The envoy whom he chose to send to Paris was the Duke of Suffolk; but he made him swear before he left that he would be nothing more to Mary than an official escort till she was back in England. Suffolk gave his oath in all sincerity; he could afford to be patient when it seemed that everything would turn out as he wished.

Mary however was under great strain, living in darkened rooms (every window had to be curtained during the seclusion of the *reine blanche*) with nothing to break the monotony except the unwelcome attentions which King Francis forced on her. Even when she heard that Suffolk was coming to bring her home there was bitterness in the news. A rumour reached her through her women that on her return to England the plan would be revived to marry her to the Archduke Charles. At last she could bear the suspense, the ordeal no longer. When Francis became too importunate she told him that she was in love with Suffolk, begged him to be their friend, to intercede on their behalf with her brother.

The risk which she took paid off. The passionate lover in Francis yielded to the astute politician. He abandoned his attempt to seduce her, devoted himself instead to foster a marriage which would put her out of reach of the Archduke Charles or any other dangerous rival in European politics. When Suffolk arrived in France he met him at Rheims, told him that Mary had let him into her secret, and assured him of his own goodwill. Suffolk who had expected opposition was jubilant. Difficulties were melting from his path. His enemies in England anxious to thwart the marriage would lose influence when it became known that it had the support of the new King of France.

He went on with an easy mind to Paris to see Mary, but he found her in low spirits, suffering from toothache. She had no trust in the lasting conversion of Francis into an ally, still feared that on her return to England she would be forced to marry someone of her brother's choosing for reasons of state. She implored Suffolk to marry her at once, told him that she would only go back with him as his wife. At first he opposed her, declared that he could not break his oath to her brother, explained how events were moving in their favour and that if only they had patience everything would be as they wished. She refused to listen, burst into tears, replied to all his arguments and remonstrances that if he cared more for his standing with Henry than for her happiness she was well rid of him, she would go into a nunnery, take the veil and never see him again.

He gave in at last to appease her, and they were secretly married. Not even King Francis was informed, although they encouraged him to write to King Henry to plead their cause. Whether in deference to French advocacy or to Henry's own inclination, the response from England was not unfavourable. Wolsey (not knowing that they had forestalled him) wrote to Suffolk that he was trying to expedite the marriage, to reconcile opponents in the council, but that much turned on the success of Suffolk's own mission in France. There were two matters of special importance to be negotiated: the renewal of the truce concluded by Louis XII for his lifetime, and restitution of the jewels and other valuables which Mary brought with her from England, together with those, a very large number, given by King Louis while she was his wife.

Both were tasks likely to provoke difficulty. The English still occupied Tournay, and the French refused to renew the truce till it was given up; no outcome of the negotiations was possible without leaving one side or the other aggrieved. As for the jewels, Francis was not the man to release them from his clutch without a struggle. Suffolk was in a painful dilemma. He needed King Francis to help him to relieve his personal worries, would need him even more when the full extent of his offence was revealed; on the other hand, unless he stood up to him, he could not placate King Henry. Francis took advantage of his dependence, exacted a stiff price for sympathy shown to the lovers.

The final blow was added to Suffolk's dismay when Mary told him that she was pregnant. Concealment could be kept up for only a few months longer. He was frank by nature, unskilled in subterfuge; inclination and necessity alike prompted him to write to Wolsey, confessing everything and begging him to intercede with the King. Mary, knowing her brother, contributed a present that would please him. It was a priceless jewel given her by King Louis, known as the "Mirror of Naples," an enormous diamond set with a pearl as large as a pigeon's egg, one of the most cherished heirlooms of the French Crown.

Confession had to be made too to King Francis. He took it very badly. It offended his vanity that the pair had used his good offices in a business whose most important aspect they kept dark. In addition he saw that Suffolk lost his value, could no longer be the means of extracting concessions if Henry's confidence in him was withdrawn. When he found out that, adding injury to insult, the "Mirror of Naples" had left France his temper was such that, in Suffolk's own phrase, Paris "stank."

Wolsey's reply when it came brought no comfort. He told Suffolk that he had passed the information on to the King, who "at the first hearing could scantly believe the same to be true." The letter dwelt with stern rebuke on the gravity of the offence; the only hope of accommodation which it offered was the advice to collect all the money due to Mary from France and make over the bulk of it to the King. Wolsey warned him that even this would not necessarily earn him pardon, he was "in the greatest danger that ever man was."

Mary tried to deflect her brother's anger; she wrote taking

148

the whole blame on to herself, explaining that she forced her husband to disobey his orders, giving him the choice of marrying at once or not at all. Her intervention however failed to exculpate him; Wolsey informed him that he was still in heavy disgrace. His crime lay not in marrying Henry's sister but, as he himself penitently admitted, in breaking his oath.

Nevertheless he obtained the consent of both Kings to a ceremony held in Paris, at which he and Mary were married a second time. The validity of their earlier vows exchanged in secret might be disputed, and Henry, as anxious as his father to protect the succession, was unwilling to risk any doubt of the legitimacy of Mary's child. The wedding was celebrated in private before carefully chosen witnesses, but the news spread quickly and without hindrance. Louise of Savoy, the French Queen Mother, recorded in her diary for the last day of March 1515 that the Duke of Suffolk, "a man of humble origin," married the sister of Henry VIII of England.

Although Francis remained bitter about the missing "Mirror of Naples" he was persuaded at last to disgorge half of the jewels which Mary claimed. Henry professed himself content and gave permission for the married pair to return to England. Apprehensive and unhappy, not knowing what reception to expect, both wrote to him before their departure to express contrition and implore mercy. They landed at Dover, and Mary travelled on ahead to Barking where he was staying, to be the first to greet him. As she approached the house a procession came to meet her, led by her brother himself. He galloped forward, dismounted, took her in his arms and kissed her. Indoors a banquet awaited her, all her favourite dishes. Music and dancing followed, the festivities lasted for the rest of the day and all the next.

No account survives of the interview when Suffolk himself met the King, but the cordial relations resumed between them bore witness to his restoration to favour. Henry insisted on yet a third wedding, a magnificent affair celebrated at Greenwich in the presence of the whole court. It seems indeed that Wolsey's letters to Suffolk gave an account deliberately exaggerated of Henry's displeasure, so that his own efforts should get all the credit for the reconciliation. Suffolk himself believed this, and he bore Wolsey a grudge which found expression many years later.

CHAPTER 11

Cortes landed in Mexico in 1519, conquered the empire of Montezuma for the Crown of Spain. All Europe was dazzled by American gold. The English remembered with regret how Columbus came looking for a patron, sought help in vain from Henry VII to equip a voyage of discovery. If the opportunity had been seized all this wealth would have poured into England. Frustration rankled, bearing fruit later in the exploits of English pirates on the Spanish Main.

In Spain King Ferdinand was dead. His successor by right was his daughter Joanna, elder sister of Queen Catherine of England; but as she was still held prisoner under a stigma of insanity a joint monarchy was created, she had to share the title with her son, the former Archduke Charles, who ruled for all effective purposes as King of Spain. On the death of his grandfather Maximilian in the following year he added the inheritance of the Habsburgs and was elected Holy Roman Emperor as Charles V. His realm stretched from the Danube to the Atlantic Ocean, and beyond the ocean into lands of El Dorado, dominions fit to compare with those of ancient Rome if they had not been split by an intervening wedge, the kingdom of France.

For the next two decades Europe was disturbed by the rivalry of the two rulers, King Francis and the Emperor Charles. They differed as greatly in character as in national interests. There was much of the showman in Francis; he loved to cut a gallant figure, to be admired for his prowess in battle and in women's beds, and in either pursuit he was heedless of any interest but his own. He was known as *le roi des gentilshommes*, which can be translated with some justice in the context as "king of cads." Yet his poses were not entirely a hollow pretence. He put his heart into his work when he went to war and fought with courage. His patronage of the arts, likewise, might comply with the fashion of the age; but it suited his tastes also, he was a man of culture. When he offered hospitality at Amboise to the ageing Leonardo da Vinci he was inspired by genuine esteem, even if he created a legend for his own glorification that the painter died in his arms.

The virtues and failings of the Emperor Charles were of an opposite sort. Where Francis was effusive he was reticent and aloof, with formal manners that earned him a reputation for frigidity. It was only in the company of intimate friends, especially of his sister, Mary Queen of Hungary, that the barrier melted and he spoke freely from his heart. The contrast between the two men is revealed in their response to danger. Francis was fearless by nature, never happier than in battle. Charles was timid; but when need arose he steeled his resolution, setting an example of courage that on more than one occasion saved his army from disaster. Francis was handsome in a manner, as Mary Tudor observed, which suggested the Devil; Charles was grotesquely ugly, a goblin with leaden pallor and elongated chin. Francis lived up to his looks, Charles did not.

In the struggle between the two it was the true interest of England to maintain good relations with the Emperor Charles for the sake of trade with the Flemish ports, the most important market for English produce; but Wolsey, to whom Henry still left the guidance of policy, cherished more ambitious aims. He had recently been promoted Cardinal by the Pope, he dreamt of attaining the Papacy itself, and meanwhile he was determined to play a leading part on the European scene. The England that he represented must match his own greatness, no mere offshore island content with commercial prosperity but an arbiter of destiny courted by the rulers of Europe, holding the balance of power between France and the Empire.

His fingers itched to manipulate the pieces on the international chessboard. No issue was so remote that he could not find an excuse to intervene, now on this side, now on that, for ever changing partners to give his influence more effect. The magnificence of the occasion has become a legend when King Henry met King Francis outside Guisnes to swear friendship on the "Field of Cloth of Gold"; but it was preceded by a visit of the Emperor Charles to England and followed by a private meeting between him and Henry at Gravelines, from which France derived no comfort. Wolsey prided himself on his skill in playing off Francis against Charles, in holding the lists without committing English forces to battle; but his success was not achieved without expense, a perpetual flow of bribes and subsidies, to keep others fighting as he wished. The wealth accumulated by Henry VII dwindled fast in the treasury.

The easygoing carelessness with which the King leant on him, unwilling to be disturbed by business of state, referring documents back to him often unread, sprang less from indolence than the slow development of a character which even at the age of thirty remained uncertain of its own strength. Henry enjoyed life, both the outdoor sports in which he excelled and the sumptuous entertainment of his leisure; but he had other interests no less cherished to which he devoted himself. As a child he had shown aptitude for scholarship so that his father had the idea, quickly dropped on Prince Arthur's death, of putting him into the Church. He retained all through his life a taste for intellectual exercise. The Dutch humanist, Erasmus, who came to live in England at his invitation, spoke with praise of the learning of the court and of the King's own readiness to discuss new ideas with an open mind. The remarkable impression made on him is described in a letter: "That King of yours may bring back the golden age, though I shall not live to enjoy it."

When Luther nailed his famous manifesto to the door of the church at Wittenberg, an action destined to introduce the Reformation, no political motive was needed to engage King Henry in the controversy. The issue appealed to him as an eager student of theology, and there can be no doubt that his book written in answer, *An Assertion of the Seven Sacraments*, was of his own composition. Even if it fails to refute Luther's arguments it does honour to the King's erudition, and its dominant theme, the respect due to authority in religion, is a principle which he upheld consistently to his death. Pope Leo X was so pleased with the book that he rewarded the author with the title, "Defender of the Faith." He would have been less content if he had foreseen that the authority which Henry supported needed no Pope, could be exercised more effectively by a King.

No one suspected that Queen Catherine's misfortunes in child-birth would provoke a breach with the Pope, the schism of the Church in England. They were peculiarly distressing, however, both to herself and to the King when so much hung on the birth of an heir. In the first seven years of her marriage she had a son and a daughter stillborn, one miscarriage, and two sons born alive who died in infancy. Concern for the succession aggravated Henry's ill-humour when her father deserted him in the middle of the campaign in France, and he threatened to get rid of her. Soon afterwards, however, she bore him a daughter who lived, called Mary after her aunt. Husband and wife were reconciled, hoping that sons would follow.

They were disappointed. The next child was stillborn, thereafter Catherine's age as well as her record left diminishing probability of living issue. It seemed that on Henry's death his daughter Mary would be his heir. The prospect dismayed him. Although nothing in theory debarred a woman from succeeding to the throne the only known example of a Queen Regnant, that of Henry I's daughter Matilda four hundred years earlier, set a dis-couraging precedent of anarchy and civil war. It would be an inglorious end to the dynasty founded by his father.

Both Catherine and he were superstitious. She believed that their marriage incurred a curse from the blood of the Earl of Warwick, on whose death her father insisted before she came to England. He for his part accused himself of incest, brooding over the text from the Book of Leviticus that "if a man shall take his brother's wife it is an unclean thing," and "they shall be childless." That was canon law, the word of God. Could even the Pope dispense him from obedience?

These doubts estranged him from his wife. Like his father, and unlike the majority of kings in his day, he was not in the habit of infidelity; but now he took Bessie Blount again for his mistress, the mother of his bastard son. Without the bar sinister the boy would have been his heir; the birth served only to aggravate his sense of frustration, the bond of his marriage was loosened be-yond repair. There were stories of his attachment to Mary Boleyn, who was back in England since the death of Louis XII, leaving her sister in France. Little evidence supports them, she had no child by him; but they indicate a change in his behaviour seldom vulnerable to scandal in the past.

This was the state of affairs at court when Wolsey, balanced so long between the contending parties in Europe, saw fit to intervene actively on the Emperor's side. England declared war on France, an expeditionary force was prepared, and even the old claim to the French throne dating from Henry V was revived. In the campaign that followed the English advanced as far as the Oise, but the Emperor failed to support them and they had to retreat. He himself, however, drew great advantage from the diversion; French resistance elsewhere was weakened, and when his generals cut off a French army led by King Francis in person in Italy and brought it to battle at Pavia they inflicted overwhelming defeat, took Francis prisoner. He remained for a year confined in a castle in Spain, obtaining release at last only on terms advantageous to the Emperor. Wolsey's policy of a balance of power lay in ruin, the Emperor Charles was left master of Europe.

A result of the outbreak of war with France was to bring home Mary Boleyn's sister, Anne. She was about seventeen when she arrived, having stayed on in Paris to complete her education under the care of the French King's sister, Margaret of Angoulême, a woman of outstanding talent, renowned for her patronage of the arts and learning of the Renaissance. Her influence fostered enlightened ideas, a taste for music and literature, graceful manners to set off Anne's natural gaiety. These were accomplishments that earned admiration at the English court, where fashion took France for its model even when the French were enemies.

Anne found a place among Queen Catherine's maids-of-honour. She aroused interest not only because of her French background; even if her features fell short of classical standards of beauty her high spirits, the sparkle of her dark eyes, the wide curve of provocative lips drew crowds of young men round her with whom she was very willing to flirt. Her chief glory however was her glossy black hair which she loved to wear loose in the French fashion, sprinkled with jewels and streaming down her back, where it set off her tall and shapely figure. It was so long that it reached to her seat.

She was already pledged to marry an Irish cousin, Sir Piers Butler, to resolve a long-standing dispute between his branch of the family and her father's. She had never met him, however, and was in no hurry to fulfil her part of the contract, content to enjoy the pleasure of life at court. It is not known when she caught the King's eye, but she was soon admitted into the exclusive circle surrounding his sister, the Duchess of Suffolk, who was eager to hear news of old friends and to recall memories of Paris. Anne's experience of King Francis was not unlike her own; no attractive nymph, however young, was safe from the Royal satyr, and as Anne's tongue was indiscreet scandal gathered round her escapades there. Jealous rivals embroidered the stories with relish; but Sir Thomas Wyatt, the poet, who was among her warmest admirers, shows better understanding of her character when he makes her describe herself as "wild for to hold though I seem tame." The philanderer was rudely undeceived who inferred from the indiscretion of her speech a like standard of behaviour.

The suitor to whom she listened most willingly was Sir Henry Percy, son and heir of the Earl of Northumberland. He was a young man of delicate health who fell short of his redoubtable ancestors in feats of arms; but he was more than their match in intellectual attainments, and even the King's old tutor, the crotchety and ribald poet, John Skelton, had kind words for him. He had a place in the service of Cardinal Wolsey, whom he accompanied on his visits to court, and while Wolsey conferred with the King he enjoyed the society of the maids-of-honour, especially of Anne Boleyn. He himself was betrothed to a daughter of the Earl of Shrewsbury as Anne was to Sir Piers Butler; but both were hopeful when they fell in love that they would be set free to marry, seeing no reason why either family should object to the match.

They were wrong. News of their purpose came to Wolsey's ears, and in the presence of the whole household assembled in the dining hall he scolded Percy for entangling himself with a "foolish girl," warned him that he had reported his disobedience to his father, who was coming to punish him. An even more humiliating scene followed when the Earl himself, Percy's father, arrived, dined with Wolsey, lingering in conversation over his wine, then rose and walked to the door where a bench was set for the convenience of attendants and messengers. Those who occupied it rose hastily as he sat down among them.

He had ignored his son hitherto; but now he beckoned to him, and as the young man stood before him he delivered a scathing tirade, accusing him of presumption and wasteful extravagance, threatening to disinherit him, and turning from time to time to the crowd of inquisitive onlookers to invite their agreement. Percy, whom he treated as a schoolboy, was in his early twenties. The injustice, the publicity crushed him. He tried to defend Anne, to insist on the excellence of her lineage; but his father shouted him down, and he was shamed into silence. He was forbidden to see Anne again, arrangements were pressed forward to marry him to the Earl of Shrewsbury's daughter.

It was peculiarly galling to the son to be accused of folly and extravagance by a father notorious for these very faults, who left the estate crippled with his debts. The old man died within three years of the scene in Wolsey's dining hall, and Henry Percy succeeded him as Earl of Northumberland; but he was married by then to a wife whom he detested, and Anne was out of his reach.

Her father removed her from court and took her to live at Hever Castle, his house in Kent. He had remarried since her mother's death, and his second wife, a countrywoman from Norfolk, was much beneath him in station; but Anne was fond of her, found her company soothing, and was glad to be alone with her out of the world while she brooded over her disappointment, burning with anger against Wolsey. The suspicion gained belief later, fostered by events, that Wolsey acted on orders from the King who desired Anne for himself. It is unlikely that the thought occurred to her; she had no reason yet to suspect who was Percy's rival, Wolsey bore the whole blame in her mind.

There is a story that the King paid a visit at this time to her father at Hever, that she refused to leave her room to meet him, but that after dinner she disguised herself as a page, sat in a dark corner of a balcony to play the lute and sing to him, slipped away when he asked whose the voice was. Her behaviour reveals distaste for social intercourse, but no resentment against the King himself, for whose pleasure she sang.

The visit was followed by others, and she avoided him no longer. Letters which he wrote have survived, and they show that he was making passionate love to her, persevering undeterred by her refusal to become his mistress. When she returned to court he made up his mind. It was no secret that he intended to take her in Catherine's place as his wife.

Wolsey was aware of his anxiety for the succession, and a possible annulment of his marriage had already been discussed between them. It could even be useful to Wolsey's plans, help to restore the balance which he himself upset when his ill-advised alliance with the Emperor led to the battle of Pavia, the destruction of French military power. King Francis was back in Paris, released from his Spanish prison, and Wolsey seeking to conciliate him, to bring England and France together again, had the idea of sealing the friendship with a marriage between King Henry and Princess Renée, younger daughter of Louis XII. Her sister Claude whom King Francis married was dead, but theirs was the senior branch of the House of Orleans.

It was a disagreeable shock to Wolsey to learn that the King wished to exchange his Queen not for a French princess but for Anne Boleyn, a girl not only without value in international politics but also bearing a fierce grudge against himself. If indeed he was acting on orders when he got rid of Henry Percy he meant to indulge the King in nothing more dangerous than fornication. He protested as vehemently as he could against so unsuitable a match; but his arguments suffered unaccustomed rebuff. This was a personal issue, King Henry asserted his will.

A plan was drawn up, and Wolsey had to obey. He sat as judge in an ecclesiastical court before which the King was summoned at his own wish to answer the charge of cohabiting with his brother's wife. When the court passed judgment declaring the marriage invalid it was expected that Papal confirmation would follow as on similar occasions without question. An event occurred, however, which upset these calculations. While Wolsey interpreted canon law the Emperor's troops aggrieved by lack of pay ran riot in Italy; they advanced on Rome in defiance of orders, stormed the city and sacked it, plundering, murdering and ravishing with a violence unmatched by Alaric the Goth. The Pope himself, Clement VII, barely escaped with his life to the castle of St. Angelo, where he was kept prisoner. He was in no position to give an unprejudiced decision on Wolsey's findings. Rome was the Emperor's captive, and Catherine against whom the Papal verdict was sought was the Emperor's aunt.

To escape from the difficulty King Henry sent Wolsey to France to form a committee of French and other sympathetic Cardinals to assume the powers which the Pope was no longer able to exercise himself. Wolsey went in great state, still hopeful of bringing off the King's marriage to the French princess, cherishing too a secret hope of his own that the Cardinals would choose him to take Clement's place; but on arrival in Paris he was unable to gather enough support, many expressed their sympathy, few were prepared for schism. He returned to England to report failure, found to his dismay that the King was more determined than ever to marry Anne Boleyn, even proposed to do so on the strength of an English annulment alone, relying on the Pope to confirm it retrospectively.

Wolsey objected with vehemence. He did not shrink from a schism which left him wearing the Papal tiara himself; but independent action of the sort desired by the King would, as he saw, isolate England from the Church, undermine his own authority as Papal legate. The escape of the Pope to Orvieto, where he was less at the Emperor's mercy, added weight to the argument that envoys should be sent to negotiate with him, that the chance of a favourable settlement should not be missed. An embassy accordingly set out for Italy. Among its leading members was Wolsey's confidential secretary, Stephen Gardiner, son of Jasper Tudor's illegitimate daughter, Ellen.

The envoys found the Pope at Orvieto dispirited and irresolute, living in rooms destitute of comfort. He listened courteously to their arguments maintaining the invalidity of the King's marriage. It is clear indeed both from his words and from his subsequent behaviour that he was impressed by them. In addition he was appalled by the prospect of schism in England when the Church was already disrupted by the Lutheran heresy in Germany. All his instinct inclined him to compromise and reconciliation, but his helplessness was apparent. He dared not offend the Emperor, he was in his own phrase "in the power of the dogs." The most that he could concede was to appoint two Papal commissioners to sit in London and try the case, and he bound himself to confirm their decision. The two chosen were Wolsey and Cardinal·Campeggio, the Italian Bishop of Salisbury.

Anne Boleyn was jubilant, supposing that her troubles were over; but King Henry distrusted the Pope's motives, feared that the appointment of the commission served only as an excuse for delay. The course of the proceedings confirmed his suspicion. They dragged on interminably, making some progress when the Emperor suffered a reverse in Europe, checked again as soon as he recovered. Even if Wolsey was faithful to his master's interests Campeggio took his orders from the Pope.

Henry waited with growing impatience. Others obtained what they sought from the Church on grounds far less cogent than his own. A peculiarly galling example was his sister Margaret, the dowager Queen of Scotland. As soon as she became a widow she outraged public opinion by her insistence on marrying the young

Earl of Angus; she joined him in stirring up civil war, fled to England to live on her brother's bounty, then on her return to Scotland she fell out with her husband, fought with him, finally asked the Church to release her to marry a new favourite. Only a month or two before Henry began his own proceedings against Catherine the Pope granted Margaret's application, and her marriage to Angus was annulled. When Henry condemned her "foolish and evil conduct," denouncing her as a disgrace to the family, his anger owed much to grievance and jealousy, a sense of injustice.

At last at the end of July 1529 the Papal commissioners in London completed their examination of the evidence, and the King himself was present in court to hear their decision. Campeggio stood up; all listened in tense expectation, but instead of giving judgment he announced that the business of the court was suspended till October for the long vacation. This was indeed the custom at Rome, but not in England, and even in Roman courts exception was made in urgent cases. The King walked out in grim silence, leaving it to Suffolk to reply, who struck the table with his fist:

"It was never merry in England while we had Cardinals among us."

An unseemly altercation followed. Wolsey reminded him of his former danger in Paris and claimed gratitude for reconciling the King to the stolen marriage. Suffolk who believed that the danger was of Wolsey's own making joined the King at dinner, more incensed against Cardinals than ever.

Anne too bore Wolsey an old grudge. No one was inclined to defend him, to exonerate him for his part in the trick played on the King, least of all when it became known that the proceedings would not be resumed, that the Pope revoked the case to Rome to be heard in the supreme court of Rota, before which, in final insult, he cited King Henry to appear. To relieve his feelings, put his troubles for the time out of his mind, the King rode off with Anne on a hunting trip into Essex.

An event occurred which had important results when the party put up for the night at Waltham Abbey. Stephen Gardiner, transferred from Wolsey's service to the King's, was among those in attendance, and as there was not room for him at the abbey he lodged in the town. He told the King of a conversation which he had over supper with his host's kinsman, a man called Thomas Cranmer, with whom he discussed the problem of the broken marriage. The views expressed by Cranmer aroused the King's interest, and he gave orders for him to be brought to see him.

The point on which Cranmer was able to throw fresh light related to the interpretation of canon law. King Henry's advocates rested their case for the nullity of the marriage on the passage already quoted from the Book of Leviticus, forbidding a man on pain of childlessness to take his brother's wife. Catherine's rejoined with the dictate from the Book of Deuteronomy, that if a woman has no child when her husband dies his brother "shall go in unto her and take her to him for wife." The law seemed to contradict itself; Cranmer argued that consistency is restored if the purpose of the second provision is understood, that the man who took to wife his brother's widow in the society for which the law was framed did so to beget children for his dead brother, not himself, so that his brother's name "be not put out of Israel." Was this Henry's purpose in marrying Catherine? Was Mary regarded as Arthur's daughter? If not, the appeal to Deuteronomy must fail.

The argument was much to the King's taste. He urged Cranmer to develop it in a book for submission to the judgment of all the principal universities at home and abroad. He liked the man, found him modest without servility and endowed with a subtlety of mind akin to his own. Anne too approved of their new champion. A friendship was founded at Waltham which lasted till Henry's death.

Meanwhile Wolsey's power was crumbling. His failure to assert the King's will against the Pope's provided the occasion; but there were other causes that prepared the event and made it inevitable. The King was approaching forty, mature at last in ability and force of character. It needed the personal issue of his marriage to draw him into political activity; but the experience left him unwilling to retire again, to rely on others. He took the lesson to heart that to get what he wanted he must do the work himself.

Wolsey depended for his eminence on Royal favour. When it was withdrawn he lay at the mercy of his enemies, powerful nobles who hated him as an upstart, resented the intrusion of a butcher's son on their hereditary privileges. The arrogance with which he asserted his importance, the ostentatious magnificence of his style of living, embittered them the more against him. Their leader, the Duke of Norfolk, victor of Flodden, had died a few years before; but the new Duke, his son, carried on the feud with unrelaxed animosity. He was a lesser man than his father, puny in body and petty in mind, but an astute politician quick to take advantage of his rival's weakness, of the influence that accrued to him as uncle of Anne Boleyn.

Wolsey was deprived of the lord chancellor's great seal, and a bill of attainder was brought against him in Parliament. He was indicted under the statute of Praemunire on the ground that in the recent negotiations he exalted the sovereignty of the Pope above that of the King in England. That offence, however, weighed less in the opinion of those who tried him than his whole conduct of foreign policy in the past twenty years. His grandiose plans to make England the arbiter of Europe could only be sustained at a cost that swallowed up all the wealth accumulated by Henry VII, and still demanded fresh taxation to fulfil his ambition. People felt that they were made to pay for what they did not want, and that the more they exhausted themselves to buy it the farther it receded from reach. Wolsey's policy left England browbeaten by the Emperor, tricked by the Pope. He was blamed for its failure, the price of his ambition.

The bill of attainder was carried in the House of Lords, but in the Commons it was vigorously opposed by Thomas Cromwell, one of Wolsey's former secretaries who had taken service with the King, and before it was put to the vote the King prorogued Parliament. His intervention saved Wolsey, who received pardon on condition that he retired to his province of York, which he had not visited in the fifteen years since he was made Archbishop. He obeyed, travelling as unobtrusively as possible, and went to live at Cawood Castle near York where his chastened demeanour earned him much sympathy.

He remained there for little more than a month. One afternoon when he was sitting upstairs over his dessert, having just finished dinner, a troop of horsemen rode up to the gate and demanded the keys from the porter in the King's name. The leader was Anne Boleyn's former lover, Henry Percy, now Earl of Northumberland, acting in his capacity as warden of the eastern marches. A private emissary from the King, Sir Walter Walshe, accompanied him. They came indoors and put a guard on the stairs so that no one should go up to warn Wolsey; but one of the servants looked over the banisters, saw them and told him who was in the hall. He rose at once and went down to greet them, met Percy midway on the stairs and invited him in, reproaching him for not sending word of his coming so that dinner could have been kept for him.

Percy had no liking for his duty. He had good reason to bear Wolsey ill-will; but it embarrassed him to have to arrest a man in whose household he lived in his youth. For a time he allowed him to suppose that this was no more than a visit of courtesy; it was not till they went into the bedroom for him to take off his coat that he laid a trembling hand on Wolsey's arm, exclaimed in a faint and faltering voice:

"My lord, I arrest you for high treason" (his words and demeanour are recorded by the only witness, Wolsey's secretary, Cavendish, who kept the door).

Soon afterwards there was a scuffle outside, and Walshe burst in, pushing and struggling with Wolsey's Italian doctor, Augustine, shouting, "Go in then, traitor." Augustine was in fact the informer to whom Wolsey owed his arrest; but Walshe hoped by this show of violence to banish any suspicion of collusion. For the same reason Augustine was sent off later to London under escort with his legs tied together under the horse's belly. Wolsey suffered no such indignity. He was allowed to ride his own mule with five of his servants to attend him, and when he found after going some way that he had left a bag which he needed, the captain of the guard sent a man back at once to fetch it. Percy remained at Cawood to take charge of the goods there; but he ordered his deputy to treat the prisoner with consideration, to make his journey as comfortable as possible.

According to the information which Augustine laid before the council Wolsey used him as intermediary to apply for help to the King of France, even to persuade the Pope to excommunicate King Henry so as to provoke an insurrection and restore Wolsey to power. Whether or not the charges were true they demanded investigation, and Wolsey was recalled to London to answer them. The mood of gloomy foreboding in which he obeyed is hard to reconcile with a clear conscience eager to prove its innocence.

He travelled by easy stages as far as Sheffield, where the Earl of Shrewsbury, acting on the King's instructions, entertained him at his house. The visit had lasted more than a fortnight when he complained after dinner one day of flatulence in his stomach and told Cavendish to get him something to relieve it. When Shrewsbury heard this he summoned an apothecary from the town and obtained a "white confection" from him, which Wolsey took. The effect was to promote violent diarrhoea.

Soon afterwards news came that Sir William Kingston was on his way to Sheffield to escort the prisoner to London. Kingston was constable of the Tower and captain of the King's guard, and Wolsey was much alarmed, declaring that the choice of such an officer boded him no good. Shrewsbury tried to reassure him, and Kingston himself on his arrival treated him with great respect. Wolsey however would not be comforted; his health grew steadily worse, the diarrhoea more frequent.

He became so weak that they put off his departure, but on the following morning he insisted on setting forth. At Nottingham where they spent the night he was very ill indeed; but still he pressed on, refusing to interrupt the journey although he was unable to sit upright on his mule without an arm to support him. When they reached Leicester they took him to the abbey, and Kingston himself carried him upstairs, staggering under the weight.

Leicester was the end of the road. Wolsey was put to bed and never got up again. He arrived on a Saturday night, on the Monday morning he died.

The suddenness with which he fell ill at Sheffield fostered a rumour that he was poisoned. The apothecary's "white confection" invites suspicion, it did him more harm than good; but as he kept the packet by him for use he was himself responsible for its repeated effect, whose virulence mounted with his fear of the danger awaiting him in London. He would have been less despondent, less addicted to the fatal confection if he had known how his enemies trembled, fearing his restoration to favour. The King was already complaining of the gap left by his absence in the council.

CHAPTER 12

Sir Thomas More succeeded Wolsey as lord chancellor. He was already over fifty, having begun his career in the King's father's reign, educated in the household of Cardinal Morton for whom he had great affection. In his early years he practised law, but he soon turned his attention to politics, rising to become Speaker of the House of Commons. The King was his friend, often his guest at his home in Chelsea; he respected his ability, enjoyed his learning and wit, but he was drawn to him most of all by the integrity of his character, the courage which underlay his gentleness and sense of humour. More had earned a reputation already among the leaders of the Renaissance as the author of *Utopia*, a satire on political institutions. The measures now introduced to mitigate abuses and restrain the overgrown power of the clergy had his wholehearted support. He and the King were at one; it was not yet apparent where the road was leading, that a point would come where they parted company.

The King still hoped for a favourable decision from the Pope on the annulment of his marriage. Cranmer's book was circulated among the universities of Europe, and in spite of lavish distribution of bribes on both sides many replied with sincere conviction, revealing weighty support for its argument. The Pope himself was known to share the opinion. He was recovering from the disaster of the sack of Rome, feeling his way cautiously to reassert his independence by alliances in Italy, overtures to France. The Emperor was less formidable than heretofore, having more pressing cares to distract him. In Germany he was at war with the

Lutheran princes leagued to resist his authority; at the same time he was threatened by the Turks in Hungary who were advancing on Vienna.

Nevertheless, the difficulty remained that the case had been revoked to Rome, that King Henry was summoned to plead in person before the court of Rota, and that nothing would induce him to submit to such an indignity. Meanwhile time was passing, he himself growing older. Anne too complained of the humiliation of her position; no one believed that she was not his mistress. He tried to comfort her by reviving the title borne by his great-uncle Jasper, creating her Marchioness of Pembroke in her own right, an almost unprecedented honour for a woman; but the effect was to harm her reputation even more, gossip regarded it as the price of her virtue.

Knowing that the French were in contact with the Pope and preparing a united front against the Emperor, he sought help from King Francis to solve his problem. A meeting was arranged at Boulogne, the first between the two Kings since the "Field of Cloth of Gold." There was less magnificence on this occasion, but on Henry's part a more earnest desire for fruitful agreement. Anne accompanied him. He wanted the French to recognise her as the future Queen of England. Since Claude's death Francis had married again, and as his new wife Eleanor was sister to the Emperor Charles she was not expected to come herself to meet her aunt's rival; but it was understood that Francis would bring his sister, Margaret of Angoulême, now Queen of Navarre, who had care of Anne in her childhood. To Anne's mortification she pleaded illness, Francis arrived without her. It was a blow the more painful coming from one on whose friendship Anne counted. To save face she left them and retired to Calais.

In spite of this rebuff the conference produced results with which both Henry and Francis were satisfied. The latter was eager to avenge his defeat at Pavia, the disgrace of his imprisonment in Spain; he sought English support for an alliance with the Pope against the Emperor, and Henry professed willingness if his own marriage to Anne Boleyn took place without delay. Dispute arose later how far the agreement extended. The French claimed that they promised only to use their utmost influence to persuade the Pope; but Henry believed that he was given a free hand, that Francis would stand by him if he waited no longer for Papal consent, and that the Pope would have to acquiesce in the marriage to save both France and England from schism. Two months after his return from Boulogne he and Anne were secretly married. In spite of precautions the news soon began to leak out. Even before this More took alarm. He could approve of reforms to check clerical arrogance and greed; but the Church itself, the hierarchy with the Pope at its head, was sacrosanct, divinely ordained. He resigned his office, pleading grounds of health, and retired into private life at Chelsea to read and write. The King parted with him regretfully, and they remained friends. Sir Thomas Audley replaced him as lord chancellor.

Another change that had important consequences arose from the death of William Warham, Archbishop of Canterbury. It was usual when a see fell vacant to wait months, even years before filling it as the revenue which accrued in the meantime went to the treasury. The promptitude with which the King acted on this occasion provoked much surprise, even more when he passed over the aspirants of episcopal rank and chose for the highest office in the Church a mere archdeacon, Thomas Cranmer, the man who made so favourable an impression on him at Waltham. Cranmer was abroad, attached as English ambassador to the court of the Emperor Charles. Henry summoned him home in haste, he relied on his cooperation to carry out an urgent task. The secret marriage to Anne, an act of impulse more in keeping with her character than his, left him no time for diplomacy. She was already pregnant; an authoritative verdict was needed at once to ensure that the child was legitimate heir to the throne. What the Pope withheld his own Archbishop of Canterbury would supply.

Cranmer sat in judgment to pronounce on the issue at Dunstable Priory. There was less danger of trouble there than in London, where jealous nobles stirred up riots in the streets to resist a policy that would strengthen Royal authority by diminishing that of the Pope. Dunstable had the advantage too that it was only a few miles from Ampthill, where Queen Catherine was established with a household of her own, finally separated from the King. It would be easy for her to attend the proceedings there in obedience to the summons served on her.

She refused, however, to obey, denied the right of the court to adjudicate on her marriage. Her refusal saved the King from a dilemma. He was unwilling on grounds of public policy and personal feeling alike to put her under arrest, but it would have been hard to avoid it if she had come herself to flout his authority.

Her absence shortened the proceedings, the case was unopposed. Even so, much time that could ill be afforded was lost in tracing indispensable witnesses and bringing them to Dunstable, and when all was in order three Rogation days intervened, followed by Ascension Day, when the court was adjourned. The date of Anne's coronation was already fixed for Whitsunday, and in the advanced state of her pregnancy it could not be postponed. Cranmer, new to his duties, had a task whose urgency might daunt the most experienced judge.

In the event he had just nine days to spare when he gave judgment, declaring the King's marriage to his brother's widow to be null *ab initio*. The rider followed that as Catherine was never the King's lawful wife his subsequent marriage to Anne Boleyn was valid. Anne was crowned with great ceremony on Whitsunday in the Abbey church at Westminster, resplendent in cloth of silver, with jewels in her long flowing hair. On occasions like this she had command of herself, could repress the impulsive levity which was her besetting fault in common life. All who saw her praised her dignity and beauty. They included nearly everyone of consequence in the realm, but not the King's sister Mary, Duchess of Suffolk. While her husband played his part in the gay festivities she lay dying at their house in Suffolk, Westropp Hall. He has been blamed for leaving her in such circumstances; but she had been poorly for some time, and there are letters of his written earlier to the King to excuse him from attendance at court so that he might stay with her. This coronation was an event at which his absence would provoke remark, no excuse could be accepted.

Thenceforward Anne bore the title of Queen, and Catherine as Prince Arthur's widow that of Princess Dowager. The repercussions abroad were more violent even than had been expected. King Francis, engaged in marrying his younger son to the Pope's cousin, Catherine de Medici, professed dismay and denied the imputation indignantly that King Henry's own annulment of his marriage was agreed between them at Boulogne. The Emperor threatened invasion to restore his aunt to her rights, and the Pope in the heat of his annoyance prepared a Bull of excommunication; he laid it aside when his temper cooled, left it unpublished till his death. Meanwhile King Henry strengthened his navy and coastal defences and awaited the outcome without alarm, following the advice of his new minister, Thomas Cromwell, whom he had taken over with Gardiner from Wolsey's service, and who assured him that his foreign enemies were too jealous of each other to unite against him.

On the 7th of September 1533 Queen Anne gave birth to her child. Much to her own and the King's disappointment it was a girl, who received the name of Elizabeth after her grandmother.

Little as Cromwell feared a united front in Europe he knew better than to underrate attempts to foment sedition in England. The Tudor dynasty was not yet fifty years old; many of the old nobility still grudged it allegiance, many could prove from their own lineage a better claim to the throne than that of the victor of Bosworth, and their discontent was aggravated by the preference shown by both Tudor Kings for ministers of humble birth, on whose loyalty they could rely. This opposition drew reinforcement now from prominent ecclesiastics, who saw in the policy pursued by Henry VIII a threat to their wealth and power. They conspired with the Emperor's agents, especially with his ambassador in London, Eugene Chapuis, who was tireless in subversive plots.

Their weakness lay however in appealing to too limited a section of the population. The new men who owed their substance to trade and industry throve under the peace and order which the King's government maintained; they cared little for Emperor or Pope, still less whom the King married. If the monarchy were in danger they would defend it to save the country from slipping back into civil war. A likelier field for troublemaking might be found beneath them in the social scale, especially among the peasants dispossessed by enclosure of the common land. Such people, however, bore little resentment against the King, whose responsibility for their suffering they failed to recognise. The tyrant in their eyes was the landlord who had turned their tillage into grazing for his flocks, and the worst offenders of this sort were the nobles, the King's secret enemies. No alliance could easily be conceived between the oppressor and the oppressed.

A solution to the difficulty was offered, and the danger to the King's government correspondingly increased, when stories spread of the miracles performed by Elizabeth Barton, known as the "Holy Maid of Kent." She had been employed as a domestic servant on a farm till a succession of awe-inspiring seizures, during which her eyes bulged, her tongue lolled out and a mysterious voice spoke from her belly, promoted her from the kitchen of the farmhouse to a nun's cell at Canterbury, the resort of curious pilgrims. The supernatural messages which she delivered in trance held nothing more remarkable at first than a conventional exhortation to piety; but under the influence of the monks of Canterbury the revelation acquired a new purpose, rebuking the King for disrespect shown to clerical privilege and warning him of divine punishment awaiting him for his association with Anne Boleyn.

For some years she was left undisturbed. Archbishop Warham, Cranmer's predecessor, was impressed by her sanctity, so too were Queen Catherine and her friends. Sir Thomas More also took an interest till he was shown a book of her prophecies which he dismissed as "a right poor production, such as any simple woman might speak of her own wit." The King himself remained unconcerned, even when she interrupted him and Anne at dinner at Canterbury on their return from Boulogne and denounced them with shrill abuse. He merely ordered his officers to remove her and take her back to the nuns.

Contempt yielded, however, to alarm when evidence emerged of a formidable plot fostered by foreign agents and many leaders of the nobility and clergy, in which her part was to kindle the superstition of the ignorant, to win their obedience. The poor could be persuaded to make common cause with the rich if they believed that God himself commanded it, speaking through the mouth of the Holy Maid. She and the monks of Canterbury, her accomplices, were arrested. For a time she insisted that her visions were divinely inspired; but when she heard that the monks had confessed to imposture, hoping to save their skins at her expense, she no longer denied her part in their designs. She was indeed less their accomplice than their dupe; her earlier seizures seem to have been genuine, the effect of epilepsy or some similar condition, but under tutelage the mysterious voice learnt to utter what the monks dictated. All were made to stand in public on a platform outside St. Paul's Cathedral in London while the preacher read out a detailed statement of their crimes, then on the following Sunday they repeated the performance at Canterbury. After that they were imprisoned in the Tower to await a final decision on their fate.

Their exposure left the Holy Maid completely discredited, and without her the plot was deprived of an essential cog. Little was done to probe deeper into its sources. Many of the highest in the realm were implicated; but the King was less anxious to bring them to justice than to disarm and deter them without disturbance of the peace. Proceedings were taken against only two men of note, Sir Thomas More and Fisher Bishop of Rochester. More wrote frankly to the King explaining that he was impressed by the nun's spiritual fervour, till the extravagance of her claims convinced him that she was deranged, and he warned her not to meddle in politics. His apology was accepted, his name struck out of the indictment.

Fisher, however, was a man of narrow views who clung to them rigidly. No reason could detach him from the persuasion that the nun was endowed with supernatural power. Unlike More he was as much interested in the political as in the spiritual purpose of her message. Cromwell had intercepted a letter written by him urging the Emperor to invade England. As Fisher refused to admit himself in the wrong he was put on trial and condemned to imprisonment and forfeiture of his goods. Both penalties were later remitted on payment of a fine.

The King was more inclined to deal leniently with his enemies because events encouraged hope of a favourable outcome to the proceedings in the court of Rota at Rome. Jean du Bellay, Bishop of Paris, had recently been appointed French ambassador; he was an enlightened prelate, a patron of Rabelais and a sincere friend of England, especially of Queen Anne whom he knew when she was a girl in France. Filled with goodwill but complaining bitterly of his sciatica, he travelled to and fro across the Alps to effect reconciliation between King Henry and the Pope. He found the Pope ready to compromise, if it could be done without disrespect to the authority of the Church or interference from the Emperor. The solution proposed was that the Pope should adjourn the court and reconvene it at Cambrai out of the Emperor's reach; that King Henry should submit to the extent of sending a proctor to represent him, on the Pope's assurance that a verdict would be given in his favour.

Many journeys were needed across the Alps to bring the parties together. King Henry shrank from any action which reopened the issue of the validity of his marriage to Queen Anne, the legitimacy of the daughter born to them, Princess Elizabeth. Meanwhile rumours of the plan leaked through to the Emperor's supporters at Rome, provoking, as du Bellay complained, a pandemonium of fury against England, of bigots shrieking "Crucifige,

crucifige." He got the court with difficulty to postpone sentence for a fortnight; this would bring the date to the Monday in Passion Week, after which there could be no further session till Easter was over.

In the course of the fortnight Henry was at last persuaded to put aside his scruples, and a messenger was sent to inform the Pope that he accepted his terms; but the passes over the Alps were snowbound, the messenger was delayed, and du Bellay was without news when the court sat on the fatal Monday. He could only trust to the habitual longwindedness of the Cardinals to keep the debate going till the court rose, and there would be time before it met after Easter to receive a reply from England and transfer the sessions to Cambrai.

The Imperial party however was aware of the trap. Never were speeches so terse, so many Cardinals content to sit silent. Even so, the dinner hour approached and still no vote had been taken. The hour struck, dinner was announced, no one answered the call. For the first time in the court's history the Cardinals were reluctant to dine. They sat for nearly seven hours; at last at five in the afternoon the doors were opened, their decision was made known. The dispensation given by Pope Julius II was upheld, King Henry's first marriage declared valid and binding.

Five days later the messenger from England was in Rome. Du Bellay pleaded in vain for the court to be reconvened. The verdict stood.

The challenge could not be left unanswered in England; it branded the King as an adulterer, his daughter as a bastard, there was good reason to fear the effect that it would have on public opinion. The Holy Maid of Kent and the monks convicted with her were brought out of prison and hanged, suffering less for their past offence than as an example to deter sedition. Soon afterwards an Act of Parliament clarified the issue, recognising Queen Anne as the King's lawful wife and vesting the succession to the throne in their descendants. The settlement which the King sought in vain from the Pope he established by law on his own authority.

The measure was so controversial and at the same time of such importance to the peace of the realm that he was not content merely to record it in the Statute Book; he insisted that everyone of any influence in the country should swear to respect its provisions, and he appointed a Royal commission to administer the oath. Few either dared or wished to defy his orders, the chief exceptions were Sir Thomas More and Bishop Fisher. Although the former was no longer active in public life his tenure of the lord chancellor's office was too recent, his reputation too eminent, to allow him to be overlooked. Fisher had still less cause to escape the obligation, having been convicted of treason and let off with comparative leniency.

Great efforts were made to overcome More's scruples. He himself was ready to recognise Anne as Queen and swear allegiance to the heir to whom she gave birth, these were matters that lay within the King's sovereign jurisdiction; but he maintained that the Pope alone could pronounce on the validity of the first marriage, denied that any English court had the right to annul it. The effect was that he recognised a Queen to whom he refused the title of wife, an heir whom he held to be a bastard. It was a distinction of which his own legal wit could approve, but which was likely to spread confusion and dismay among the common people. Cranmer pleaded with him in vain, even offered a compromise which would allow him to subscribe to the oath in a truncated form; but More's conscience was inflexible, and the King feared the example that it set for the disaffected. More was imprisoned in the Tower, where Fisher soon afterwards joined him.

As much as possible was done for their comfort. Cromwell who liked and admired More saw to it that he enjoyed many privileges, including frequent visits from his friends and even permission to go out into the town himself to see them. The general opinion was that both would be kept under restraint till the danger was over, and then released. The King spoke kindly of More, and Fisher was too old and frail to be a formidable enemy; he bordered already on dotage.

The death of Pope Clement VII set events in motion which thwarted these hopes. Cardinal Farnese who succeeded him as Paul III had been among King Henry's supporters in the court of Rota and was anxious to effect reconciliation with England. He announced his intention to call a general council of the Church, and so that England might be represented with dignity he looked for a suitably eminent Englishman on whom to bestow a Cardinal's hat. By irony of fate his choice fell on Fisher. His own motive seems to have been genuinely conciliatory, he was either unaware of the disgrace in which Fisher lay or underrated its importance; but his advisers included many who were better informed and less concerned to heal the schism.

Fisher's promotion had the effect that might have been foreseen. King Henry took it as a studied insult. He was liable to moods of brooding suspicion whose stress found relief in sudden fits of rage. These increased in violence as he grew older, more impatient of control, and although they seldom lasted long they left devastation in their wake. When the Pope's emissary arrived with the Cardinal's hat he told him to take it back to Rome, and that the head would follow. The threat was not fulfilled to the letter, but Fisher had no cause to rejoice. His head was struck off, impaled above London Bridge.

More too was beheaded. There was nothing to implicate him in the Pope's action, to cast doubt on his loyalty; but the King was beside himself, suspecting everyone, and no reason could prevail. More enjoyed international esteem; learning, humanity, religion suffered irreparable loss. His death did more harm to King Henry's cause in Europe than anything that had happened since the dispute with Rome began.

The replacement of Queen Catherine by Queen Anne, reducing the former to the rank of Princess Dowager, was safely accomplished; but the dynasty was still without a male heir. It was of little use to bar Princess Mary from the succession if she made way only for another girl. She and her mother were parted to their great sorrow. The Princess Dowager was removed to Kimbolton Castle in Huntingdonshire, Mary aged eighteen went to live with Queen Anne's aunt, Lady Shelton, who had charge also of little Princess Elizabeth. It was an uneasy household; Lady Shelton was too gentle and ineffective to control a stubborn girl who bitterly resented the humiliation put on her and brooded sullenly over her own and her mother's wrongs. The King's purpose in parting mother and daughter was to keep Mary from influences prejudiced against himself; his dictate, however, defeated its own ends, fomenting passionate devotion to her mother's cause and to that of Papal supremacy. It is a tribute to the goodness of her heart that she vented no grudge on her baby sister, played with her, behaved with unfailing kindness.

Little more than a year later the Princess Dowager's troubles were over. She died at Kimbolton in January 1536 shortly after her fiftieth birthday. Both the King and the Queen offended good taste by the gratification that they betrayed; but the King always ambivalent in his feeling for her, torn between affectionate memories and his longing for freedom, showed remorse in his subsequent behaviour, and he ordered her to be buried at Peterborough with fitting solemnity. The Queen too regarded the death with less complacency when she had time to consider its effect. It released her from a rival of whom she had long ceased to be afraid; but it left the King in the eyes of all who accepted the verdict of the court of Rota an eligible widower free to marry again. Her own marriage was not recognised by the Pope; he had no need even to annul it.

She could no longer count with confidence on the King's love. The prize for which she strove was hers; but she was less happy in her victory than among the anxieties and disappointments of the struggle when nothing was certain except that he loved her, could not bear her to leave him, wrote complaining of the "great elengeness [dreariness] that I find here since your departing." It was her turn now to feel "elengeness," the more so since she suspected that he was absent not on affairs of state but in the company of Lady Jane Seymour. The attention which he paid to this woman already attracted remark. She was of about the Queen's age, approaching thirty; but her excessive pallor, the tightness of her mouth, pinched and thin-lipped, and the sour expression of her blue eyes were in such contrast to the Queen's impulsive warmth that many expressed surprise at his preference.

Some months before the Princess Dowager's death Jane Seymour left the court and returned to her home in Wiltshire. The King seemed to recover his old affection for the Queen, and the reason became clear when it was known that she was pregnant. She would be invulnerable to Jane Seymour or any other rival if she bore a son, able to relieve the King of his fears for the succession. It is certain that he ardently desired this, probable too that while he awaited the event he meant to remain faithful; but he visited his daughter Mary after her mother's death to comfort her, and she and Jane Seymour were friends. The opportunity was afforded there to renew the intrigue.

On the day of the Princess Dowager's funeral he and the Queen were at Greenwich. As the afternoon wore on he left her, telling her that he was going to the chapel to pray; he lingered there so long that she grew uneasy and went to look for him. The wintry light was fading, it was almost dark when she entered. She found him on a seat in the chancel, with Jane Seymour on his knee.

The shock was so great, her agitation so violent that her pangs came on prematurely. She had barely strength to return to her room, nothing could avert a miscarriage. The child born dead was a boy.

For three more months she remained Queen; but the misadventure convinced the King that the annulment of his first marriage failed to absolve him, he still lay under a curse that denied him a son. On May Day she accompanied him to attend the traditional tournament to celebrate the festival at Greenwich. The incident has often been described when she dropped her handkerchief from the balcony, and a knight picked it up, Sir Henry Norris, a close friend of the King's, one of the witnesses three years before at her secret wedding. He wiped his face with it, then passed it back to her on the point of his lance. A few minutes later the King rose abruptly, called Norris to his side and rode with him to London, leaving her alone.

The incident was trivial, a pretext apparently rather than a cause; but when the charges brought against her were published Norris was among those cited as her accomplices in acts of adultery. She learnt of them on the following day after an unhappy night spent alone, interrupted at dinner by a commission of lords of the council headed by her uncle, the Duke of Norfolk, who told her that she was under arrest. She was brought back to London by river and lodged in the Tower, not in a cell but in the apartments of state which she occupied just before her coronation.

Those accused of adultery with her included as well as Norris another knight, Sir Francis Weston, and a musician, Mark Smeaton, who was her servant. Two other counts were added to the indictment, incest with her brother, Lord Rochford, and conspiracy against the King's life. No attempt was made to proceed with the last of these; she stood to gain nothing from the King's death, her position depended on his survival. Even on the charges that were pressed no evidence of substance was offered, nothing more incriminating than reports of idle and indiscreet words. She was habitually unguarded and often flippant in speech, she was vain too and fond of admiration; but all this was a long way from adultery or any behaviour inconsistent with the impetuous loyalty of her character.

The arrested knights denied to the last that they had been her lovers. The only confession obtained was Smeaton's; but as he was of humble rank he was questioned under torture, till he was ready in the agony of his pain to admit anything suggested. The case against her brother was so weak that his friends attending his trial laid odds of ten to one on his acquittal. He defended himself with feeling and wit, asking whether natural affection deserved punishment in a family, whether no man was safe from a charge of incest who was fond of his sister. Nevertheless a mocking spirit which he shared with her cost him his life. A note was shown him bearing what purported to be a remark made to him by her and overheard. He was told to confirm that the words were hers, but on no account to divulge them. He retorted by reading them aloud; they referred to the King and were indelicate as well as defamatory.

At the last moment new evidence was added to buttress the inadequacy of that on which the case rested. A statement was submitted that Lady Wingfield, a former attendant on the Queen, had been a witness of conduct leading to adultery. This was testimony relating to deeds, not merely to words; but Lady Wingfield was unable to swear to its truth in person, she was dead. The deposition read in court was the work of a woman who attended her in her last illness and professed to be repeating what she told her.

The story left room for many questions, but none were asked. All the prisoners were found guilty, all condemned to death. Among the peers sitting in judgment was Anne's old suitor, Henry Percy, Earl of Northumberland; but in the middle of the proceedings he was taken ill and allowed to leave. He never recovered from the shock of the ordeal; he died a few months later, the last of his line.

There is much mystery about this trial which has never been cleared up. None of the evidence produced against Anne is of a sort on which she could reasonably be convicted; yet if the King had only wished to be rid of her, to exchange her for another wife, he had the judgment of the court of Rota to support him in denying that he was married to her, and he could have relegated her without unsavoury publicity to a convent or similar retreat, while he remarried with the blessing of the Church. An explanation has been suggested by the late Dr. Margaret Murray in her book, *The Divine King in England,* and although it rests on conjecture it provokes interest by the congruity with which it fits together otherwise inexplicable facts. Dr. Murray contends that the rites survived in England of a pre-Christian religion denounced by the Church as witchcraft, that their purpose was to promote fertility by human sacrifice, for which a willing victim was chosen, raised to honour, then suffered degradation and death.

There is only space to mention a few of the arguments: the shameful charges so carelessly pressed, the odd mixture of humility and dignity, fear and exhilaration in Anne's own demeanour. Sir William Kingston, the constable of the Tower, the same who arrested Wolsey, wrote to Cromwell: "I have seen many men and also women executed and they have been in great sorrow, but to my knowledge this lady has much joy and pleasure in death."

The King himself showed unexpected feeling. He assigned her the apartments of state to be her prison, sent for an expert swordsman from France so that no clumsiness would protract her agony on the scaffold. These concessions are less in keeping with the punishment of a guilty wife than with the sacrifice of a victim whose blood has miraculous power to fertilise the womb of her successor, conjure forth a male heir.

The arguments nowhere mount up to proof, but they offer a plausible reconstruction of the motives that inspired the ritual on Tower green, when Queen Anne laid her head on the block and her eyes were covered with a bandage to spare the headsman their brightness.

On the day following her execution the King married Jane Seymour and seventeen months later she bore him a son, Prince Edward. If the King imputed supernatural power to the grisly rite preceding his wedding he had reason to believe that it was effective; but in granting his prayer it took its revenge on the new Queen. Within a fortnight of the birth of her child she died, succumbing, according to Cromwell, to "the neglect of those about her, who suffered her to take cold and eat such things as her fantasy in sickness called for." The King gave her a magnificent funeral as befitted the mother of the heir to the throne; he even put the court into mourning in spite of his own hatred of black clothes. This display of grief failed to impress the Imperial ambassador, Eugene Chapuis, who recalled an occasion when two pretty girls were introduced to the King after his marriage to Jane, and the regret that he expressed that he met them too late.

CHAPTER 13

King Henry was forty-six years old when his son was born. The handsome and easygoing young man who left Wolsey to govern his kingdom while he hunted and jousted, composed music or read theology, had grown into an autocrat, dominant and formidable, fully determined to manage his own affairs. Cromwell was his capable servant, but there was no longer doubt as in Wolsey's time who gave the orders. The change in the King's character was partly the fruit of slow growth to maturity; but it had dangerous aspects also, the aggravation of faults latent in the boy, flourishing unchecked in the man whose will no one dared to oppose. His temper had always been uncertain, liable to sudden outbursts of rage. Even at the age of ten in his father's lifetime he provoked scandal at court by his fierce refusal to pay respect to his sister Margaret whom he disliked, when she was betrothed to the King of Scotland. The habit grew on him, fostered by sulky brooding; but he made up for it by the geniality of his intervening moods, his easy charm and good nature.

Although he had none of his father's scruples against shedding blood, and seldom shrank from the execution of a prisoner if it suited his policy, he took no pleasure in cruelty, was capable of genuine compassion when circumstances sufficiently outrageous were brought to his notice. Nevertheless he could be murderous in his fury, as he showed in his treatment of More and of Queen Anne. On such occasions he was as uncontrollable as a force of nature. When the storm was over he himself often regarded the result with dismay.

It can be argued that the deterioration of his character had its origin in the disastrous outcome of his second marriage, that whatever the motives were that prompted him to put Anne to death they left an incurable wound. There is another cause, however, which cannot be excluded. Early in 1537 he suffered the first attack of a painful ailment, an ulcer in his leg, which afflicted him for the rest of his life. Many explanations have been put forward; that offered by Professor Shrewsbury in his essay, *Henry VIII, a Medical Study*, covers the symptoms best when he describes them as a form of gout, which Henry inherited from his father and which his own indulgence in food and drink aggravated. Crystals of sodium biurate developing in the tissue of the leg at one of the joints, hip, knee or ankle, work their way to the surface, forming ulcers where they emerge. While the discharge lasts the patient is in excruciating pain; but afterwards the lesion heals and he resumes his normal health, till—if he is constitutionally predisposed and takes no precaution in his diet—the whole process begins again.

The description fits what is known of Henry's illness. It was intermittent; almost to the end he enjoyed periods of relief during which he could find pleasure in active sports, make strenuous journeys on business of state. When the pain came on it goaded him to passionate irritability, like the picador's darts maddening a bull; but the power of his mind never failed him, he governed the country with strength and sagacity till his death.

His vagaries of temper made life uncomfortable for his courtiers; but his firm government, orderly administration earned him the respect and gratitude of his people, of all who wished to live in peace. Lacking any standing army, threatened by disaffected nobles and ecclesiastics who conspired with his enemies abroad, he could rely on popular support for his authority to carry out radical reforms in Church and state. He knew how far to go with safety, when to strike, when to yield. His ambition was to exalt the dynasty founded by his father, to leave it securely established in a prosperous and contented realm. If he pursued his own glory he put his vanity to constructive use.

The most celebrated of his reforms are those which he carried out in the Church, the substitution of Royal for Papal authority and the dissolution of the monastic system. Personal motives played a part in the former; schism could have been avoided if the Pope had annulled his marriage to Catherine, accepted Anne as his wife.

That is not to say that England would have remained untouched by the Reformation, devoted to the see of Rome. Henry was cautious by temperament, in no hurry to reject the old and adopt the new. He punished impatient reformers as harshly as treasonable reaction. His policy, however, served a consistent purpose, resistance to foreign dictation. He was determined to be master in his own house, claiming undivided allegiance from his subjects whether laymen or clerics.

This motive had its part in his treatment of the monasteries, which were an enclave of Papal influence, subject not even to the authority of a diocesan Bishop but to the Pope alone. The system, however, called for reform as much on social as on political grounds, and action was in fact taken in his father's reign and earlier by the most orthodox to suppress some of the worst abuses. During the millennium or so of their existence these communities dedicated to religion often filled a useful place in society, feeding and comforting the needy and providing refuge for learning and the arts; but as times changed and more settled conditions were established much of the work became superfluous or was neglected. Scholars were no longer driven to seek ecclesiastical protection, and as monastic wealth accumulated the abbot appeared to his neighbours less a friend in need than an arrogant and rapacious landlord. Few monks took vows of celibacy from a sense of vocation; the appeal of the monastery lay in an easy livelihood, an honourable standing in the neighbourhood.

The strain of the cloister unsweetened by religious inspiration was more than flesh could endure. There is nothing surprising in the scandals revealed by the King's agents who carried out a visitation to report on prevailing conditions. Many of these officers were overbearing in their manners, ruthless in demanding and seizing treasure. Their methods were often violent and unjust, but their evidence rings true of the vices which flourish in a segregated community. The monastic life had outlasted its usefulness, was ripe to be dissolved.

The smaller houses were the first to suffer dissolution, but the larger did not long enjoy reprieve. The process was carried on till the whole system was eradicated. The result was to denude the face of England of a traditional feature often of great architectural beauty, a multitude of abbeys and priories with their churches adorning the bank of a river, a secluded valley or the outskirts of a town. It was the King's intention to convert the buildings into schools, hospitals and almshouses, and when he put the treasures of the monks up for sale he retained the fabric in his own hands; but years went by, nothing was done, no money was available for the purpose, and meanwhile the buildings fell into ruin, neighbours stripped the roof of lead, the walls of stone, using the house of religion as a convenient quarry. The end of the story was that the King sold the site for what it would fetch, and a new owner took possession concerned only to make a profit. The King had the consolation in this, that it contributed to the permanence of his reform of the Church. A vested interest grew up in the country immovably opposed to the restoration of ecclesiastical land.

The administrative reforms which date from King Henry's reign belong rather to constitutional history than to this portrait of the dynasty. An exception is his work in Wales, of which some account is needed to show that like his father he was not unmindful of the land of his ancestors. On two occasions in the past the Welsh had been offered a prospect of orderly government, an end to the anarchy and tyranny of the marcher lords. When Edward IV sent his son and heir to live at Ludlow it was so that he should grow up to be Prince of Wales in fact as well as name; but the father died too soon, the boy became Edward V and vanished in the Tower of London, and the Council of the Marches in Wales remained as far as ever from effective power. Henry VII repeated the attempt, setting up his own son, Prince Arthur, to rule the principality; but misfortune dogged Ludlow Castle, Prince Arthur died of the plague, and the King was too discouraged or too preoccupied elsewhere to persevere.

Wales had to wait for a lasting settlement till the latter years of the reign of Henry VIII. When the presidency of the Council of the Marches fell vacant in 1534 he appointed Rowland Lee, Bishop of Lichfield, a swashbuckling prelate more at home in armour than in the pulpit. Lee imposed order by force, hanging malefactors by the thousand without respect for forms of law; but the terror on which he relied was impartial, Welshman and marcher lord suffered alike. He prepared the way, little as he knew it and little as he approved when it was known, for an Act of Parliament whose clemency could have been mistaken for weakness without this savage prelude. The scheme which the King enacted in Parliament gave Wales the same administration as England, abolished the quarrelling fiefs in the marches, divided the whole country into shires. Welsh law was superseded by English; but Welshmen and Englishmen enjoyed the same rights, were equally eligible for office under the Crown. The act of a Tudor King relieved Wales from the stigma of the penal laws of Henry IV. There was complaint, it is true, over his insistence on English for the conduct of official business. The Welsh pleaded in vain for their language, arguing in a petition submitted to him that "it is that which was spoken anciently not only in this island but in France," and that he should not blame it for its harsh pronunciation, should believe rather that "words that sound so deep proceed from the heart." The plea was rejected; nevertheless the language persisted, and as most of the justices of the peace appointed under the new constitution spoke it as their mother tongue the provisions banning it from the courts were seldom enforced in practice.

In England many expressed alarm at the King's policy, reproached him for putting trust in "the Welshery." Lee especially was indignant; but he died, and his repressive methods were not resumed. The King's wisdom was proved by events. Wales, enjoying law and order, settled government almost for the first time in its history, repaid him with grateful loyalty, remained at peace no matter what troubles distracted other parts of the realm.

In the summer of 1536 these broke into open rebellion in the north of England. The rebels, professing religious motives and protesting against the breach with Rome and the dissolution of the monasteries, called their insurrection the "Pilgrimage of Grace"; but it received inspiration and support from the same group of disaffected nobles who conspired with the Emperor and prompted the "Holy Maid" earlier to treason. Since her imposture was exposed they could rely no longer on her miracles to appeal to popular credulity; they made up for the lack by fomenting social and political grievances, many of which had just cause. The north complained of corrupt administration, neglected trade, bitterly quoting the proverb, "Out of sight, out of mind."

The rebellion began in Lincolnshire and spread quickly across the Humber into Yorkshire, gaining strength with the capture of York and the surrender of Pontefract Castle. For a time there was great danger; the rebels were said to be looking for a suitable claimant of Plantagenet blood to marry Princess Mary and replace her father on the throne. Levies hastily raised were put under the command of the Duke of Norfolk, who advanced north to restore the King's authority; but in Yorkshire he found himself so heavily outnumbered that he chose rather to negotiate than to fight. He met the rebel leaders at Doncaster, and terms were agreed. Robert Aske, their spokesman, accompanied him back to London to have them confirmed by the King.

The terms were not carried out. When Aske returned to the north jealous rivals disowned, defied him. They took up arms again, and this time Norfolk no longer shrank from battle. His enemies were too disunited to follow a concerted plan, and he was able to intercept their marauding bands and eliminate each in turn. All the leaders were captured and sentenced to death, not even Aske was spared; but when the danger was over many changes were made in the administration of the north, many of the grievances which provoked the rebellion found redress.

The threat of the Pilgrimage of Grace revealed how dangerously the King depended on loyal nobles willing to defend his interests. The forces commanded by the Duke of Norfolk were drawn from his own estates or contributed by other territorial magnates; the King was without adequate resources of his own to support him. He was reminded of his insecurity in the following year when a plot came to light involving two powerful families, Pole and Courtenay, both of which traced their descent from the House of York. The Poles, Henry, Reginald and Geoffrey, were grandsons of Edward IV's brother, George Duke of Clarence. The most active in sedition was Reginald, who from deacon's orders had recently been made a Cardinal. He urged his brothers to seize the opportunity to revolt when Pope Paul published the bull of deposition prepared against King Henry but held in abeyance by Pope Clement. The plot was discovered in time, the eldest of the brothers beheaded. Geoffrey, the youngest, saved his life by betraying his accomplices. Reginald escaped altogether, never venturing into danger from his refuge in Flanders.

As long as enemies of this sort threatened King Henry's throne he could afford no quarrel with the party of nobles led by the Duke of Norfolk. They supported him to further their own interests, but they had no love for the reforms on which he was engaged, and they hated his minister Cromwell as a vulgar upstart. The King kept control by holding the balance. Cromwell's policy was his own; but he restrained, even opposed it when feeling rose too violently in the council.

Norfolk and Cromwell were too unlike to understand or respect each other. The former inherited prestige from his father, the victor of Flodden, but was himself without distinction either as soldier or statesman. He was a pillar of the Church, a powerful champion of its privileges, retaining a reputation for piety even when his treatment of his wife drove her out of her mind, and he installed his mistress, the children's nursemaid, to preside in her place in his house. When his niece, Queen Anne, fell into disgrace he condemned her sternly, careful to preserve himself unspotted by ties of blood.

Cromwell in contrast, the son of a Putney brewer, owed his fortune to his own efforts. After a youth spent in raffish adventure in Italy he entered Wolsey's service, where his ability earned him rapid promotion. Wolsey himself before his fall recommended him to the King, and Cromwell till his death cherished the memory of his old master with affection; but with this exception—to which later he added Cranmer—he held all churchmen in distrust, a layman to the depths of his soul, ardent supporter and instrument of the King's plans to subordinate ecclesiastical to secular authority. His numerous enemies found much in him to denounce, he was ambitious and ruthless and retained the habit learnt at an early age among the Italian banditry of enriching himself at the public expense; but if he had the vices he had also many of the virtues of a self-made man of the Renaissance, cultured tastes, zest and wit, and his modest house in London in Throgmorton Street was the favoured resort of needy beggars, among whom he loved to distribute generous bounty from his ill-gotten wealth.

He was at one with the King not only in curtailing the power of the Church but also in his concern for mercantile interests, and in the struggle on the Continent between France and the Emperor he favoured alliance with the latter because of the dependence of English trade on markets in the Netherlands. This was a policy difficult to maintain after the publication of the Papal Bull of deposition; the Pope was the King's enemy, the Emperor the Pope's friend. It was the opinion of many that the King's best retort was to seek help from France and seal the understanding by marrying a French princess.

The French responded with alacrity, offering him his choice from a bevy of nubile beauties; but Cromwell who distrusted King Francis did his best to discourage this "Judgment of Paris," and sent Holbein to the duchy of Cleves on the lower Rhine to paint the portrait of the Duke's sister Anne. When the likeness was shown to King Henry he was greatly attracted, impatient to make her acquaintance, and negotiations began with a view to marriage. The ducal family followed the Catholic tradition, professing spiritual allegiance to the Pope; but as an elder sister was the wife of the Elector of Saxony, leader of the German Lutheran princes, the Duke kept a foot in either camp. He was a young man, who had recently succeeded to the title, Anne herself was only twenty-four. The marriage seemed to offer everything that Cromwell wanted, a close connection with Protestant Germany at which the Emperor need not take offence.

When Anne of Cleves landed in England Henry was so eager that he rode to meet her with a party of friends. They set off without formality and intercepted her at Rochester; but when he saw her he sustained a shocking disappointment, was so upset by her unlikeness to her portrait, her lack of charm that he forgot even to give her the sable muff and tippet which he brought as a present. He returned at once to Greenwich, where he vented his anger on Cromwell. At first he demanded that the contract be repudiated, the bride sent back to her brother. Cromwell pointed out that such a rebuff would estrange not only the Duke himself but also the Elector of Saxony and other princely kinsmen in Germany, leave England stripped of allies in Europe. His arguments prevailed; the King agreed to go through with the wedding, but his dissatisfaction persisted.

The political fruits of the match were as disappointing as the bride. The Duke of Cleves fell out with the Emperor over conflicting claims to the province of Gelderland, and he appealed to England for help. King Henry found himself burdened not only with an unloved wife but also with her brother's quarrel. Cromwell's enemies in the council made the most of these misfortunes, hoping to overthrow him. The balance of power was already swinging in their favour. They had recently persuaded the King to enact a measure, the Act of Six Articles, to check the pace of religious reform and impose fierce penalties on the heterodox. They had means too of exerting influence on him through the passion which he conceived for Catherine Howard, one of the new Queen's maids-of-honour. Catherine, like Anne Boleyn before her, was a niece of the Duke of Norfolk, and Stephen Gardiner, now Bishop of Winchester and leader of the conservative party in the Church, did his best to foster the attachment by offering his house at Southwark, the official residence of the see of Winchester, for clandestine meetings.

Nevertheless Cromwell retained the King's confidence. His position seemed to be impregnable when he opened the parliamentary session with a plea for mutual toleration and charity, and a few days later he was created Earl of Essex. That was in April 1540; in the following June proceedings in the council were interrupted by the captain of the guard, who arrested him on a charge of treason. His enemies crowded round, abusing him; the Duke of Norfolk himself snatched the George star, emblem of the Order of the Garter, from his neck. He was dragged away by the soldiers, conveyed by boat to the Tower.

Cranmer, Archbishop of Canterbury, who was his friend, wrote to the King to plead for him, urging that he was "such a servant in my judgment, in wisdom, diligence, faithfulness and experience, as no prince in this realm ever had." The King himself hesitated; twice he sent emissaries to the Tower to put questions to the prisoner, and he listened to the answers with evident emotion. There could indeed be few men less deserving a charge of treason than Cromwell, whose political creed sought fulfilment in extending and exalting the King's authority. The failure of his efforts to fulfil it cost him his life; the King was too dependent on the opposing party to be able to save him. A bill of attainder was carried in Parliament, received Royal assent, and Cromwell was beheaded. In later years the King expressed his regret.

While Cromwell was in the Tower the King summoned a convocation of clergy to pronounce on the validity of his marriage to Anne of Cleves. There was little difficulty in finding ground for annulment when it became known that after four months of cohabitation she remained a virgin. He shielded his vanity by unflattering remarks at her expense; but a more probable explanation is indicated by the scandalous secret which the former Queen Anne confided to her brother, Lord Rochford, and he blurted out defiantly in court. The King was not impotent in 1536, he was able to beget a son on his marriage to Jane Seymour; but failure of virility is often a gradual process, and it is reasonable to suppose that four years later, when he was forty-nine, he was an even less effective partner. If there was no hope of issue from Anne of Cleves the fault was not hers.

She was distraught with terror when she heard that her marriage was annulled, she expected to share the fate of her namesake; but her spirits revived quickly when she was assured that the King intended her no harm, and that if she submitted to the Act of Parliament he would make generous provision for her maintenance. The only condition imposed was that she must remain in England, a hostage to deter her brother from avenging her wrongs. She agreed without demur, her reward was an ample income and estates at Richmond and Bletchingley, where she lived in comfort and honour, happier in exile than in the dull obscurity of her brother's court at Cleves. There were occasions even when the King visited her; they could enjoy each other's company when they were no longer husband and wife.

Meanwhile he married Catherine Howard. She was only eighteen, first cousin to Anne Boleyn, but a great deal younger. Her attraction owed more to the high spirits of youth than to her tawny complexion, round face and short and dumpy figure. The King, however, was much enamoured, he called her his "rose without a thorn." It flattered him to succeed in wooing so young a girl. She herself was not of a type long to resist the temptation of a Royal wooer.

She was the most unsophisticated, least dignified of his wives, never outgrowing the effects of her neglected upbringing. Her mother died when she was a child, and her father, left with a large family on his hands, put her in charge of his stepmother, the dowager Duchess of Norfolk, second wife of the victor of Flodden. The old Duchess took no trouble to look after her, let her run wild with the servants and friends of disreputable character. There was much in her record already that would not bear the light; but the King knew nothing of it, and she herself was of sanguine temperament, able to believe that she could hush it up. It is clear, however, that as soon as she became Queen she was pestered by former companions anxious to take advantage of her position and reminding her with thinly veiled blackmail of escapades shared with them in the past.

In the spring there was trouble in Yorkshire, an abortive rebellion fomented from abroad by Cardinal Pole, of which the chief victim was his mother, the aged Countess of Salisbury, daughter of Clarence and niece of Edward IV, who was put to death for her part in it. After its suppression the King set out on a progress of state through the north to restore loyalty and confidence, and the Queen accompanied him. He left the government in his absence in the hands of a triumvirate consisting of Cranmer, Lord

Audley and Edward Seymour, Queen Jane's brother, who had been created Earl of Hertford.

While he was away evidence came to them of the Queen's unchastity before marriage. The informer was a woman, Mary Lassels, who had been employed in the house of the dowager Duchess of Norfolk where she was a witness of amorous romps. As reward for holding her tongue she had applied to the Queen for a profitable situation and was now taking revenge for her lack of success. The most damaging of her stories was that the Queen pledged troth to a lover, Francis Derham, and that the betrothal was physically consummated so that she became his wife.

The King returned in radiant good humour, delighted with his reception in the north and his young bride, his companion. The unenviable task fell on Cranmer of telling him what Mary Lassels had reported. He took the news at first with incredulity, but supporting evidence was shown him. Even then there was no outburst of rage; the shock was too painful, he wept heartbroken.

If the Queen was less surprised by the charges her response to them was more violent. She became hysterical, sobbed and screamed, contradicted herself in answer to questions, declaring at one moment that the whole story was untrue, at another that Derham raped her. To pacify her Cranmer promised with the King's authority that her life would be spared. Meanwhile, however, fresh evidence came to light, relating to events after her marriage to the King. She was accused of resuming acquaintance with her former lovers, in particular that on her recent journey with the King in the north while they were staying at Lincoln she left her room to spend the night with one of them. Her offence was no longer just perjury, marriage contracted on a false pretence of virginity; she was put on trial for adultery, warned that this was treason in a Queen, that the penalty was death.

Found guilty, she died under the headsman's axe. Her faults were those of youth and ignorance, of an education that denied her the chance to strengthen her character. Her execution, however, is free from the suspicion attaching to that of her cousin Anne. The grounds on which she was condemned were proved beyond reasonable doubt.

The dowager Duchess, her stepgrandmother, suffered confiscation of her estates and a year's imprisonment for her failure to warn the King that his bride was no virgin. Few others were punished, although most of those in the council who encouraged the marriage were well aware of the girl's background. The Duke of Norfolk, uncle of two beheaded Queens, wrote in fulsome terms to express his abhorrence of their guilt, and his excuses were accepted. The King could not afford to quarrel with him, the dynasty was not yet secure.

Foreign war after long respite again threatened England, but the pieces on the board were rearranged. The Emperor in incongruous alliance with the Protestant princes of Germany urged and persuaded King Henry to make common cause with them against France. It was the policy advocated by Cromwell, fulfilled after his death. War with France as usual disturbed relations between England and Scotland; tradition founded on ancient treaties bound the Scots to intervene on the French side. Thirty years had passed since James IV was defeated and killed at Flodden, leaving a son of only a year old to succeed him as James V. Scotland was recovering strength; James V, a grown man, married to a French wife, was ready to support his ally, avenge his father's defeat. As long as his mother, King Henry's sister Margaret, was alive English interests had her surreptitious help, less through influence exerted on her son—from whom she became as bitterly estranged as from the two husbands who in rapid succession consoled her widowhood—than by a flow of secret information with which she kept her brother supplied in return for his gifts of money. She died, however, in 1541, and King Henry no longer knew in advance what was planned in Edinburgh.

Suspicion mounted on both sides, and when a meeting was proposed between uncle and nephew the Scots smelt a trap and refused. The English, in fact, were the first to break the peace. The Duke of Norfolk led a raid across the border, devastated the valley of the Tweed; he achieved nothing else, was driven back into England. King James gathered an army to retaliate; but the war was unpopular, there were many even among the leaders who feared another Flodden, many attracted by the ideas of the Reformation who admired King Henry for his defiance of the Pope. To avert mutiny the army was disbanded, another raised in its place, a tumultuous host, ill-organised, ill-led. King James, taken ill with pleurisy, was unable to accompany it. The Scots advanced into Cumberland where they met strong resistance, were brought to battle in the marshes by the Solway and suffered calamitous defeat, many killed by the English, many drowned by the incoming tide.

King James returned to Edinburgh, a broken man. Both his sons had died in infancy; but his wife again was pregnant. He left her to await her delivery at Linlithgow while he himself withdrew into Fife to his palace of Falkland. He was desperately ill; the affection of the lungs from which he suffered before the invasion was the prelude to tuberculosis, and he was too depressed to exert his will to recover health. He lived long enough to receive the news that the Queen had given birth, that the child was a girl. His dying words are recorded: "It came from a lass, it will end with a lass." His family owed the throne to marriage with the daughter and heiress of Robert the Bruce, King of Scotland.

The new-born baby Mary became Queen of the Scots. For the second time in a generation the unhappy realm was condemned to the dangers and weakness of a long regency.

In the summer of 1543 King Henry decided to marry again. His sixth wife was Catherine Parr, who herself had already been twice widowed although she was not yet thirty-one. Her former husbands were both much older than she, so old indeed that they needed less a wife than a sick-nurse. On the death of the second, Lord Latimer, she looked forward at last to a marriage of love, responding gladly when she was wooed by Thomas Seymour, brother of the Earl of Hertford and Queen Jane, a man whom few women could resist. The King's intervention destroyed her hopes; Seymour dared not oppose him, relinquished her without demur. For the third time she was condemned to marry an ageing invalid. The King's attacks of gout were becoming more frequent, and while they lasted he was often beside himself from the pain.

Her second husband, Lord Latimer, had been a devout champion of the traditional order in the Church, and it was generally expected that his widow would use her position as Queen to promote views of the same sort. The expectation was not fulfilled. She was a woman of much wit and intelligence, attracted by the new learning, but careful while Latimer was alive to disguise her tastes. In the King she found a mind more in tune with her own; he enjoyed the discussion of ideas, she had greater freedom to say what she thought, and her influence became apparent in the favour shown to many reformers.

Not to those, however, who forced the pace, advanced faster than suited his policy. Heterodoxy was a man's own concern if he kept it to himself; but the public advocacy of forbidden doctrines still invited savage punishment, and heretic and papist alike were burnt at the stake. Close friends of hers were among the victims, and she was unable to save them. To be associated with her increased their danger, attracted the attention of informers. Her enemies, of whom she had many in the conservative faction in the council, were looking for an opportunity to entrap her; they hoped by condemning her acquaintance to involve her in the disgrace.

Stephen Gardiner, Bishop of Winchester, who disapproved of the spread of radical views, nearly succeeded in provoking her downfall. It was said of him that, when he hunted, it was his habit "to bend his bow to bring down the head deer" and spare the does and fawns; but the Queen was of too exalted rank to be spared as a doe, he classed her among the stags. An opportunity came when she was more than usually bold with her tongue, and the King irritable from gout took offence. Gardiner fanned the King's ill temper, played on his mood so skilfully that he obtained permission to draw up articles for her indictment. A document was prepared and given to the lord chancellor; but as he carried it in his pocket it fell out by accident on the floor. A young page saw it there, picked it up, and when he read what was written he took it to the Queen, to whom he was devoted.

Her alarm was such that she fainted, and even when she recovered consciousness her agitation was still so violent that her attendants, fearing serious illness, put her to bed. They informed the King of her condition, explaining that it was brought on by distress of mind, and although he was in great pain from his gout, and had to be carried in a chair, he came at once to see her. His mood was already calmer, he regretted his hasty decision, and as he sat at her bedside all his fondness for her returned; she was a woman of great charm.

He said nothing of the threat hanging over her head, and she herself was too exhausted to plead with him; but the kindness of his manner reassured her, and on the following day she took courage to go to him to ask how she had offended. His anger began to kindle again, he told her that she laid down the law to him, exalted her judgment over his own; but her ready wit appeased him when she declared that she only opposed her views to his for the sake of argument, to take his mind off the pain which he suffered from his ulcered leg.

"Is it so, sweetheart?" he replied. "Then are we perfect friends."

Meanwhile the lord chancellor had made a fresh copy of the

missing indictment, and he came with it to arrest her. He found her walking in the garden with the King, who had his arm round her waist. When he announced the purpose of his visit a bellow of Royal fury interrupted him. He clutched his papers and fled.

The King's illness was intermittent. There were times when he enjoyed much of his old vigour, went hunting, was as capable as most men in their fifties of strenuous recreation out of doors. In the summer of 1544 he took command in person of the forces carrying on war in France and was present at the siege and capture of Boulogne. Soon afterwards his health compelled him to return to England; but he was active again in the following year, organising naval defence in the Spithead to repel a French invasion. Nevertheless, as relapses grew more frequent and the intervals between them shorter, he knew that he was approaching the end of his life, and he brooded anxiously over the dangers threatening his son who would inherit the throne so young.

In August while his navy was driving the French from the Channel he lost his oldest friend, Charles Brandon, Duke of Suffolk, his companion since childhood and his brother-in-law. Many familiar faces were missing at court, and among those left there were few in whose wisdom and loyalty he had confidence when he was no longer there to watch them. The most trusted were Archbishop Cranmer and the Earl of Hertford, the young Prince's uncle. Hertford was a man of great integrity; he was also an able commander on the field of battle, leading a successful expedition against the Scots and appointed to supersede Norfolk in France to save Boulogne from recapture.

These advisers on whom the King relied to guide his son through the difficult years of his minority belonged to the reforming party in the Church. Ever since the boy was old enough to understand he had been brought up in the principles of the Reformation; his tutor, John Cheke, was among the foremost scholars of the new learning. Cautiously as King Henry proceeded in public affairs, suiting his pace to the needs and limitations of his people, he looked forward to a time when the new ideas would triumph, and he was careful to educate his son for the coming climate of opinion. His own policy was moving more surely in that direction; the Queen's influence made itself felt, she was never in danger again from her enemies. On Christmas Eve, 1545, he prorogued Parliament, and his words were long remembered even if few acted on their precept. He reproached the assembled peers for lack of love between man and man, which is "the special foundation of our religion," for dissensions "the occasions whereof are opinions only." Some, he went on, "are called Papists, some Lutherans and some Anabaptists, names devised of the devil for the severing of one man's heart by conceit of opinion from the other." He implored them to heal their divisions, to bear in mind that a man's first task is to strive "for his own amendment." His voice shook with feeling as he spoke, his eyes filled with tears. It was the last speech that he was destined to make in the House.

In the autumn of the following year it was evident that he was dying. He was too weak to enjoy the few recreations left him, to be wheeled out into the garden to fish in the pond or to play on his lute while his fool, Will Somers, sang. So that he should not be deprived entirely of music, Somers himself had to take the lute and play to him. While he was in this condition stories reached him of the behaviour of the Duke of Norfolk and his son, the Earl of Surrey, an ambitious young man whose arrogance earned him many enemies, but whose poetry written in his spare time was and still is greatly admired. The immediate charge against Surrey was that of changing the quartering on his shield, transferring the Royal arms—to which he was entitled through his mother's Plantagenet blood—from the second quarter to the prominent position reserved for the heir to the throne. The offence might have been trivial enough in other circumstances; but the gesture carried dangerous implications when the King was on the point of death, and his heir a child.

Further evidence was brought against him, that he boasted that as soon as the King was dead his father would seize control of the council of regency, even that he plotted with Cardinal Pole in Italy to deny the crown to Prince Edward, usurp it for Princess Mary whom he himself would marry. True or false, the charges were of a sort to prey on the King's fears. For years he had borne with the Duke of Norfolk, making concessions to retain his support and that of his party in the state; but now a firm decision was needed, the challenge could no longer be avoided without danger to the little Prince, his son. Surrey was arrested, put on trial, found guilty of treason and beheaded.

Norfolk who admitted that he knew of his son's plans tried to save his own life by pleading that he did his best to dissuade him, that his only crime lay in failing to report them to the King. He was arraigned before Parliament to answer to a bill of attainder, and in spite of his plea it was carried and he was sentenced to death. Only the Royal signature was lacking; but the King lay barely conscious, too ill to attend to business of any sort. It was the afternoon of the 27th of January, 1547; just after midnight he died. There was no King, no Parliament, the bill lapsed. Norfolk was left alive in prison.

CHAPTER 14

Edward VI was nine years old when he began to reign. His father mindful of the dangers to be feared when "the cat is a kitten" left detailed instructions in his will for the constitution of a council of regency. Its membership, a total of sixteen, included Cranmer and Hertford; but Stephen Gardiner who had held higher office than many of them was omitted. When King Henry was asked the reason he replied: "If he were one of you he would cumber you all, and you could never rule him." It needed his own strength to harness Gardiner's will, to command his loyal service. They shared Tudor blood, were second cousins, even if Gardiner's heredity lacked the blessing of the Church.

The principal regents received fresh titles. Hertford became Duke of Somerset, the name by which he is generally known to history. He had a natural advantage over the others as the young King's uncle, and the motion was carried with only one dissenting voice that he should be recognised as their leader, appointed Lord Protector to exercise sovereign authority during the King's minority. The council was too large a body to be an effective instrument of government.

There was provision also in the will to regulate the order of succession. If the new King died without issue his elder sister Mary would succeed him, or failing her, his younger sister Elizabeth. If the direct line failed altogether the crown would go to the descendants of King Henry's younger sister Mary by her marriage with his friend, the Duke of Suffolk. The little Queen of Scotland or anyone else claiming through his elder sister Margaret was excluded, partly because he was unwilling to put a Scotsman on the English throne, still more perhaps because Margaret exasperated him.

The contingent remainders seemed very remote at the time. King Edward was a healthy boy. His only serious illness, a quartan fever at the age of four (in the middle of his father's distress over Catherine Howard's infidelity), had passed without lasting harm, and in spite of the heavy strain of his education, his tutor's insistence on application to his books, he remained active in body, sharing his father's love of athletic exercise. There was every reason to suppose that he would grow up and marry and have children of his own to inherit the throne.

For the present his uncle, the Duke of Somerset, held control, guardian of his person as well as Lord Protector of the kingdom. The strict discipline that he imposed estranged him from his ward, who much preferred his younger uncle, Thomas Seymour, a boisterous extrovert, something of a braggart but a brilliant performer in the tilt-yard. While the elder uncle, stern and grave, discouraged any indulgence that could tempt to levity and extravagance, the younger dazzled the boy with stories of his adventures and exploits, brought him presents, lent him money. There was a shrewd purpose in Thomas Seymour's behaviour; he was jealous of his brother's eminence, dissatisfied with his own share of the rewards, although this included the title of Baron Seymour of Sudeley and the office of Lord High Admiral. He hoped to make good the setback to his ambition by influence established at an early age on the King.

In the previous reign he had been a suitor for the hand of the widowed Lady Latimer, Catherine Parr, till King Henry claimed her in marriage and made her his Queen. She was a widow again now; but Seymour aspired higher. He preferred if he could to marry Princess Elizabeth; she was not yet fifteen, Somerset refused his consent. Disappointment inflamed Seymour's anger more bitterly than ever against his brother, but he consoled himself with his old love, Queen Catherine. She was still fond of him, and they were married in private. Somerset, kept in ignorance till the wedding was over, found fault with her for remarrying so soon after King Henry's death.

Her three stepchildren stood up for her. She was the first in their father's lifetime to be a mother to them all, to draw them together into a united family, and they rewarded her with loyal affection. The King expressed jubilation at her marriage to his favourite uncle. Princess Elizabeth who was living with her moved with her into Seymour's house.

This arrangement was of a sort needing tact and prudence to escape scandal. Seymour possessed neither, and the stories lost nothing in the telling of his freedom with the girl, of romps in her bedroom when he pulled her out of bed and spanked her, with peals of laughter, her own as well as his. Queen Catherine ignorant of his earlier proposal refused at first to believe any ill; but swelling gossip compelled her to intervene, and she arranged for the Princess to move elsewhere into a house of her own. Her place was taken by her ten-year-old cousin, Lady Jane Grey, granddaughter of King Henry's sister Mary and the Duke of Suffolk. Under King Henry's will Lady Jane followed Princess Elizabeth as heir presumptive to the throne.

Somerset could afford to make light of his brother's jealousy, his own predominance in the council was assured. Even Gardiner, excluded from the government, respected the harmony of the new reign, contenting himself with an appeal "not to trouble the realm with novelties" while the King was a child. His words received little attention. Radical plans were put into effect at once to reform the Church, to permit marriage of the clergy, remove images and abolish ceremonies condemned as idolatrous. Harsh laws were repealed, those especially which condemned heretics to be burnt at the stake. The new legislation bore the stamp of Somerset's character, his philanthropy, his hatred of cruelty and superstition; it was no less typical of him in its high-handedness, its impetuous haste. He was incapable of listening to objections, too sure that he was right.

Except for Gardiner there were few who dared or were able to object. The Duke of Norfolk, saved from the axe by King Henry's death, gained life but not freedom; he remained a prisoner in the Tower. All thought of his release was abandoned when the Pope declared that King Edward was born in schism, and that it was the duty of the faithful to depose him and put his sister Mary on the throne. If the plan attracted little support in Europe the reason was, as the Emperor's advisers warned him, that it had no chance of success since the execution of the Earl of Surrey. King Henry's foresight had its reward, Surrey was dead. Norfolk survived, but was kept where he could do no mischief.

France was a source of greater anxiety. Before his death King

Henry made peace there on favourable terms; but King Francis followed him to the grave within two months, and his son who succeeded as Henry II was eager to recover Boulogne, take revenge on the English. There were many matters in dispute which held the making of a quarrel, and when a French ambassador came over to discuss them Somerset's own temper was far from conciliatory; he despised negotiation, thought it dishonest to haggle. He was so peremptory indeed that he might have provoked a declaration of war if the Frenchman had not been drawn aside by a tall dark stranger, who advised him not to pay attention to the Protector because "within these three years we shall see an end of his greatness."

The author of this prophecy, whom the Frenchman failed to recognise, was John Dudley, recently ennobled as Earl of Warwick, a leading member of the Protector's council. He was son of Henry VII's minister, Edmund Dudley, who earned unpopularity by his extortionate practices and was convicted of embezzlement and beheaded on the accession of Henry VIII. John Dudley, starting life under the shadow of his father's disgrace, owed his advancement to his own ability. He showed great skill in command of troops, personal courage on the battlefield, and was equally successful at sea when he was appointed Lord High Admiral to repel the French invasion in 1545. He knew too how to make his influence felt in the council chamber. Imperious by nature, intensely ambitious, he was careful not to betray himself; his voice and manner were so suave that men submitted unaware of the pressure to his inflexible will.

This was the rival already laying his plans for Somerset's downfall. He enjoyed the advantage in the struggle that he was unburdened by principles.

Somerset turned his attention to Scotland, behaving as tactlessly there as with the French. The little Queen was already five years old. It was King Henry's wish that she should be married to his son, to unite the English and Scottish crowns; but her mother, the Queen regent, a Frenchwoman, could not be persuaded. Somerset now revived the plan; conditions were more favourable, the Scots were tired of supporting France in distant quarrels and craved for peace. There was a strong party among them in favour of the marriage; but they feared for their independence under the united monarchy and sought assurances from Somerset, asking him whether he would not be anxious himself "if your lad were a lass and our lass a lad." The appeal was in vain; he was too sure of his own benevolence to have any sympathy for those who doubted it. When they rejected his terms he mustered an army, crossed the Tweed and advanced up the coast to devastate Scotland.

His generalship was as skilful as ever. The Scottish forces awaiting him on Pinkie Cleugh near Musselburgh suffered crushing defeat. He won the battle, lost the war. A French ship picked up the little Queen of Scots in the Clyde and carried her off to Brest out of his reach. When it was too late he offered concessions which might have averted the war and obtained Scottish approval for the match; but by then the child was in Paris, betrothed to the Dauphin. As usual his second thoughts were wise, as usual his own haste frustrated them.

King Edward wept bitterly over the loss of his Scottish bride. He was in no mood to listen to Lord Seymour, who proposed that he should console himself with his cousin, Lady Jane Grey. She was Seymour's ward living in his house, and he hoped to gain advantage from the match; but Edward was less amenable than his favourite uncle expected. His cousin Jane was his companion since the nursery, no substitute for the charms of the unknown, for a cloud-castle in Scotland.

Although Seymour held the office of Lord High Admiral, succeeding Warwick at the beginning of the reign, he let his ships sail without him to invest the Firth of Forth in the Scottish war. He himself stayed behind in London, taking advantage of his brother's absence to foster plans to grasp power. The King's tutor Cheke watched him with growing suspicion, found out about the loans of money with which he kept the King in dependence. On Somerset's return from the war Cheke went to him and told him what he knew. Somerset, enraged, sent for his brother, rebuked him sternly for deserting his command at sea and abusing the King's confidence; but after this tirade he relented, offered reconciliation and forgiveness. He had great affection in his heart for his brother, who took advantage of it and laughed at him behind his back.

Some restraint was exercised on Seymour by Queen Catherine, his wife. When she was about to bear him a child an improvement was noted in his behaviour, as if he resigned himself to his station in life, accepted its responsibilities. She was thirty-five years old; this was her first pregnancy in four marriages, and he awaited the outcome with anxiety. When she was safely delivered his relief was such that he forgot even to be disappointed that the child was a girl.

The rejoicing was premature. Within a week of the birth she contracted a fever and died. Seymour resumed his pursuit of restless ambition, unrestrained by her influence, unprotected by the prestige attaching to her name. To provide the resources that he needed, he leagued himself with the pirates whom as admiral he was employed to suppress. He conspired with the master of the Bristol mint to coin money for his private use. While Somerset remained ignorant his enemies in the council gathered evidence, eager to discredit not one brother only but both.

An incident at Hampton Court late on a January night in 1549 brought the trouble to a climax. The palace awoke to the loud report of an explosion; soldiers and servants came running, found Seymour outside the King's bedroom with a smoking pistol in his hand. The King himself bewildered and frightened stood at the door in his nightshirt, his dog lay dead at his feet. Seymour's own story was that he wished to test how well the King was guarded, that the dog attacked him, and he shot it in self-defence. No one believed him; he was arrested, charged with an attempt to murder the King and imprisoned in the Tower to await trial. He had nothing to gain from the King's death, no motive for murder; his purpose seems to have been to seize the King's person so that the rising which he planned could claim Royal authority.

Somerset wished to visit him in prison; but Warwick dissuaded him, fearing that if the brothers met the younger would plead for mercy, the elder relent and pardon him. The examination was carried out by a deputation of peers from the council, who found nothing to mitigate the offence, and a bill of attainder introduced into Parliament was quickly enacted, awaited only the signature of the Lord Protector assenting on the King's behalf. For weeks Somerset hesitated. When at last he signed the warrant his hand trembled so that his name was barely legible.

Seymour was beheaded. Somerset's enemies stirred up feeling against him for signing away his brother's life.

He was popular, however, among the poor, known to them as the "Good Duke." He encouraged them to come to him personally with their grievances and listened to them with compassion. He set an example by giving away land of his own in Middlesex to the farmers who occupied it. Nevertheless, the evils that he deplored went on undiminished. The common field was enclosed to provide pasture for the rich man's flocks, and the dispossessed peasants were left to starve or steal. The coinage was debased, and the cost of living rose inexorably. The powerful interests that throve on these practices were beyond the control even of the Lord Protector.

His good intentions raised hopes that he was unable to fulfil, and the exasperated victims took the law into their own hands. There were risings in the west country, in East Anglia too. Religious grounds of complaint were added; many resented the suppression of traditional forms of worship and the replacement of the Latin liturgy by Cranmer's Book of Common Prayer. The government had German mercenaries at its disposal, recruited for the war in Scotland; but Somerset was unwilling to use them against his fellow countrymen. At last alarmed by the spread of rebellion he yielded to military advice, sent effective reinforcements with whose help the loyal gentry prevailed; but he incurred blame on both counts, for his delay in restoring order and for letting loose a rabble of foreigners in England. Warwick on the other hand emerged with credit, victorious commander of the forces fighting in Norfolk.

Somerset's enemies in the council waited for a month to strike. Then they wrote to the Emperor to inform him of the dissatisfaction felt in England with the present government and prepare him for coming changes. The letter was sent in secret, but Somerset got to know of it and denounced such correspondence with a foreign power as treason. He made haste to join the King at Hampton Court so as to have him in his care. Less prudently he ordered leaflets to be distributed in the streets of London appealing to the people to rally to his support. Men of substance were alarmed, fearing a renewal of the violence of the past summer.

Meanwhile the conspirators met at Warwick's house in Holborn, and when news reached Hampton Court of the armed forces gathered there an envoy was sent to demand an account of their intentions. The envoy did not return. Somerset waited all day, increasingly agitated. Hampton Court was built for amenity, not to withstand a siege. When night fell he could bear the suspense no longer, decided to move the King to a place of greater safety. Edward was already in bed, he was woken up, came downstairs, found the courtyard full of flaring torches, anxious people. An observer has described how his spirit rose to the occasion; he had a jewelled dagger, a toy given him by his father, he waved it in the air, called to the crowd to follow him against his enemies.

"God save your Grace," they shouted. "We all would die for you."

In the chronicle which he himself composed of his reign he tells the story without comment: "That night with all the people at nine or ten o'clock at night I went to Windsor, and there was watch and ward kept every night." Other sources supply the details, the raw autumn night, the long ride through the rain to Windsor Castle, the bare rooms, the lack of comfort in the ancient fortress which had not been used as a Royal residence since the death of Henry VII. In the morning Edward was suffering from a bad cold.

Somerset's confidence was shaken by these misadventures, especially by the risk to the King's health. His first impulse to furious action was wearing off, and as was his habit he was stirred by belated regret, in a mood for moderation. When a message came from the council inviting him to surrender his office peacefully his friends persuaded him to negotiate. The alternative was civil war, renewal of the disorders from which the country had barely recovered. He did not swallow his pride without a struggle; there were moments when he threatened to escape with the King to Wales, uphold his cause there by invoking ancestral loyalty to the Tudors. These fantasies passed; he agreed to the council's terms, to resign his power and give himself up on condition that his life was spared.

He was imprisoned in the Tower where he remained for three months, then he was released and allowed to take his place again in the council, sitting there in fallen glory while his enemy presided. Warwick did not yet feel strong enough to eliminate the people's "Good Duke."

The title of Lord Protector was allowed to lapse. Edward, not yet thirteen, was encouraged to think that he played a more active part in the government. The belief was without foundation, Warwick who became his guardian kept jealous control; but the suavity of his manner contrasted agreeably with Somerset's avuncular sternness, the boy was less inclined to revolt, readier to absorb his influence. It was at about this time that Edward began the chronicle already quoted. Its style is factual and terse; he records events, never interposes his own comments. Where issues arise involving controversy as in his account of Somerset's downfall he presents always Warwick's point of view, his only source of information.

There is no reason to accuse him of heartlessness for his dry precision. From childhood he had been taught not to betray his feelings, least of all in a document vulnerable to prying eyes. The chronicle was an exercise undertaken at first with his tutor's help, later from his own resources, to fit him for his duties when he came to reign in fact as well as in name. It pays earnest attention to the fluctuations in value of the currency and to plans for the reform of the council, matters which were much on his mind; the tone remains equally dispassionate when he reports an uncle's execution or the denial to his sister Mary of the right to hear Mass. There is no place in it for his own emotions; he neither reveals nor intends to reveal them.

Accounts of his behaviour from observers who knew him show him in a very different light. The dispute with his sister of which he writes so coldly included a visit which she paid him in person, when her tears of distress provoked his own, and if Warwick had not intervened she would have had her will from his ready sympathy. His heart was more susceptible to persuasion than his mind. Another example is his attitude to the anabaptist, Joan Bocher, of whom he was content to record that she "was burnt for holding that Christ was not incarnate of the Virgin Mary, being condemned the year before but kept in hope of conversion." Behind this bare statement lie his passionate tears, his bewildered cry, when Cranmer brought the death warrant for his signature: "How can I send her to the Devil in all her error?" There is no lack of evidence that he shared his grandfather's hatred of cruelty.

Somerset had persuaded Parliament to abolish the death penalty for heresy, and in reintroducing it Warwick acted without legal authority. His purpose was to court the approval of orthodox rulers abroad by burning women of no importance like Joan Bocher, while he strengthened his position at home by alliance with reformers who commanded a substantial following. His religious policy disappointed the conservatives who, encouraged by his conformity in the past, supported his accession to power to restore their party's influence. The two most eminent were the Duke of Norfolk and Stephen Gardiner, and both were prisoners in the Tower, the former since King Henry's reign, the latter since the summer of 1548 when he broke with Somerset and defied his orders by preaching a sermon in favour of transsubstantiation before the King. Warwick was determined that they should stay there; both were rivals to be feared, Norfolk for his wealth and social standing, Gardiner for his ability. The leaders of the opposite persuasion offered no such danger. Even a Dudley could hold up his head among them, and they were glad to pay him honour. In their company he became more Protestant than the Protestants.

Any reform was acceptable whose advocates could be useful to him.

The new order in the Church was not content only to remove abuses which brought religion into disrepute; the attack was extended to doctrines and observances so closely woven into men's lives that society lost cohesion without them. Ancient habits of thought were deprived of sanctity, and there was nothing to take their place. Among rich and poor alike manners were corrupted, lacking an accepted standard of conduct. Landlords evicted their tenants, merchants swindled their customers, the victims of injustice turned to crime for a living. Anarchy invaded the home, broke up marriages, kindled strife. The spirit was starved, the only gods whose worship survived safe from doubt were those of money and power.

Many sincere reformers were appalled by what they saw; they deplored the haste with which the work was carried out. In retrospect they could appreciate King Henry's wisdom in holding a careful balance between tradition and change. Somerset was among those who expressed the bitterest dissatisfaction, having been deposed himself on a charge of misgovernment by the very men now leading the country into chaos. He formed a plan with Archbishop Cranmer and others of like mind to come to an understanding with Gardiner and obtain his release from the Tower. Although Gardiner was their resolute opponent in King Henry's reign, and it was Somerset as Lord Protector who imprisoned him, they respected his ability and strength of character. His restraining influence could be useful in the prevailing condition of affairs.

The opportunity came when Warwick was absent in France. The war, renewed by Somerset soon after King Edward's accession, strained resources, crippled trade, and its fruit was a disheartening series of reverses. The purpose of Warwick's journey was to conclude peace, the terms of which he had agreed. In comparison with those won by King Henry they were humiliating to English pride, involving the immediate surrender of Boulogne, but as a French delegate pointed out during the negotiations: "Then was then, now is now." The old cat was dead, the new a kitten.

While Warwick watched the French reoccupy Boulogne a deputation from the council led by Somerset visited Gardiner in the Tower, offering to set him free if he accepted a number of reforms in the Church including the new prayer book. His reply was conciliatory, willing to compromise. He was so sure indeed of the outcome that he ordered his servants to get his house ready for him at Southwark, and he even invited the officers of the Tower and their wives to a farewell supper, at which he kept them all laughing with jovial stories of his imprisonment.

News of these doings reached Warwick in France, enraged and alarmed him. He made haste to return, and when he saw the conditions on which Gardiner was to be released he insisted on adding others of a sort which no one but a Protestant of the strongest persuasion could accept. Gardiner's own comment was, "I'd sooner tumble myself into the Thames." The disappointment left him worse off than before. He spent the rest of the reign in prison, deprived of his see of Winchester, his revenues and estates.

Warwick was not content. His power remained insecure as long as Somerset lived. He waited for nearly a year, however, before he was ready to strike. In the summer of 1551 there was a serious epidemic of the "sweating sickness," and the lords of the council scattered to their country seats to escape infection. Business of state could still be carried on by travelling to and fro between each other's homes. The arrangement suited Warwick's plans. He could make sure that Somerset was not present by failing to inform him where a meeting would be held.

Among other matters discussed at these informal gatherings was the grant of a batch of new titles, which the leaders conferred on themselves under the Royal authority committed to them. Warwick's own prize was the highest, he became Duke of Northumberland. It was a name made famous by the Percys, to whom it belonged; but they were Earls only, not Dukes, and the direct line became extinct when Henry Percy, the last Earl of Northumberland, Anne Boleyn's suitor, died childless. A collateral branch of the family survived; there was great indignation when the title was usurped and exalted into a dukedom by the upstart, John Dudley.

Somerset had no share in these honours, he was not even consulted when they were awarded. This was more than a rebuff to his dignity, it was a threat to his life; the newly ennobled were without exception his enemies. In his dismay he turned for advice to his former secretary, William Cecil, to whom he had shown kindness in the past, putting opportunity in his way to raise him from obscurity and start him on a successful career. After Somerset's fall from power Cecil offered his services to the new government, obtaining high office and a knighthood. He was better informed almost than anyone about the Duke of Northumberland's plans, the recruitment of suborned witnesses, the relentless will hunting Somerset to his death. When his old benefactor confided his fear to him he replied coldly:

"If your Grace be not guilty you may be of good courage. If you are I have nothing to say but to lament you."

The cautious Cecil was destined to play a leading part in events in the years that followed.

The plague had abated, the lords sat again in the council chamber at Westminster, and on a morning when little business was expected Somerset arrived late, shortly before the hour for dinner. As he took his seat the lord treasurer leapt up, accused him of treason, and Northumberland (as Warwick must now be called) beckoned to an officer waiting with a posse of guards at the door, who entered, arrested Somerset and led him away to the Tower. The scene closely resembled that of Cromwell's arrest, as if it followed a precedent.

When the prisoner was put on trial he was charged with plotting to murder the Duke of Northumberland and other lords of the council at a banquet given in their honour, to assume authority again as Lord Protector and marry the King to his daughter, Lady Jane Seymour, a union of first cousins. Somerset was habitually indiscreet in speech, there was no lack of evidence of wild words, fulminations against the government; but it fell far short of proving him guilty of a plot to seize control of the state, in which the only accomplices which the indictment could suggest were his wife and family. Two years later when Northumberland himself came to die he confessed that the charges were false.

Nevertheless, Somerset was condemned to death. In spite of the firm measures taken to suppress it there was great lamentation among the people, who refused to believe ill of their "Good Duke." On the day of the execution crowds flocked to Tower Hill from London and the country around, and at one moment it even seemed that the prisoner would be saved; armed men came running up, onlookers shouted "Rescue," "Reprieve." It was only a detachment of guards arriving late on duty. He himself betrayed neither hope nor disappointment. He appealed from the scaffold for silence. "Through your quietness," he told his friends, "I shall be much quieter."

King Edward's entry for that day in his chronicle records: "The Duke of Somerset had his head cut off upon Tower Hill between eight and nine o'clock in the morning." The terse and factual style is in keeping with the rest of the document, revealing nothing of the boy's own feelings. It is clear that he believed the story told of his uncle's guilt; but there is nothing to show exultation over the fate of a stern guardian whose discipline he used to resent. Seven weeks were allowed to elapse between the trial and the execution; the delay was attributed by those in touch with the court to Edward's reluctance. The French ambassador who spoke to him reported his anxiety to save his uncle's life.

The removal of Somerset left Northumberland without an enemy who dared to oppose him. The discontented resigned themselves to wait till the King came of age, trusting that he would follow his father's example, that John Dudley would share the fate of his own father, Edmund Dudley, when the extent of his peculation was revealed. There was hope indeed that the time might not be far off. Edward was growing up fast, had a maturity of mind beyond his fourteen years, and although still dominated by Northumberland's mixture of cajolery and intimidation he was beginning to chafe against his dependence, impatient to put his own ideas into effect.

The direction which these were taking is shown by his behaviour about a month after Somerset's death when Ridley Bishop of London preached a sermon before him at Westminster, describing and deploring the miserable condition of the poor. After the service when the Bishop was about to go he was told that the King wished to see him. He found Edward waiting alone, who made him sit beside him and read the notes which he had taken of the sermon while he was listening. To every case of hardship cited by Ridley he had appended an appropriate remedy; in particular he named two empty houses of religion, the priory of St. Thomas in Southwark and the convent of the Grey Friars close to Newgate, which could suitably be converted to uses of social welfare. With Ridley's encouragement and advice his wishes were carried out; the former became a hospital for the sick, the latter a school for the children of needy parents—known as Christ's Hospital, it stood as a lasting memorial to his benevolence for three hundred years, when the site was sold and the school transferred to Horsham.

The hopes aroused of a golden reign when he was old enough to govern helped people to endure with patience the misgovernment of the regency. There was great rejoicing when the council agreed in response to his own urgent demand to let him assume power as soon as he reached the age of sixteen, without waiting for the legal term of his majority. If doubt was felt it was on account of his health, his slightness of build made him look frail to those who remembered his father's burly strength; but his body was wiry and active, and the anxious were reassured by the enthusiasm with which he took part in foot races, archery and other athletic sports.

Then in the spring of that year he suffered from a severe attack of measles, his first serious illness since the fever at the age of four. He seemed to make a complete recovery, was well enough in the summer to set out on a progress of state through the southwestern counties. There was lively entertainment at the great houses where he stayed, and he enjoyed it the more because Northumberland was not with him. A glimpse is afforded by the antiquary, John Aubrey, who lived nearly a hundred years later and tells in his *Natural History of Wiltshire* a story heard from a very old woman whom he knew. She remembered how as a girl of sixteen she met a boy riding alone on the hill; he had lost his way and asked her to direct him, and while they were talking the other riders of the hunt galloped up and greeted him. Even before they addressed him she knew that it was King Edward.

In addition to hunting parties there were visits of state to occupy him, including an inspection of the dockyard at Portsmouth. It was an exhausting programme so soon after his illness in the spring. He himself refused to admit that he felt the strain; but those who were with him observed evident signs of fatigue and grew uneasy. They decided to shorten the tour, making the excuse to him that it put too heavy a financial burden on these parts of the country. Even so, his weakness persisted, and when Northumberland joined them at Salisbury he was greatly alarmed, insisted that on their return to London the King should see Girolamo Cardano, a celebrated Italian doctor.

The doctor's report was reassuring, the patient only needed rest to recover his accustomed vigour; but Cardano was an astrologer as well as a physician, he confessed in secret that he read in Edward's horoscope "the omens of a great calamity."

At the end of January, Princess Mary was invited to stay at the palace of Westminster to see a masque acted by children at Candlemas. She arrived to find her brother in bed, with a high fever. She left the next day; the festivities were cancelled, the young actors dismissed. For weeks the King lay gravely ill, suffering from a tubercular infection of the lungs. He was at the dangerous age for the Tudors, the age at which his uncle, Prince Arthur, died at Ludlow of the plague.

In March he rallied, was able to open Parliament in person; but everyone was shocked to see how much the effort cost him, and when the session was over he left for Greenwich in the hope that fresher air and quiet would restore him to health. Encouraging bulletins were issued, but they failed to relieve the suspense, to banish foreboding. He was kept indoors hidden from sight.

Northumberland was haunted by anxiety. If the illness proved fatal all his plans were threatened with ruin. As he racked his brain to think what to do, his only chance of safety seemed to lie in linking himself by marriage with the Royal Family. He proposed that his fourth son, Lord Guildford Dudley, should marry Lady Jane Grey, the King's cousin, who had gone back to live with her parents after Lord Seymour's death. She was granddaughter to King Henry's sister Mary, heir presumptive to the throne after her mother if King Henry's own line failed. The Tudors, like the House of Lancaster before them, were desperately short of male heirs. Jane's mother, born Lady Frances Brandon, was the elder of two daughters, and her own family consisted of three girls of whom Jane was the eldest.

Since the failure of the plan to betroth Jane to King Edward himself, a marriage had been arranged for her with Edward Seymour, eldest son of the Duke of Somerset; but her parents foresaw little difficulty in breaking it off, Somerset's execution left the family without influence. All concerned were amazed and indignant when Jane not quite sixteen refused to accept the exchange, less attached, it seems, to Seymour than unattracted by Guildford Dudley. Her father swore, her mother whipped her. Her behaviour recalled that of her grandmother, Mary Tudor, when she was told to marry the King of France. Her grandmother was eighteen at the time, and even she was forced to yield. Jane's defiance suffered a like fate; but it was an early warning to Northumberland that his new daughter-in-law had a will of her own, no amenable pawn in the game that he directed.

The wedding was celebrated in London with a lavish display that jarred on public opinion at a time when the King lay dying at Greenwich. It was important however to Northumberland's plans to invest the ceremony with magnificence, to impress it on everyone that his son was acquiring royalty, that the great-grandson of Lady Guildford, governess to the King's children in Henry

VII's reign—the boy was called Guildford after her—was marrying the granddaughter of her Royal pupil.

King Edward was sinking fast. His doctors themselves gave up hope, and Northumberland dismissed them, installing a woman in their place, a charlatan, in whom he professed to have faith. She could do nothing to heal, but the stimulants which she administered (probably containing arsenic) prolonged life at the cost of great suffering. In the respite. thus gained Northumberland applied ruthless pressure to persuade the dying boy to alter the terms of his father's will, disinherit his sisters Mary and Elizabeth and appoint as successor his cousin, Lady Jane Dudley. He had arguments on which he could rely to make an impression. Although Edward was fond of his sisters he knew and feared the bigotry of Mary's views.

Nothing of this was revealed in public; but Northumberland summoned the lords of the council and the legal officers of the Crown to a secret meeting at Greenwich, where the King, lying in bed, barely able to speak, informed them of the new device for the succession and ordered them to swear to uphold it. His haggard face and weakness appalled them; no less so, the oath which he demanded. They foresaw the outburst of popular indignation which it would provoke. Northumberland was detested, many even of the reforming party preferred Mary as the lesser evil. They argued in vain, however; King Edward pleaded, Northumberland blustered and threatened, and at last they signed the deed of settlement, ready with excuses for use when the time came to repudiate their signatures. Cranmer alone swore without secret reservations, too full of pity for the King to disappoint his dying wish.

Less than a month afterwards, on the 6th of July, 1553, King Edward died, aged fifteen, the last King of the House of Tudor. It was a night wild with thunder and lightning, of hailstones red like clotted blood.

CHAPTER 15

Northumberland kept the King's death secret as long as he could. He wrote to Princess Mary who was living at Hunsdon in Hertfordshire and told her that her brother was asking for her, that her presence would comfort him; meanwhile he sent two of his sons with an armed escort to intercept her on her way and arrest her. She set off at once in response to the appeal; but at Hoddesdon before she could fall into the trap a horseman, better mounted than the Dudleys and outdistancing them, galloped to meet her. It was her goldsmith from London; she loved pretty jewels and was a frequent visitor to his shop. He came now with a message from Sir Nicholas Throckmorton, an officer in the palace of Greenwich, to warn her that her brother was dead. When the Dudleys reached Hoddesdon she was already in flight for Newmarket and the coast, with a party of only two women and six men to attend her.

For nearly two days Northumberland waited in vain for news of her capture, then, as rumours were spreading, he dared maintain the pretence no longer. He summoned the lord mayor and aldermen of London to Greenwich and informed them, swearing them to secrecy, that the King was dead, and that his successor appointed by letters patent under his own hand was his cousin, Lady Jane. On the following Sunday, having occupied the city with a formidable garrison, he ordered the announcement to be made in public and suitable sermons to be preached in the churches. There was little active expression of discontent; the people were too bewildered, and the precautions that he had taken cowed them.

The lords of the council gathered in the Tower, a fortress strong enough to protect them from insurrection. Meanwhile Northumberland with a few others to support him, including the new Queen's father and mother, took a barge up the river to Isleworth to fetch her from Syon House. She was still unaware of King Edward's death, much bewildered by the honour with which she was received. Northumberland led her to a dais, knelt to her and informed her that the King was dead, that before his death he had disinherited his sisters, and that as her mother renounced her claim she herself was next in succession to the throne. He invited her to accept the title of Queen of England.

Her reply was to burst into tears, and the only words that could be distinguished through her sobs were, "so noble a prince." She had known her cousin Edward from childhood and was fond of him. The assembled conspirators were taken aback; they waited respectfully till she composed herself. Then Northumberland repeated his offer of the Crown. Her answer came uttered with conviction:

"The Lady Mary is the rightful heir."

Again there was a battle of wills as when she refused to marry Guildford Dudley. Other means of persuasion were needed, her mother was unable to whip her; but the voices of the most eminent in the land were raised in chorus, imploring, inveighing, expostulating, to break her spirit. For a time she remained silent; according to her own account given later she was praying for a sign from heaven, and as no sign came she took it that God meant her to do what her parents said. She yielded, Northumberland and his lords prevailed; but it was not a victory to inspire confidence in her docility.

Her independence of character was the result of prolonged struggle against her upbringing. Her father, easygoing and good-natured when no interest was at stake, owed his career to his wife's influential connections; he submitted without effort to her dictation, and she herself was unrelenting in pursuit of wealth and power. In the early days she cherished great hope of marrying her eldest daughter to King Edward and insisted therefore on educating her strictly to equip her for her place in society. The child grew up accustomed to carping vigilance and reproof, often to corporal punishment.

It was not enough for the future planned for her that she should acquire the usual feminine accomplishments; under the influence

of the Renaissance a cultivated mind was demanded in a woman no
less than in a man, in Jane especially because, in her mother's
opinion, she was unlikely to travel far on her beauty. Her brown
eyes widely spaced held a pleasing frankness, her features were
delicate and her smile revealed the whiteness and regularity of her
teeth; on the other hand she was well below the normal stature,
and although her complexion was fresh and healthy it suffered from
freckles. A tutor was engaged for her when she was barely out of
the nursery to instil the rudiments of classical learning, Latin,
Greek and Hebrew. She was an apt pupil and made rapid progress.

This erudition was merely intended to be the means to social
advancement; but it had an effect on her which had not been
foreseen. The tutor was kind and patient, he inspired her with
his love of scholarship, treated her with an affection of which she
was starved elsewhere. In every task or recreation that she shared
with the family, at meals, at play, sewing or dancing, she was under
her mother's stern eye, liable to harsh abuse for the smallest fault,
to pinches and blows. She came to look on the hours spent in study
as a rapturous interval of peace, lived only for the opportunity to
escape there. Academic speculation, including her tutor's Protestant doctrine, acquired warmth and radiance; worldly aims and
amusements left her cold, she associated them with her mother's
tyranny.

The devotion with which she cherished her principles was
illustrated soon after her arrival in state to join the council in the
Tower. Everything possible was done to make it an impressive
occasion. She wore thick-soled buskins to raise her stature, so that
she should not be dwarfed by her attendants. Heralds proclaimed
her accession in the streets, and the escorting trumpeters responded
with an exultant blast to make up for the glum silence of the
onlookers. When she entered the presence chamber the crown with
its appropriate jewels was brought out for her inspection. She
gazed reverently; in her eyes it was the sacred emblem of sovereignty which she would receive in trust from God at her coronation, and she was indignant when one of the lords present
offered to put it on her head. He excused himself, explaining that
his purpose was only to try whether it fitted, and he was ill-
advised enough to add that another would be made to fit her husband. She said nothing, waited till the rest had gone and she and her
husband were alone, then she told him that no one could wear the

crown but herself, that she had no right to make him King, she could offer him nothing more than the title of Duke.

Guildford Dudley was the spoilt darling of his family, unaccustomed to be thwarted. He lost his temper, stormed at her, and when she remained stubbornly silent he burst into tears and ran out of the room to find his mother. They returned together, but the Duchess of Northumberland was no better able than her twenty-year-old son to bring Jane to order. Recriminations and threats fell on deaf ears. When her husband and mother-in-law paused at last for breath she repeated that Guildford could be a Duke, but unless Parliament wished it she would never make him King. The Duchess retorted that her son could no longer sleep with so undutiful a wife, and she led him away announcing that she was taking him back to Syon House. They packed up and were ready to depart, but officers sent by Jane stopped them from leaving the Tower. She had no need of her husband in bed, she said, but in daytime his place was at her side. Crestfallen he obeyed the Queen's orders.

Meanwhile disturbing news reached the council. It became known not only that Northumberland's two sons had failed to intercept Princess Mary at Hoddesdon, but worse still that when they tried to pursue her their men deserted, and they themselves barely escaped with their lives. She was already in Suffolk, finding safe refuge at Framlingham Castle, a fortress belonging to the Howards on whose allegiance she could count. She sent a letter from there to the council skilfully framed in conciliatory terms, offering to restore to favour anyone willing even now to recognize her claim to the throne.

Northumberland dictated a defiant reply. He had control of the government of the kingdom, was supported by a well-equipped army. His position indeed looked so strong that even the Emperor's ambassador, whose master was Mary's first cousin and could expect great advantage from her success, advised her to give up the attempt and save her life by flight. She paid no attention, better informed than he of Northumberland's hidden weakness, his well-founded distrust of his followers, whom he had induced by threats to accept King Edward's new device for the succession, and who were likely to uphold it only as long as it served their interest. Most of them feared and hated him, there were few in the country who did not.

He was well aware of the danger of disaffection, burdened with two conflicting tasks, to be more vigilant than ever to forestall betrayal by his friends, at the same time to crush the rebel princess before her cause attracted too formidable a body of support from his enemies. Unable to undertake both himself, he decided that his own place was in London at the seat of power, and that Jane's father—now Duke of Suffolk, since the death of his wife's two half-brothers—should command the army destined for the eastern counties.

It was an arrangement not at all to Jane's liking. She was afraid to be left with her father-in-law. Even her father was better protection, at least she knew what to expect. She refused to sign the commission which would send him away from her. Northumberland did not coerce her, unwilling to let it be seen how little he regarded the Royal authority which he himself had set up. The tasks were redistributed; he was in any case the more competent general, and when the army set out from London he and his sons, except Guildford, rode at the head. Crowds watched them go; no one, as he observed bitterly, wished them "God-speed."

Before his departure he reminded the lords left in the Tower of their oath of allegiance to Queen Jane, and warned them that if Mary prevailed their lives would be forfeited like his own. As soon as his back was turned their behaviour showed how much reason he had to distrust them. Emissaries travelled between the Tower and Mary's secret supporters in the city. Everyone was concerned to save his own skin; Jane might retain the title of Queen, but no one cared what happened to her. It was a blessing for her that she could retire into a world of the mind, of divinity and philosophy, scarcely aware of events round her.

Meanwhile Northumberland's campaign was dogged by misfortune. The fleet sent to watch the coast to prevent Mary from escaping was driven by adverse winds into Yarmouth, where the crews declared for her, compelled their officers to join them and reinforced the garrison at Framlingham. There was mutiny, too, in the army, and Northumberland's urgent request for money to allay the discontent received no attention in London. He had just enough left to bribe the men into surly obedience, and they advanced as far as Bury St. Edmunds; but there they mutinied again, and he blustered and pleaded without effect. His cause was too unpopular.

His discredit was completed by the arrest of his cousin, Sir Henry Dudley, at Calais with a train of waggons loaded with plate and jewels stolen from the treasury. He confessed that his purpose was to bribe the French King to invade England, with a promise to cede Calais added as a final inducement.

The lords in the Tower hesitated no longer. They sent a deputation to confer with the lord mayor and officers of the city, then the keys of the Tower were handed over, and all went together to proclaim Queen Mary in Cheapside. Jane's father himself tore the Royal canopy from the chair in which she was sitting. She expressed no regret, there was relief in her voice as she asked, "May I go home?" She received no answer; her father left her alone there, rushed out to declare his loyalty to Queen Mary to the crowds on Tower Hill. Queen Jane's reign was over, having lasted for nine days.

Northumberland surrendered, Queen Mary entered London in triumph, receiving an enthusiastic welcome. She owed much to the discontent provoked by his misgovernment, it was enough to earn popular favour that she opposed him; but support arose too from the nostalgic lustre clinging to her father's memory, people rejoiced to see his daughter on the throne, the usurpation thwarted. The very obstacles which she had overcome took their minds off the disadvantage which her father most feared, reconciled them to a female sovereign, the first to wear the Crown of England since the disastrous precedent set by Queen Matilda four centuries before.

Her known devotion to the ancient tradition of the Church, to the Pope and the Mass, troubled few except the extreme Protestants; many admired her for the staunchness with which she clung to her faith in the previous reign. The ideas of the Reformation had no firm root yet in England, and anxiety was allayed by her promise given in her first declaration to the council that she would put no constraint on men's consciences. The only apparent danger arising from her religious views threatened those in possession of estates of the Church, which they had acquired by gift or purchase after the dissolution of the monasteries. They included men from every rank in society, powerful nobles, rich merchants, working farmers, and no government could afford to offend them. Mary undertook that whatever else she restored to the Church there would be no disturbance of existing titles to the land, and this promise unlike the former was strictly kept. King Henry's reforms were too securely founded.

Mary was thirty-seven years old when she came to the throne. The happiness of her early childhood while her father and mother lived together in peace, and she herself was petted and honoured as heir to the throne, enhanced in retrospect the pain of the years that followed, sorrow after sorrow, the separation from her mother, the humiliation of bastardy, danger even to her life. As a young woman she was seldom free from anxiety, and the religion in which she sought consolation aggravated her troubles, involving her in struggle with her father and after his death with those ruling in her brother's name. It is remarkable how little this experience soured her; her nature remained gentle and affectionate, quick to anger but easily mollified, ready to trust and show mercy.

The nickname by which she is known to history, "Bloody Mary," is quite untrue of her character. If it can be applied without injustice to events for which she was responsible the reason lies in a habit of mind which she shared with her cousin Jane. Both sought relief from the present in an ideal world, Jane's the academic calm of the intellect, Mary's the warm shelter of Catholic piety. The ritual and doctrines of the Church recalled her mother, her childhood; they were a door giving access to bygone happiness. The veneration that she felt for them grew into bigotry, turned a kindhearted woman into a persecutor. Her victims were no longer human in her eyes, vandals who desecrated the beauty of the holy mountain.

Her reign, however, began in a spirit of conciliation. On arrival at the Tower she made haste to release two eminent prisoners, Gardiner and the Duke of Norfolk. She shed tears over them, kissed them as martyrs who suffered for religion. Both were indeed on her side against the reformers; but in her father's reign both collaborated with him actively to annul his marriage to her mother and defy the claims of the Pope. Norfolk was not even imprisoned on religious grounds; his offence was treason, a plot to deprive her brother of the throne. Nevertheless, he recovered his title and estates. Gardiner she not only restored to his see of Winchester, she made him her chancellor.

Another prisoner set free was Edward Courtenay, whose grandmother was daughter to Edward IV, sister to Mary's own grandmother, Elizabeth of York. His father was involved in the conspiracy instigated against King Henry by Cardinal Pole after the Pilgrimage of Grace; a fellow conspirator, Pole's younger brother, betrayed him, and he was sentenced to death. His son, a child at the time, was confined thenceforward in the Tower, a danger to the dynasty because of his Plantagenet blood. He lived there in comfort, received a good education; but when Mary allowed him to return, a grown man nearly thirty, to take his place in society he had no experience of the world outside his prison, could not even ride a horse.

Her clemency was not limited to those who suffered under her predecessors. Few victims paid the penalty for the usurpation which nearly deprived her of the throne. Most of the leaders who submitted were pardoned and reinstated in office; she accepted their excuse that they put their names to the new device for the succession under constraint. She was even ready to spare Northumberland himself when he announced that he repented of his heresy and asked to be received back into the Catholic Church. Her advisers, however, overruled her, insisting that he was too dangerous to leave alive, and he was beheaded.

His recantation provoked dismay among Protestants, shocked them the more because he had never lacked courage and was too worldly wise seriously to expect a reprieve. Those who knew him declared that he acted with customary foresight, seeking credentials for a successful career in the kingdom of heaven.

Two of the most hated of his supporters died with him; but that was all, no further vengeance was taken. Jane, the nine-day queen, was not allowed her wish to go home, she was kept in the Tower; but she wrote a letter which, without palliating her fault, described in detail how her brief authority was forced on her, and Mary was much impressed by its honesty and refused to listen to any suggestion that she should put her defeated rival to death. Jane's life in the Tower was not uncongenial; she was parted from her husband but not from her books. She could read and write to her heart's content, indomitable in her Protestant opinions, denouncing the Mass as "the swill of strangers," a renegade scholar as a "white-livered milksop." She looked foward when things settled down to her release.

At first it seemed that the government would establish its authority without further upheaval. All laws directed against the old doctrines and rites of the Church were repealed; Catholic bishops replaced Protestant, and similar changes followed in other ranks of the hierarchy. The Latin liturgy including the Mass was restored. There was opposition in some parts of the country, especially in London, where a priest was murdered as he consecrated the host. Such zeal, however, found little support in the population at large. The Queen's religion was no secret, her behaviour no surprise. Few wished to make trouble by resisting her. Women rebuked in the previous reign by austere disciples of Calvin for anything smacking of frivolity in their dress applauded the new fashion that she set. She herself loved jewels and gay colours, and she encouraged others to follow her example.

The Protestants were in any case discredited by Northumberland's recantation, and Gardiner who controlled religious policy pressed the advantage with resolution and skill. He lived up to his reputation, drew his bow at the head deer, sparing the does and fawns. Leaders of the reforming movement were arrested, but as long as he had his will in the council the humble were ignored. Even those whose importance exposed them to danger were given every chance to avoid it. He took care that they had warning of the proceedings intended against them, and if they used the delay to escape abroad nothing was done to stop them. He was content to be rid of them, glad to end the hunt without kill.

The effect was, however, to foster the growth of hostile communities in exile, useful instruments for a foreign power anxious to stir up rebellion in England. The refugees were often men of learning and distinction; they included King Edward's old tutor, Sir John Cheke. Among the few who stayed at home was Archbishop Cranmer, who refused to desert his post.

Queen Mary, like her father, was worried about the succession. If she had followed her own inclination she would probably have remained unmarried; but she was unwilling to die childless and leave her sister Elizabeth as her heir. There was no jealousy in this of a younger woman. Elizabeth was in the bloom of youth, not yet twenty when the reign began; but Mary's piety would not allow her to grudge another her good looks, or to complain that her own faded prematurely. The lack of sympathy between the sisters had its source in early memories. Mary could never forgive the wrong done to her mother by Anne Boleyn. She had too much conscience to avenge it on Elizabeth, she went out of her way indeed to treat her with sisterly affection; nonetheless the ancient grief persisted, casting its shadow unexorcised between Catherine's daughter and Anne's. If they had been more compatible in temperament it would have been easier to forget the past; but Mary's burning interest lay in religion, Elizabeth preferred this world to the next, speculation to unquestioning faith. In her brother's lifetime she had been on good terms with the reformers, and if she conformed now on occasions to the Mass it was from expediency rather than conviction. Mary feared that, if Elizabeth became Queen, all her own work for the restoration of the Church would be undone.

The only way to avert this was to take a husband, and there was no time to be lost. She was already at an age dangerously near the limit for childbearing, especially for a woman of her far from robust constitution. She discussed the matter with Gardiner, and he had a candidate to propose, her cousin, Edward Courtenay, whose company he had shared for many years in the Tower. He spoke highly of his mind and character, pointed out that by marrying him she would gratify public opinion, draw the bond closer between the Tudors and the House of York. The proposal was not at all to her liking. Courtenay annoyed her; she found him callow and unbalanced, his ignorance of the world made him seem even younger than he was. When Gardiner persisted in his advocacy she retorted that she could not see why she should be forced to marry a man "because a Bishop has made friends with him in prison."

An adviser to whom she paid more attention was the Emperor's ambassador, Simon Renard. She had great respect for the Emperor, the champion of her mother's cause. She was drawn to him too by his Spanish blood; his mother and hers were sisters. Spain, her mother's country, held enchantment for her; she found refuge there in imagination from harsh reality in England. When she was six years old and the Emperor twenty-three she had been betrothed to him; it seemed right to her that she should turn to him now for advice on her marriage. Renard to whom she explained her feelings encouraged them eagerly. He informed the Emperor, who proposed for her husband his son and heir, Prince Philip, a man eleven years younger than herself.

Gardiner tried in vain to dissuade her from the match, foreseeing what protest it would arouse. It was the main objection to a female sovereign in England that, if she married a foreigner, he would use the country to promote the interests of his own. The prospect was the more alarming when the proposed consort was heir to Spain and the Netherlands and all the wealth of the newly discovered Americas. Spain was already taking the place of France as the inevitable enemy in English eyes. Merchants resented the monopoly claimed by the Spaniards on the western ocean, adventurers were impatient to encroach on the coveted trade. Although acts of trespass were not frequent enough yet to lead to war they were a source of dangerous friction between the two nations.

There was violent outcry, therefore, when it became known in England that the Queen intended to marry the Spanish Prince, and the effect was a grave setback to her religious policy. Hitherto there had been little active opposition to her attempt to restore traditional rites; even Protestants submitted, resigned to her authority. The feeling changed quickly now; the Catholic cause became tainted with foreign influence, that of the reformers gained credit among patriots. It was no longer a struggle between rival creeds, but between Spanish aggression and English independence.

Former supporters of Northumberland's party, who gave Mary no thanks for the mercy shown them when it kept them debarred from power, grasped the chance to avenge their defeat, to take advantage of the resentment fomenting against the Spanish match. Plans were laid for simultaneous risings to break out in the early months of 1554 in Devonshire, the midlands and Kent, to overthrow her, put Elizabeth on the throne and marry her to Courtenay.

Courtenay himself, vain and garrulous, upset the arrangements. His boastful talk of coming greatness aroused suspicion, and Gardiner wheedled the whole story out of him. He made humble confession, begged Mary to pardon him. News of the betrayal forestalled the rising in Devonshire, and the leader, Sir Peter Carew, fled to France; but in the midlands the Duke of Suffolk, father of the erstwhile Queen Jane, raised a small force to capture Leicester. He was beaten off and taken prisoner in his own park, hiding in a hollow tree.

The only rising that came near to success was that in Kent, led by Sir Thomas Wyatt, son of the poet, Anne Boleyn's friend. The rebels defeated the army sent against them and advanced to the Thames at Southwark, barred from London only by the guard on Tower Bridge. Queen Mary refused to take flight; she rode to the Guildhall and addressed the citizens in person, appealing to their loyalty to defend her from her enemies and promising to submit the question of her marriage to Parliament. Her courage turned public opinion in her favour, and when Wyatt made a circuit, crossed the river at Kingston and threatened London from the west he met fierce resistance. He reached Ludgate; but his followers were cut off, and at Charing Cross he was surrounded and yielded.

Severe punishment was exacted for the rebellion. The government frightened by its narrow escape was in no mood to repeat the clemency shown after Northumberland's defeat. Suffolk could expect no second forgiveness and was beheaded, as were Wyatt and most of the other leaders who were caught. Elizabeth herself was put in the Tower under arrest; but no evidence of her complicity could be found, she denied it stoutly and spoke of Courtenay with such contempt that Mary believed and released her. Courtenay obtained pardon in reward for his confession, but he was told to travel abroad. He left the country and never came back. He caught a chill in a gondola at Venice; pneumonia set in, and he died of it at Padua.

The most innocent victim of the rebellion was the Queen's cousin Jane. She knew nothing of it, except for a glimpse from the Tower of the rebels encamped at Southwark; but her father was manifestly guilty, and no one could forget that she herself once bore the title of Queen. As long as she lived her name encouraged revolt, little as she wished it. The Emperor declared that his son would not come to England till the danger was removed. Jane's execution was the price that Mary paid for her Spanish bridegroom.

At last, in the following July, he arrived. The terms were settled, Parliament gave reluctant consent, and Mary and he were married. She was not a wife to suit his taste, so much older than himself that he spoke of her behind her back as "Aunt"; but a strong sense of duty urged him, he obeyed his father's wishes to promote the interests of Spain. A hard task lay before him in England to overcome the suspicion with which he was regarded, a task for which he was ill fitted by nature, reticent and indrawn, a man to whom the effort did not come easily to ingratiate himself. While he was in the Netherlands he was much disliked, accused of arrogance. His father wrote anxiously to the Duke of Alva who was in charge of the retinue at the wedding, imploring him to see that "my son behaves in the right manner."

The Emperor's fears were quickly allayed. Philip kept his feelings under strict control, behaved with such amiability at the English court that prejudice was disarmed and he was able to exert an effective influence on public affairs. He failed, however, to achieve his main purpose; neither his own blandishments nor Mary's expostulations could reconcile the council to the proposal to crown him King of England. He remained a mere consort without sovereign authority.

With Mary herself he had great success. Not least of the

problems arising from his marriage was that of cohabiting with a woman who had preserved her virginity into middle age, and whose religion taught her to eschew carnal impulse. It is a tribute to his skill that she responded with passionate devotion, came to depend adoringly on his judgment. She was happier than at any time since her childhood, thankful that she had rejected Courtenay, free from sentimental regret even when Cardinal Pole, indefatigable champion of orthodoxy and instigator of rebellions against her father, returned from exile, arriving in state as Papal legate. He was her cousin, a grandson of Edward IV's brother, the Duke of Clarence, and long ago when both were children their mothers had planned to unite them—a plan revived just before the Spanish marriage (he was in deacon's orders only, and the Pope would dispense him from his vows) in the hope of thwarting it. He refused the part, yielded her to Philip without demur; he was fifty-four, scholarly and ascetic, better equipped to offer spiritual advice than to beget an heir.

Although she did not want him as a husband she enjoyed his company, and he helped to direct her policy for the rest of her reign. Soon after his arrival the religious persecution began in earnest for which her name is notorious; the fires were lit at Smithfield and more than 1300 victims were burnt. Part of the blame lies with Wyatt's rebellion. Heresy became associated with treason, Catholic orthodoxy a test of loyalty to the Queen's government. Even so, it is clear that the harshness of the tribunals owed more to bigotry than political expediency. At first the policy had Gardiner's approval and active support. He believed that if a stern example were made of the leaders, especially the bishops of the reforming movement, their followers would lose zeal; but when the martyrdom of the "head deer" served only to provoke more stubborn resistance, and multitudes of "does and fawns" were herded to the stake, he protested in disgust that the cruelty achieved no useful purpose. His protest came too late; he was out of favour, overshadowed by Philip and Pole, and his health was failing. He died as the holocaust mounted.

The persecution seems indeed to have been inspired and fostered chiefly by Philip, a relentless champion of the Inquisition in Spain, who approved of the extermination of Protestants. His wisdom was infallible in Mary's eyes.

She was the more bound in devotion to him because she believed that she was about to bear his child, sure enough of her condition in the spring of 1555 to allow the news to be published. In April she retired to Hampton Court for the last stages of her pregnancy; nurses were engaged and a gorgeous cradle was prepared for the child whose birth would unite the crowns of Spain and England. May passed, June too; she still expected to be a mother. Ever since puberty she had been liable to dysmenorrhoea, and while she was a virgin she recognised it for what it was; but when the symptoms reappeared after her marriage the longing of her heart deceived her, and she was convinced beyond doubt when her breasts swelled with milk. She did not know that a false pregnancy can induce the secretion.

At last in August she gave up hope. It seems that the menstrual flow was resumed; she left Hampton Court, took part again in public affairs. Then as if the disappointment were not enough she heard from Philip that he must go to the Netherlands to visit his father. She stormed, pleaded, wept, but he insisted. He was tired of the strain of conciliating the English, of making love to a woman who did not attract him. In spite of his efforts he remained uncrowned. He saw no reason to endure his humiliating position any longer if she was unable to bear him an heir. He told her that he was leaving her for six weeks at most; he was away for nearly two years.

She had her father's temper when she was provoked. In her rage she ordered Philip's portrait to be removed from her room; but the mood soon passed, she missed him too painfully to harbour a grudge against him. She cherished his policy the more devoutly indeed in his absence; it was a bond left to draw them together that she could still regard him as her mentor. The persecution of heretics continued as fiercely as ever. Among those consigned to the flames the most eminent was Cranmer, in whose condemnation she filled the double part of Philip's disciple and her mother's avenger. She appointed Pole in his place as Archbishop of Canterbury.

Even if those punished were seldom the guilty there was reason to suspect the Protestants of sedition. Inflammatory pamphlets composed abroad were distributed by secret agents denouncing Mary as the "Jezebel of England" and calling on the people to revolt, and in the spring of 1556 a plot came to light threatening consequences scarcely less dangerous than Wyatt's rebellion two years before. Sir Henry Dudley—the same cousin of Northumberland's who offered Calais to the French if they would intervene on behalf of Queen Jane—was collecting a force of armed exiles to land on the Isle of Wight and advance on London, where accomplices were ready to rise in his favour. He relied, however, on a type of man easily induced by rewards or threats to betray him. Informers warned the government in time, and before the conspirators could act most of them were arrested. Dudley himself escaped, remaining out of reach in France.

The plot owed much to French support. Although England and France were nominally at peace relations between the two were dangerously strained by recent events in Europe. Philip's father, the Emperor Charles, prematurely old at fifty-six, almost crippled by arterial sclerosis, decided to abdicate and spend the rest of his life in comfortable retirement in a monastery in Estremadura. It was to announce this decision that he summoned his son to his side. Philip became King of Spain, a protagonist in the ancient struggle with France for European hegemony, and he urged Mary that it was her duty to engage England actively on his behalf. Her council did its best to restrain her, insisting that the nation, impoverished and disunited, was in no condition for war.

She herself hesitated when her husband added the Pope to his enemies. The new Pope, Paul IV, eager to assert himself in Italy, joined the French in a campaign to expel the Spaniards from Naples. Mary was torn between her love for Philip and lifelong veneration for the Papacy. How could she who condemned heretics to the stake declare war on the citadel of the Catholic faith? Philip wrote to assure her that the quarrel was none of his making, that the Pope attacked him unprovoked, and he argued that in chastising an unruly pontiff he defended the dignity of the Apostolic see. He made up for any inconsistency in the argument with the news that he was coming to England to plead his cause in person.

He arrived at last in March 1557, and she greeted him with rapture, accepted his explanations without demur when she heard them from his own mouth. The lords of the council however listened less willingly, they grudged the expenditure of English lives and money to fight battles for the King of Spain. Almost his only support among them came from those of Protestant views who could reconcile themselves even to alliance with the Spaniard when the common enemy was the Pope. Nevertheless his own and the Queen's voice prevailed. When he left the country after a visit of little more than three months England and France were at war.

She accompanied him to Dover to see him off, and they parted on the quay never to meet again. The King of Spain, the Netherlands and the western Indies neither could nor wished to spare the time to revisit his ailing and ageing wife. The months spent with her had achieved their only purpose, committed England to fight for him against the French. He had nothing more to gain from her company.

She paid a heavy price for that glimpse of him. The course of the war was as disastrous as those in her council foretold whose advice she rejected when they warned her not to intervene. England was unprepared and lacked resources for the struggle, and when the French moved at once to besiege Calais, to rid themselves of a humiliation that had rankled for more than two centuries, since the capture of the town by the English King Edward III, the defending garrison outnumbered and outfought appealed in vain for reinforcements. In little more than a week Calais surrendered. The adjacent fortress of Guisnes held out for another fortnight, then it too was taken by storm. Nothing was left of the English dominions in France. The exploits of Henry V, the coronation of his son in Paris dwindled, a barren effort, into the shadows of history.

Tradition has preserved Mary's words, that "when I am dead and opened you will find Calais lying in my heart." She lived for ten more months, in pain both of body and of mind, denied the child for whom she longed, denied the love of her husband, condemned to failure at home and abroad. Her sister would succeed her and undo all her work for the restoration of the old religion, on which she had set her heart, hardening it to acts of cruelty foreign to her nature. Her reign was dogged by a succession of cold wet summers, and that of 1558 was no exception. There was an epidemic of fever resembling influenza which lasted on into the autumn, and she herself, weakened by the pain of a malignant tumour on the ovary, was in no state to resist infection. She died in the morning of 17 November, and in the evening of the same day Cardinal Pole, her friend and mentor, died at Lambeth.

PART III

Gloriana

CHAPTER 16

Queen Elizabeth I is among the most celebrated monarchs in English history, and it would neither do her justice nor satisfy the reader to try to compress the details of her long reign into the concluding chapters of this book. The bare facts are well known: that inheriting a position diminished by the weakness of her brother and sister who preceded her, she restored it to a dignity worthy of her father, Henry VIII; that reversing her sister's religious policy she accepted many of the principles of the Reformation and steered the Church on a course midway between doctrinal extremes; finally, that in her foreign relations she sought a balance of power in Europe, avoiding war till late in her reign when the King of Spain was provoked to attempt invasion. The defeat inflicted on the Spanish Armada raised England to the first rank among European nations. These are events which have been described and discussed by many historians; it is more relevant to the present purpose to show what sort of woman Elizabeth was, on whom the achievement depended.

A dark shadow lay over her childhood. She was nearly three when her mother was beheaded, old enough to retain some impression of the closing stages of the broken marriage when her mother carried her in her arms to the King in the hope of rekindling his affection. During the years that followed she suffered neglect and even privation; but when she was eight her father married his fifth wife, Catherine Howard, who was her mother's cousin and went out of her way to treat her with kindness. The shock was all the greater when this Queen shared the other's fate on the headsman's block. Elizabeth was at an age to know and understand what had happened. Her father's sixth and last marriage brought more comfort. Catherine Parr did her best to draw her three stepchildren together, to give them a common life. Elizabeth became very fond of her, and after the King's death when she was fourteen she went to live with her.

The arrangement had the disadvantage that Lord Seymour, the Protector's younger brother, was a frequent visitor, renewing his courtship of Queen Catherine which her marriage with King Henry had interrupted. The girl living under her care caught his eye. To a man of his long-sighted ambition the princess was a better match than the Queen Dowager, and he sought the consent of his brother, the Lord Protector, who was her guardian. To his disappointment this was refused; he consoled himself therefore with his old love, who accepted and married him and, unaware of his earlier plan, kept Elizabeth with her under his roof. Although he no longer needed a bride he found the young girl attractive, her proximity encouraged amorous romps. His behaviour indeed provoked so much scandal that Queen Catherine at last intervened, and Elizabeth was removed to Cheshunt where she was given an establishment of her own.

Loyalty was a trait which Elizabeth inherited from her mother. Her disgrace and the distress caused to her stepmother left her bitterly ashamed, and her contrition was aggravated a couple of months later when Queen Catherine died of puerperal fever after giving birth to a daughter. On the other hand Seymour was the type of man, handsome, ostentatious, vigorous and bold, whom she was least able to resist. As a widower he resumed his designs on her, and although his brother intervened again to thwart him it is clear that she regarded him with favour, became much attached. In the following year he was arrested, convicted of treason and beheaded. Among the charges against him was that of conspiring to seduce Elizabeth, marry her and put himself on the throne.

She was not yet sixteen. Her governess, Catherine Ashley, who had been with her since she was four and to whom she was devoted, was taken from her and imprisoned in the Tower as an accomplice. She herself had to submit to examination by a commission appointed by the council. She defended herself with skill and spirit, denying any improper association with Seymour, and when a rumour was spread that she was pregnant she wrote to the Lord Protector to denounce it as "shameful slander" and asked leave to come to court "that I may show myself there as I am." Barely past adolescence she was pitting her wits against those of the most powerful men in the land, fighting alone for her reputation and prospects.

Even with so much at stake she was careful to shield her governess, Mrs. Ashley, whose indiscretion had been much to blame, and she pleaded for her release. It was a habit that endeared her through her life to those who served her that she was always ready to stand up for them.

The strain which the experience put on her was aggravated by Seymour's execution. When the news reached her she preserved her self-command, gave the eager spies nothing to report but her comment: "A man has died of much wit and little judgment." Her true feelings, however, were revealed to those in her confidence, witnesses of her passionate tears and of the vehemence with which she resented anything said to his discredit. His death recalled her mother's and her cousin's; it was as if any attachment that she formed lay under the shadow of the headsman's block. Lasting harm was done both to her emotions and to her physical health. For the rest of Edward VI's reign she lived for the most part in retirement, prevented by a succession of illnesses from attending functions at court.

Although her life was long by the standard of the times, seventy years, she was far from robust, seldom free from ailment. Like her sister Mary she suffered from dysmenorrhoea, and the uterine weakness probably fostered many of the digestive and similar troubles, ranging from sick headaches to jaundice, to which she was liable. In middle age she developed an intermittent ulcer on her leg, of gouty origin like her father's; but while his owed much to the imprudence of his diet she herself was remarkably temperate in her habits, neither ate nor drank to excess. She had a liver intolerant of strong liquor. An occasion is recorded early in her reign when she was travelling to Kenilworth and arrived hot and thirsty to find that the only ale available was of more than the usual strength. She refused to quench her thirst, fearing to provoke a liver attack, and her host bore the brunt of her impatience while horsemen were sent scouring the neighbourhood for a less potent brew. It scarcely needed the memorandum added in the records of the castle to remind the steward in future: "If the ale of the country will not please the Queen, then it must come from London."

She had a quick temper, was capable like her father of ungovernable fits of rage; but hers seldom lasted long. There was more hysteria than ill-will in her outbursts; they sprang from an emotional instability, much of which she owed to the troubles of her childhood culminating in Seymour's disastrous courtship. A similar source may be found for another trait destined to play an important part in her career, her fear of sexual intercourse. She had all her mother's vanity, loved to flirt with men, to bask in their admiration; but an instinct of neurotic intensity checked her when they wished to carry the suit to its conclusion. At the age of eight she told Robert Dudley, who shared a tutor with her: "I'll never marry." He quoted the words himself years later when he was her powerful favourite, the closest companion of her throne. He had better reason than any to deplore her refusal to change her mind.

She was twenty when her brother died and her sister Mary succeeded him. Poor health continued to trouble her, aggravated by fresh anxieties. She herself was the heir if Mary failed to bear a child, and the prospect did nothing to improve relations between the sisters estranged already by the grudge which Mary bore to Elizabeth's mother. Opponents of Mary's religious policy and her Spanish marriage looked to Elizabeth as the champion of the Protestant cause, and when Wyatt's rebellion broke out its declared purpose was to put her on the throne. She herself denied any part in the plot, apparently with truth; she was cautious by temperament, had youth on her side and could afford to wait for events to take their course. In addition, while the rebels used her name to foment insurrection, she lay seriously ill at her house at Ashridge in Buckinghamshire.

After Wyatt's defeat she was summoned to London for questioning and she pleaded that she was too ill to travel. Queen Mary's own doctors sent to visit her confirmed that the illness was genuine. Even so, the council insisted that she must come; but she was allowed to make the journey by easy stages, breaking it four times at suitable houses to spend the night on the way. When at last she reached London the French ambassador reported that she had "some swelling which has attacked her whole body and even her face," he described her as "a pitiful sight." In this condition she was committed to the Tower, the scene of her mother's execution. She remained there for two months awaiting a decision on her fate. Then her sister relented, and she was removed to Woodstock where she lived under supervision.

Among her fellow prisoners in the Tower was Robert Dudley, the friend of her childhood, who was of the same age as herself. He was the fifth and youngest son of the Duke of Northumberland and had given active support to his father during the brief interlude of the reign of Queen Jane, sharing in the abortive attempt to seize Mary before King Edward's death became known. Like his father and brothers he was imprisoned on Mary's accession. The Duke himself and Guildford Dudley, Queen Jane's husband, were beheaded; but the others were granted pardon after a time and released.

Although Elizabeth shared a prison with Robert Dudley there is no evidence of their meeting there. She herself was strictly watched, in poor health and preoccupied with cares of her own, in no mood to run risks to enjoy the company of a former playmate, even if she were able to bribe the guards. Four years before this he had married Amy Robsart, the daughter of a landowner in Norfolk, whom he met when he accompanied his father to the eastern counties to suppress an insurrection against the Lord Protector's government. It was a match without lustre even for a youngest son, falling far short of the standard set by the brides chosen for his brothers, connecting them with the noblest families; but the Duke was an indulgent father, Robin was much in love, Amy a pretty girl of seventeen, and they were given a magnificent wedding attended by King Edward in person.

When the Dudleys fell into disgrace Amy remained loyal to her husband. She begged permission to visit him in the Tower and took advantage of it as often as she could. Elizabeth can have felt no temptation to intrude.

During the last years of Mary's reign Elizabeth recovered her freedom of movement and the position due to her rank. To appease her sister she even attended Mass, but the occasions were as few as possible for fear of offending her Protestant supporters. Perfunctory conformity of this sort sat lightly on her own conscience. She was very far from being an irreligious woman, but she was born with a sense of proportion. Later in life she summed up her creed: "There is one faith and one Christ Jesus, the rest is a dispute about trifles."

Dudley too lived unmolested. He was a Protestant himself, destined when he grew older to be regarded as leader of the extreme party of Puritans, and now as Mary's victims accumulated at the stake he was sufficiently moved by the persecution to go with his brothers to attend meetings of protest at St. Paul's Cross; but a stern warning from the government deterred him from further effort, and he retired to his wife's property in Norfolk. A less compromising outlet for his energies was offered in 1557 when King Philip returned to England and persuaded Mary to declare war on France. This was an enterprise after Robert Dudley's own heart, combining military adventure with opportunities of advancement. He raised a company of men at his own expense to join the English and Spanish forces besieging St. Quentin, where his ability and courage earned favourable notice from Philip himself. His brother Henry, who accompanied him, was killed in action. Of the Duke of Northumberland's five sons only Ambrose, the third, and Robert, the youngest, remained. Ambrose became head of the family.

These were probably the years during which the acquaintance between Robert Dudley and Elizabeth warmed into close friendship, even love. No record of their association survives; but the lives of both at the time were unobtrusive, neither desiring nor likely to invite public attention. Each was of a type to attract the other, he tall and well-built with a forcefulness recalling Seymour's but held more firmly in check, she owing less to beauty of features than to expression and high spirit, a charm described by her enemies as witchcraft, and making up for the pallor of her complexion by the red-gold splendour of her hair, her Tudor inheritance. If he had been insusceptible hitherto he could hardly fail to respond when Mary's proved·inability to bear a child left the throne to his former playmate, to become Queen of England.

As soon as the news of Queen Mary's death reached him he mounted a white horse and rode to Hatfield, where Elizabeth was staying, to pay homage to the new monarch. She rewarded him by appointing him on the spot her master of the horse.

Their intimacy could no longer escape notice, and gossip throve. Elizabeth, cautious and secretive in affairs of state, was governed by impulse in her personal behaviour, incapable of disguising the affection that she felt for the favourite. Even if his wife was not already aware of it tongues were soon chattering too loudly for her to close her ears. She had moved from Norfolk to Berkshire, where he took a house for her, Cumnor Place, near Abingdon, which she shared with his married steward and two women who were her friends. It may be that she preferred to live there rather than to join him at court. She had congenial company, travelled often on visits to friends, and she never seems to have been short of money. From time to time her husband came to stay with her. Many wives suffered greater neglect. None but she had the mortification of knowing that when her husband was away he was wooing the Queen. Even if the malicious stories put about were untrue that he wished to poison her, it was only too clear to her that she was an embarrassment to him, that her death would afford him relief. A phrase in one of her few surviving letters, a business note to an agent about the sale of some wool, provides a glimpse of her state of mind; she apologises for forgetting to obtain her husband's instructions, "he being sore troubled with weighty affairs, and I not being altogether in quiet for his sudden departing." She was an unhappy woman, a sick woman too. The Spanish ambassador, writing to King Philip about the scandal, added the information that "they go so far as to say that his wife has a malady in one of her breasts, and the Queen is only waiting for her death to marry Lord Robert."

The climax came on a Sunday when the servants returning from Abingdon fair, where she had sent them all in the morning, found her lying dead at the foot of the stairs with a broken neck.

Much defied explanation. The stairs were not steep; it was an odd chance for a fall of that sort to kill her. The means chosen suited neither murder nor suicide. Those who argued nevertheless for the latter pointed to the care with which she contrived to be alone, dismissing everyone to the fair, much annoyed when a friend wished to stay behind because on Sundays the booths were so crowded. There was evidence too from her tirewoman who admitted under examination that she had heard her mistress "pray to God to deliver her from desperation."

The fact remained, however, that when her body was found the hood that she wore was not disarranged. This seemed to exclude not only suicide but murder also; still public opinion was unconvinced, refusing to believe that an event so favourable to her husband's plans could happen without his contrivance. He himself foresaw what construction would be put on it when the messenger came to him at Windsor bringing the news. He ordered strict investigation to be made, was eager for an inquest to be held with a properly qualified jury. It was as if he hoped for some clue to be found which would absolve him. His attitude was that of a man taken by surprise, frightened for his reputation. If this was a murder carried out at his command he was ill prepared for the success of his crime.

He had the sense at least to refrain from any profession of grief; the hypocrisy would have provoked derision. The jury at the inquest brought in a verdict of accidental death without trying to explain how it came about; but in the eyes of most people in the country he was a murderer, and for years the infamy cast a shadow on his career.

The mystery of Amy Robsart's death has invited speculation ever since. Sir Walter Scott heaped added obloquy on her husband's name by his treatment of the theme in his novel, *Kenilworth*. In recent times, however, medical evidence has been offered which throws light on much that was obscure. Professor Ian Aird writing in the *English Historical Review* (Vol. 71, 1956) shows that malignant cells from a cancerous tumour are liable to be carried by the blood to the spine, whose structure they corrode till the affected bone becomes so brittle that the least strain is enough to break it. If Amy, as it seems, was dying of cancer of the breast the bones of her neck could have been in the condition described, and walking downstairs, taking a step perhaps too heavily, she would sustain a sudden fracture followed by paralysis, unconsciousness, a collapse too gentle to disarrange her hood.

This interpretation gives good ground for her feeling of "desperation." It may still be asked why she insisted on sending everyone out of the house, but it is not unknown in great pain to crave for peace and solitude.

The scandal surrounding his wife's death deprived Robert Dudley of his chance of marrying the Queen, if that was ever her intention. There is little reason, however, to suppose that it was. She was fond of him, liked to have him near her, and he continued to enjoy her favour; but she knew him too well to believe that as her husband he would be content to remain Prince Consort, would not try to be King himself. She described her feeling for him frankly when she told the French ambassador:

"I cannot live without seeing him every day; he is like my little dog, as soon as he is seen anywhere they know I am coming."

If this was a humiliating relation for him it was sweetened by many titles of honour and rich perquisites.

So familiar an association between a Queen and her subject

invited ribald comment. Stories spread through the country and overseas into Europe, according to which Dudley was her lover, shared her bed, had even got her with child. Many people were sent to gaol for repeating them; but still the rumours persisted, flavoured with racy detail. Years afterwards in 1588 when England was at war with Spain a young man calling himself Arthur Dudley appeared at the Spanish court; he was about twenty-seven at the time, he claimed that his mother was Elizabeth of England. His account of his early life held the traditional episodes of romance: the baby smuggled out of the palace, given to trusted retainers to bring up, the education that distinguished him from his foster-brothers, the secret influence of a powerful nobleman.

Great advantage could accrue to Spanish policy from revelations so damaging to Elizabeth's character. King Philip's interest was aroused; he examined Arthur Dudley's claims with care, dismissed them with contempt. Even Perkin Warbeck inspired more belief, challenging Elizabeth's grandfather.

If her relations with her favourite were misrepresented much of the fault lay with her own indiscretion. She made no effort to hide her partiality, flaunted it in public. At Michaelmas 1564 she invested him with the title of Earl of Leicester. It was an occasion of state attended by the greatest in the land and many dignitaries from Europe. All had their eyes on her as he knelt before her and she draped him in the insignia of nobility. They saw her lean forward and tickle his neck.

Such behaviour indeed argues for her virtue. Knowing that suspicions had no ground she had no fear of affronting decorum. There is weightier evidence, however, in support of her virginity. The closer a witness stood to reliable sources of information the less his reports incline to scandal. A noteworthy example is William Cecil whom she created Lord Burghley, the same who began his career as secretary to the Protector Somerset, abandoned his service for Northumberland's, and now after discreetly lying low through Mary's reign enjoyed Elizabeth's confidence as secretary of state, her principal adviser in domestic and foreign affairs. Burghley had no love for Leicester, he was jealous of his influence with the Queen; but writing in confidence to his friend, Sir Thomas Smith, sent on a mission to France, he assures him that the tales of the court are "fond and untrue," and that "the Queen's Majesty may be by malicious tongues not well reported, but in

237

truth she herself is blameless and has no spot of evil intent." He expresses regret nonetheless for her lack of "circumspection." Her attachment to Leicester did not deter her from receiving and considering proposals of marriage from foreign royalty. In her sister's reign King Philip had urged her to marry his cousin, the Archduke Charles, a nephew of the former Emperor Charles V, her mother's old enemy, and Spanish efforts were renewed after her accession to promote the alliance. She was careful neither to reject nor to accept the Archduke's suit. Although Mary's war with France was concluded and peace restored, relations remained uneasy; English pride was embittered by the loss of Calais. At the beginning of her reign Elizabeth was anxious to be on good terms with Spain, to keep the French busy on other frontiers.

Important changes, however, were about to take place in Europe. In 1559, the year after she came to the throne, the King of France, Henry II (son of that Francis I, at whose court her mother was brought up), was killed accidentally in a tournament, and his son who succeeded as Francis II was a boy of fifteen married to the young Mary Queen of Scots, Elizabeth's own cousin and heir presumptive. The effect was to leave France weakened, with a King technically of age but in fact too young to rule. His mother, Catherine de Medici, would have liked to take control of affairs; but it was held against her that she was Italian, even more that she came of a mercantile family, in spite of the fact that it was the wealthiest and most powerful in Florence, that her cousin had been Pope Clement VII, her uncle Pope Leo X, and her grandfather Lorenzo the Magnificent. The faction opposed to her was led by the two brothers of the House of Guise, the one a Duke and the other a Cardinal. They were uncles to Mary Queen of Scots, and through her they exerted great influence on the young King. He was devoted to her, although the marriage was unconsummated and his doctors pronounced him impotent.

The two Guises became virtual rulers of France. They taught Mary to jeer at her mother-in-law as a "Florentine shopkeeper," and in proof of their zeal for religion they proclaimed her Queen of England, denouncing Elizabeth as a bastard and heretic. It was a challenge which Elizabeth did not have to endure for long. In the following year Francis II died from a mastoid infection of the ear; his brother who succeeded as Charles IX was barely ten, and during his minority the Queen Mother exercised the functions of regent by constitutional right. Mary, a widow at eighteen, was sent back to Scotland; the power of the Guises suffered a rebuff. Rival forces were able to assert themselves in the country, especially the Protestants who made up for their lack of numbers by the wealth and quality of their following among the landed gentry and small nobility.

Catherine de Medici herself was no bigot. She preferred to settle disputes by compromise, to rely on her skill in intrigue. While contending factions struggled, embittered by religious intolerance, she tried with the inadequate means at her disposal to preserve her son's heritage, to restore peace. There were occasions when she succeeded in bringing the opponents together, getting them to agree to mutual concessions; but their intransigence quickly defeated her again, armed incursion from one side provoked reprisal from the other, and slaughter and destruction were resumed. The result was civil war lasting, with a few uneasy intermissions, till the end of the century.

In these circumstances she looked for foreign alliances to make good the weakness of the Royal government. She herself had no quarrel with Elizabeth, played no part in pressing her daughter-in-law's claim to the English throne. Elizabeth's religion was less an offence to her than an inconvenience which would yield to negotiation; the all-important fact in her eyes was that here was an unmarried Queen, an eligible bride for a prince of the House of France. She had two sons, small boys, in addition to the reigning King Charles. Their defect was their age. Even Henry, the elder, was eighteen years younger than Elizabeth.

She waited to propose the match till he grew up. He was her favourite son, with whom she had most in common, and she relied on him to share her concern for the interests of France; but at twenty he had already a will of his own, fastidious tastes. When his mother urged him he refused stubbornly to take a wife of thirty-eight, who, as he protested, "is not only an old creature but has a sore leg." In spite of the efforts of the French to hush them up his words were carried to England, and the French ambassador was put to much embarrassment to explain them away.

Elizabeth was sensitive above all things to any aspersion on her age and beauty. Nevertheless she allowed herself to be appeased, and when the French Prince under pressure from his mother and his brother, King Charles, reluctantly agreed to let his suit go forward she received it with apparent favour and discussed the terms as if she had marriage seriously in view. It helped her to swallow her pride that she was playing a part. Only three years before this a rising of hostile nobles in Scotland had overthrown Mary Stuart, obliged her to seek refuge in England, where she was held more as a prisoner than a guest. Her presence was an embarrassment to the English government, an encouragement to the disaffected who craved for a Catholic Queen; already a dangerous rebellion had broken out, barely suppressed in the north, aiming to put her on the English throne. Elizabeth feared that further plots of the sort would receive support from France, reviving the old alliance between France and Scotland. Which would Catherine de Medici prefer—the doubtful cause of the widow of her dead son Francis, the undutiful daughter-in-law who called her the "Florentine shopkeeper," or the glorious prospect of a new daughter-in-law, the reigning Queen of England, married to her favourite son Henry?

The negotiations proceeded so smoothly that Henry himself took alarm. He did not want to marry her, only seemed to acquiesce because he trusted that the obstacles were insuperable. Seeking excuses to withdraw he complained of her reputation, the stories reaching Paris of her familiarity with Leicester. His mother tried to reassure him, she gave an account of the conversation to Sir Francis Walsingham, Elizabeth's envoy:

"I told him that all the hurt which evil men can do to noble and royal women is to spread abroad lies and dishonourable tales of us, and that we princes who be women are of all persons liable to be slandered wrongfully by them who be our adversaries, other hurt they cannot do us."

She added for Walsingham's benefit that her arguments had effect, that her son became fully convinced of Elizabeth's virtue. A less invidious reason was found for breaking off the match, that he had religious scruples, was dissatisfied with the conditions restricting him after marriage to private attendance at Mass. Elizabeth retorted that her own conscience was no less uneasy about marrying a papist.

Catherine's defence of Elizabeth's reputation is of interest as her own has suffered even worse treatment from history. In the year following the rejection of her son's suit an event occurred in France which has been remembered ever afterwards with horror. On St. Bartholomew's Day, 1572, the Catholic mob ran riot in Paris, killing the Huguenots (as the Protestants were called), men, women and children alike, with maniac cruelty. The bloodshed went on in Paris for three weeks, and the provinces caught and propagated its fury. The massacre of St. Bartholomew claimed more than 12,000 victims.

The blame for these atrocities has been laid on Catherine although they were, in fact, a disaster to her, utter defeat to her hopes of reconciling the sects, ending the civil war. Unwittingly, however, she lit the flame which set off the explosion. Coligny, the Huguenot leader, formerly her ally in support of concession and compromise, had been turned by Calvinist preaching into an unyielding fanatic; there was no one on either side more opposed to a settlement that fell short of his full demands. To her dismay she saw that he dominated the impressionable mind of the young King, who admired his bellicose manners, and it seemed to her that France could find no peace while he lived. In her native Florence there was a traditional solution for problems of this sort, a blow in secret from an unknown assassin.

Her daughter Margot was about to be married to the King of Navarre, the future Henry IV of France, and Coligny came to Paris with other Huguenot leaders for the wedding. Towards the end of the celebrations a reception was held at the Louvre, and as Coligny left it a musket was fired in the street, the bullet hit but failed to kill him. Wounded but very much alive, he prepared his revenge. He could guess who had instigated the attack, employed the unskilful assassin.

There was consternation in the palace. The King, indignant at first at the attempt on his hero's life, veered to panic when his mother told him that his own life was in danger from the avenging Huguenots. He gave her authority to resist them by armed force. Even so, she tried to limit the slaughter, made a list of Coligny's chief friends to be sought out and killed; the violence, it was hoped, would die down if the rank and file had no one to lead them. She underrated the ferocity of the passions engaged on both sides. All Paris, overwhelmingly Catholic, was agog at the news of the attempted assassination, eager to follow the example and fall on the heretics. When Catherine's emissaries went to pick off the Huguenot leaders hordes of ruffians gathered to join them, killed without discrimination, without mercy. Nothing could check the massacre.

Public opinion in England was appalled. The French ambassador complained that no one would speak to him; but Elizabeth herself, after thinking it over for three days, received him with diplomatic courtesy and accepted his description of the affair as a regrettable accident. She saw that France weakened by civil war could be used with safety as counterpoise to Spain, and when the indefatigable Queen Mother reminded her that she had another son available, more amenable than Henry, the unpopularity of a French marriage was not allowed to hinder negotiations. The new suitor was four years younger than Henry, twenty-two years younger than Elizabeth. At birth he received the name of Hercules; but it was so inappropriate to his stunted body that he changed it when he was confirmed, took that of his eldest brother Francis who by then was dead. He had a face wizened even in youth, pitted with smallpox, adorned with an enormous nose which consorted oddly with his diminutive figure.

In spite of his mother's efforts to palliate his physical disadvantages they were too notorious in France to remain long unknown in England. Ugliness was hateful to Elizabeth, and she could not bear to have anyone deformed near her. Nevertheless she expressed interest in his proposal of marriage, and prolonged discussion followed between London and Paris to arrange the terms. He was less exacting than his brother, raised few difficulties either on religious grounds or about suspected rivals at the English court. His appearance lacked charm for brides of his own age, he was very willing to console himself with the hand of the Queen of England.

Elizabeth was in no hurry to disappoint him. She enjoyed being wooed no matter what she thought of the wooer, and it suited her policy to encourage hopes of alliance in France. It is possible that she was uncertain of her own mind, torn between fear of domination, of physical surrender, and the desire to bear a child to carry on the Tudor dynasty. In 1574 when Charles IX died prematurely of tuberculosis and his brother Henry, her former suitor, succeeded to the French throne as Henry III she declared that if he renewed his proposal she would accept him. He was good-looking, intelligent, a husband worthy of her; but he made haste to marry the dowerless and unassuming Louise de Vaudemont, with whom he was in love. Elizabeth bitterly offended was cast back again on his younger brother.

For years Leicester had watched a succession of foreign Princes apply for her hand. His own position at court, his hold on her affection remained unshaken; but he knew by this time that he was as unlikely as they to win her, and meanwhile he was entering middle age without a wife or an heir. Cautiously without arousing her suspicion he took steps to make up for lost opportunities. He was attracted by Lady Essex, a granddaughter of Mary Boleyn, the Queen's aunt, and when her husband died he proposed to her, intending that the marriage should be kept secret till a time came when it could safely be revealed. Lady Essex accepted the condition, but she insisted on the presence of responsible witnesses at the wedding so that no doubt of its validity could arise.

For an uneasy year he succeeded in keeping the Queen in ignorance, faithfully celibate in her presence, wedded at home. He did not dare to confess to her that tired of waiting he had consoled himself with someone else; her vanity demanded unchanging devotion for ever unrewarded. It was a precarious position, and in spite of his efforts rumours spread. The witnesses at the wedding were not all as discreet as he wished, and his wife herself was ill content to live in obscurity, impatient to enjoy her new eminence.

Meanwhile Elizabeth still flirted with proposals of marriage from the French Prince. He sent his friend, Jean de Simier, to plead on his behalf. Simier was an accomplished courtier; she was much taken with him, more attracted by the envoy's charm than his master's cause. Their evident enjoyment of each other's company provoked Leicester's jealousy; he had enough on his mind already without this Frenchman to outshine him. He suspected with reason that Simier was trying to undermine his influence, seeking means to discredit him, hot already on the scent of his dangerous secret. The enmity between the two reached a climax when Simier travelling in a barge on the Thames with the Queen narrowly escaped injury from a musket-shot fired from a neighbouring boat. It was an accident, the musket was discharged unintentionally when the boat lurched. The Queen laughed it off and pardoned the culprit, but Simier remained convinced that Leicester plotted to murder him.

By this time he had ferreted out the details of the secret marriage; he took his evidence to the Queen and showed it to her. When she understood that there was no room for doubt she burst into tears, her anger with Leicester was beyond control. It was bad enough that he should marry without her consent; it cut her to the heart that through all these months he had been playing a part to deceive her. At first she wished to commit him to the Tower; but the scandal would have been too great, and she was dissuaded. He was warned to avoid her presence. Then her rage passed, she allowed him to retire to his seat in the country and his wife, eventually even to resume his duties at court; but her manner was cold when they met, and his wife was forbidden to accompany him.

Simier returned to France with cordial messages from the Queen of England to his Royal master, Francis Duke of Anjou, who was so encouraged that he crossed the sea in disguise and arrived unheralded to visit her in person. Report did him no injustice; seen in the flesh, he was even uglier than the English courtiers expected, and they could hardly believe the evidence of their eyes when the Queen, whose taste was so fastidious, greeted him with delight, professed to be overcome by his fascination. She herself was tall and stately, nearly twice his age; the contrast was ridiculous with the grotesque and ungainly dwarf, his vast nose.

About ten years after these events, not so long that they could be forgotten, Shakespeare produced the play, *A Midsummer Night's Dream*, with its scene where Titania, the fairy Queen, falls by enchantment into love with Bottom, the ass-headed weaver. "What angel wakes me from my flowery bed?" she exclaims when she sees him, and Puck reports to Oberon: "My mistress with a monster is in love." No audience of the time could miss the allusion, fail to be reminded of Queen Elizabeth's absurd-looking suitor.

She was not under a spell. Unlike Titania, she knew very well what she was doing, making up to the French Prince to discourage plots hatched against her in France in favour of Mary Stuart, and at the same time punishing Leicester for his unfaithfulness, tormenting him with jealousy and the prospect of permanent exclusion from power. In the following year Anjou paid her another visit, attended on this occasion with due ceremony, an impressive retinue of French lords. She received him with the same benevolence, kept him at her side, called him affectionately her "frog," teasing him for his puny stature. On an occasion when the whole court was assembled she put her ring on his finger. It seemed that at last she had made up her mind to marry, and discussion began on the terms of the treaty of marriage. Her advisers warned her anxiously of the danger likely to arise from his religion, the execration still aroused in England by the memory of St. Bartholomew's Day 1572, France's disgrace.

She dismissed their advice with angry disdain, then proceeded to follow it. The negotiations with the French dragged on interminably; as soon as one point of dispute was settled she found another no less hard to resolve. Anjou grew impatient, threatened to return to France; but she implored him with tears to stay, and he was persuaded. The entertainments were resumed, the blandishments; still no terms were agreed. Already he had wasted three months in England. Urgent business claimed his attention at home, ambitious intrigues against his brother, Henry III. In spite of Elizabeth's protests he tore himself away, better fitted by nature for treason than courtship.

She accompanied him to Chatham to see him off, taking care on the way to show him the formidable fleet that she was building there. Then he embarked for France; his prodigious nose and goblin frame were lost to her for ever. To Leicester his departure was a source of thankful relief. As for her own feelings, Shakespeare is as likely as anyone to be right:

> And the imperial votaress passed on
> In maiden meditation, fancy-free.

CHAPTER 17

Under the will of Henry VIII, given statutory force by Act of Parliament, the succession to the throne vested on his death in his son Edward, then in default of a direct heir in his daughters Mary and Elizabeth in turn, and if they too died childless the line of his younger sister Mary inherited to the exclusion of that of his elder sister Margaret, Queen of Scotland. On the accession of Elizabeth still unmarried this contingent remainder, seemingly remote when her father devised it, became of living importance. Her heir presumptive was to be sought among the surviving descendants of her aunt Mary, the widowed Queen of France who eloped with Charles Brandon, Duke of Suffolk.

Two daughters were born of that marriage, Lady Frances and Lady Eleanor Brandon. The former married Henry Grey, Marquess of Dorset, who in time through deaths in the family obtained the title of Duke of Suffolk for himself. They in their turn had daughters only, Jane, Catherine and Mary, of whom the eldest, married to Northumberland's son, Lord Guildford Dudley, reigned for nine days after King Edward's death as Queen Jane, was dethroned by Queen Mary and beheaded. Her mother had already renounced her place in the succession. This left Lady Catherine Grey, the second daughter, as heir.

Catherine had to endure in her childhood the same tyranny at home as her sister, but she was less eager to escape from it to the tutor who gave them their lessons. She was no scholar, preferred dancing to reading, and was less often, therefore, the butt of her mother's harshness, unaccustomed like Jane to betray contempt for her parents by studious habits and pert retorts. She had the advantage, too, of an appearance more in accord with accepted standards of beauty, tall and slim while Jane was short and plump. Jane's, however, was not only the abler mind but also the stronger character. Catherine was much under her influence.

In 1553 the celebration of Jane's wedding to Guildford Dudley served as occasion also for the betrothal of Catherine to Lord Herbert, heir to the Earl of Pembroke; she was thirteen, he nineteen. As was usual, the child was taken afterwards to stay with her future husband's parents so that he might get to know her better, and she him. The Herberts lived at Baynard's Castle just outside the wall of the city of London at the mouth of the Fleet. Catherine was present there through her sister's brief reign, accompanied the family to the Tower to pay homage to the new Queen, saw the lords come surreptitiously to Baynard's Castle a few days later for a meeting at which Queen Jane was deposed, Queen Mary proclaimed. Pembroke, anxious to vindicate himself, made haste to annul his son's betrothal, and Catherine was sent back to her mother.

It is probable that the lamentable end of the story made less impression on her imagination than the glorious scene with which it began, her sister enthroned as Queen of England, her formidable mother making obeisance, holding the train of the daughter whom formerly she bullied and whipped. At thirteen Catherine learnt what it meant to be of Royal blood, in direct line of succession to the Crown.

She was too young to understand where her sister's sudden promotion, sudden fall could lead. At first indeed the course of events was reassuring. Although Queen Mary kept Jane a prisoner she regarded her as the innocent victim of Northumberland's ambition, fully intended to release her as soon as she could do so without danger to her own authority. If she had mercy even for the eldest, the usurper of her crown, she had still more for the younger girls. Catherine was invited to her court, treated with the honour due to a princess of the blood, and rode in red velvet in the procession at the coronation, taking precedence of everyone in the retinue except Princess Elizabeth.

In the following year Wyatt's rebellion broke out, with fatal consequences both for her sister Jane and for her father. It brought no change, however, to her own position at court, where she was likely to hear, and at fourteen believe, only a version of the story favourable to the government. She was much attached to Jane, admired her intellectual brilliance; but Jane herself would have been the last to approve of any questioning of the Queen's judgment. Just before her execution she sent Catherine a letter written on the blank pages of her Greek Testament, full of pious exhortation. Catherine kept and cherished the little book. Many of the words have been effaced by her tears; but the message which it carried, the duty demanded by loyalty to her sister's memory, was one of piety, resignation to the will of God, nothing inconsistent with continued service to the Queen. She became indeed devoted to Queen Mary and looked back afterwards on her reign as the happiest time of her life.

Within three weeks of her father's execution her mother married again, choosing for husband her equerry, Adrian Stokes, known already to scandal as her "fancy man." She was thirty-seven, he twenty-one, far beneath her in rank; but he had a handsome face and figure and a charm made the more irresistible by the pains which he took to exert it. Nevertheless he was an odd choice for the ambitious and dominating Duchess of Suffolk, unless recent experience had frightened her, souring the fruit of political success. Queen Mary allowed the newly wedded pair to present themselves at court; but she did not approve of the match and removed Catherine and her nine-year-old sister Mary, putting them in charge of the Duchess of Somerset, widow of Edward VI's uncle, the Lord Protector. The child Mary was almost a dwarf, deformed with a hunchback.

The Duchess of Somerset had her only unmarried daughter, Jane, and her two sons, Edward and Henry, living with her at her house at Hanworth in Middlesex. Lady Jane Seymour was nineteen when Catherine joined the household. She had the delicacy of colouring, the zest that often go with a tendency to consumption, she had her father's impulsive temperament and love of learning; he himself had plans before his fall to marry her to King Edward. There was much in her to recall her namesake, Catherine's sister, her intellectual interests and force of character; but Jane Seymour was less serious-minded than Jane Grey, readily kindled to romantic ardour. She had great influence on Catherine, they became close friends.

Edward Seymour, the elder of the boys, was no stranger to Catherine. In King Edward's reign he was betrothed to her sister Jane, and it was the custom after betrothal to allow the two to visit and get to know each other. The contract however was annulled when Northumberland proposed one more advantageous, Jane's marriage to his own son, Guildford Dudley. Edward Seymour bore the stigma of his father's disgrace and execution, and the titles to which he was heir were forfeited. On Queen Mary's accession the positions were reversed, Northumberland suffered attainder while Seymour's was removed by Act of Parliament; but it was not till the year after her death that he recovered the title of Earl of Hertford, that of Duke of Somerset was never restored to him.

At the time of Catherine's arrival at Hanworth he was seventeen, sparely built, dark and hawklike, but unfashionably short in stature so that in later life he was known as "Little Hertford." Catherine was at a susceptible age, growing up, no longer a child, and she was in daily contact with him. At last his mother grew uneasy, seeing them so much together, and she questioned him. "Mother," he told her, "young folks meaning well may well accompany." She reported this reply to the Queen, but nothing was done to interrupt the attachment. Queen Mary, married to Philip, was expecting to give birth to an heir. If all went as she hoped and prayed Catherine could marry whom she chose, she was no longer in the direct line of succession to the throne.

No child was born, Catherine's place in the order of succession gained fresh importance. It was even suggested that Queen Mary should declare her her heir, to the exclusion of Elizabeth. In spite of the Protestant tradition in her family Catherine conformed without demur to the established rites, she told the Spanish ambassador that she was "as good a Catholic as any." Her piety was sincere; but it had none of Jane's intellectual framework, she cared nothing for dogma. Biddable by nature, she did what she was told, till an issue arose too important to submit to dictation.

As long as Mary lived that issue provoked no struggle. Edward Seymour was Catherine's accepted suitor, waiting only till she was old enough for marriage. Both her mother and his gave consent, the latter uneasily expressing the fear that so dangerous a connection would be her son's "undoing." The Queen, however, did not oppose it; she was resigned to the prospect of Elizabeth's accession after her death.

Queen Mary died, Queen Elizabeth reigned in her place. The prospect for the lovers changed for the worse. As long as the new Queen remained unmarried Catherine was her immediate heir, no intervening life stood between her and the succession. She became an important piece on the international chessboard. Spanish influence, relying too hopefully on her conformity in the previous reign, supported her claim in the interests of Catholic religion. There was even talk of a plot to kidnap her, carry her off to Spain and marry her to Don Carlos, King Philip's eldest son, in spite of the insanity with which he was afflicted.

Elizabeth herself, ready at no time to consider who should succeed her, professed contempt for Catherine's right. She denied her even the rank of Royal Princess which she had enjoyed at court under Mary, and reduced her to employment in her service as a lady of the bedchamber. Catherine, cherishing memories of her sister's brief reign, resented the slight put on her. There was no love lost between her and the Queen. A scene is recorded by a foreign envoy when, usually demure and submissive, she lost her temper in the Queen's presence and spoke "very arrogant and unseemly words." What they were his report does not divulge, but she told the Spanish ambassador, on whom she could rely for astute sympathy: "The late Queen showed me much favour, the present Queen bears me no good will."

Elizabeth did not forget the outburst; but she did nothing to pursue the quarrel, she was scrupulous in her respect for ties of blood. Catherine retained her position at court which, short as it might fall of her expectations, ensured her comfort and honour, and her young sister Mary was invited in spite of her deformity to join her. Whether or not Elizabeth knew of the understanding with Seymour she showed no displeasure in her treatment of him. She restored him his father's lower title of Earl of Hertford.

The death of Henry II of France in 1559 evoked a threat destined to haunt Elizabeth for most of her reign. His son, who succeeded as Francis II, was married to Mary Stuart, and the opportunity was taken to assert her claim to reign as Queen of England. Elizabeth had an answer readily available to eliminate her, to recognise Catherine Grey as her heir in accordance with the Act of Succession; but she disliked Catherine, disliked even more any appointment of her own successor. She took to heart the lesson learnt in her sister's reign when she herself was the heir whose star waxed as the old Queen's waned. She had no intention of letting Catherine Grey enjoy such advantage; she was determined to keep her in her place, above all to keep her a spinster.

Meanwhile, Catherine and the newly ennobled Earl of Hertford, unaware or heedless of the issues at stake, still hoped that she would consent to their marriage. They discussed it with Catherine's mother and stepfather, who were all the more favourable to the match since Hertford's recovery of his title. Mr. Stokes, the more accomplished scribe, composed a letter for his wife to sign, imploring the Queen to be gracious to the wishes of the young couple and their parents. The terms of the letter were agreed, but from month to month they put off sending it. Hertford took fright, mindful perhaps of his father's fate. Then the Duchess, Catherine's mother, fell ill, and they decided to wait till her health was better; but instead it grew worse, and she died with the letter still in her possession. The chance to use her influence with the Queen was lost.

This setback seems to have inspired the courage of despair, a mood ready to listen when Jane Seymour, Hertford's sister and Catherine's close friend, proposed an enterprise more appropriate to her favourite legends of romance than to the court of Queen Elizabeth, a secret wedding of which the Queen would be kept in ignorance till conditions changed in their favour. The probability of any such change owed more to sanguine hope than to prudent reason; nevertheless her ardour overcame their hesitation.

The chance came early in December 1560 when the Queen ordered the court to accompany her on an expedition to Eltham. Jane pleaded a headache, Catherine a toothache; both received permission to stay behind at Westminster. Meanwhile, Hertford was making preparations at his house in Cannon Row; a cold meal was laid out in his bedroom, the servants were sent off to their own quarters. He was alone when the girls arrived unattended and on foot, approaching in the wintry dawn by the path beside the river. They were in a hurry, time was short; if they were not back at the palace for dinner their absence would attract remark.

He had disturbing news for them. The priest on whom he was relying to perform the ceremony was not yet in the house. They waited for him to come, waited in vain. Lady Jane refused to lose heart; she set forth herself into the street braving inquisitive eyes to find another to officiate, while Catherine and her brother stayed hidden in the room. She returned at last with a stout, red-bearded man wearing a black gown of the sort favoured by reformers from Geneva; that was all that any of them could remember about him afterwards, she herself did not know his name. He conducted the service according to the Protestant rite, then Jane showed him out and dismissed him with a fee of ten pounds.

When she joined the other two again she led them to the table and poured out wine to drink to the occasion; but none of them was in convivial mood, they barely sipped from their glasses, left the food untouched. After a few minutes she went out, and the bride and bridegroom alone together took their clothes off.

Two hours later they rose and dressed in panic-stricken haste. The morning was already far advanced, dinner at noon. They went to look for Jane, then all ran together downstairs to the water gate. The incoming tide overflowed the bank, and the path was under water; but they were able to hail a passing wherry, on which the girls embarked. It carried them swiftly on the tide to Westminster, and they were in their places when those left at court sat down to dine.

All this story came to light when a judicial inquiry was held, but that was not till several months later. At first they succeeded well enough in keeping their secret, able to meet without difficulty as Hertford had the excuse of a visit to his sister to admit him to the rooms in the palace belonging to the maids-of-honour, and Jane herself visited him at Cannon Row, taking Catherine with her and leaving them alone together. He gave Catherine a keepsake that had belonged to his father, the Lord Protector, a little note-book bound in red velvet and inscribed in the Protector's own hands; she cherished it with her sister's Greek Testament and kept them both safe till her death. A more valuable gift was a deed conveying land to her, all the more important as it was written evidence of her marriage, acknowledging her as his wife. She put it away, forgot about it and lost it.

In the spring she told him she thought that she was pregnant, and they agreed that if it were true they could maintain the deception no longer, must confess to the Queen and trust to her mercy; but shortly afterwards to her dismay he received orders sending him to Paris on a diplomatic mission. It may be that the Queen already suspected something and was anxious to part them. To refuse to go was out of the question; but he arranged for Catherine to write to him regularly and engaged a servant to carry their letters to and fro. He promised that if she became certain of her pregnancy and it could no longer be concealed he would come home at once to be with her.

Before his departure she sustained an even harder blow. Jane

Seymour, always delicate, succumbed to an acute infection of the lungs and died in a few days. Catherine lost her closest friend on whose advice and comfort she depended, she lost, too, the only witness of her wedding.

She was right in thinking that she was about to bear a child. The symptoms were soon unmistakable, and she wrote in distress to her husband begging him to return in accordance with his promise. She received no answer, she wrote again and still he was silent; she had no news of him beyond rumours of his gay life in Paris. In fact he wrote to her often; but the servant employed as messenger was in the pay of the government, their letters were intercepted, hers withheld from him and his from her. The stories of his amusements were put about merely to discredit him.

Believing that he no longer cared for her and left by Jane's death with no one in whom to confide, she was desolate; already it was barely possible to disguise her condition. She dared not go to the Queen herself; she sought in her despair the mediation of the powerful favourite, Robert Dudley (he was not yet Earl of Leicester), relying on the tie between them that her sister had been his brother's wife. With the rest of the court she was attending the Queen on a progress through Suffolk, and they spent the night at Ipswich. Having made up her mind and unable to bear the suspense any longer she went on a sudden impulse to Dudley's bedroom, fell on her knees and poured the whole story out to him.

His chief concern was to get her out of the room. The Queen's own room was not far off, and the fear appalled him that she might hear the noise, come to see what was happening, and find him with Catherine in compromising association. He put her off with soothing promises and sent her away, and on the following morning he made haste to tell the Queen everything, to convince her that he himself had no part in the affair. Elizabeth, unwilling to mar the festivities prepared for her, kept her knowledge to herself till the itinerary was completed; but on their return to London she ordered Catherine Grey to be arrested and committed to the Tower.

Meanwhile, Hertford was recalled from Paris. His friends in France advised him to stay abroad; but he made light of his danger, insisting that if Dudley could woo the Queen he himself had as good a right to wed her heir. He returned to England and was arrested as soon as he landed at Dover. Like Catherine he was committed to the Tower, but they were kept apart, he in the White Tower, she in the Belfry. They were left there to await the findings of an official inquiry, which on Cecil's advice was postponed till Catherine was delivered of her child. If Cecil hoped that she would not survive the experience he was disappointed. Her labour was short, she gave birth to a healthy boy who received the name of Edward Seymour and the title, if his claim to legitimacy prevailed, of Viscount Beauchamp. He was great-great-grandson to Henry VII.

When the council held its inquiry the stories told by the two were consistent; both described in detail the events related of the morning of their secret wedding. The evidence of the servants corroborated them; the cook was peeping from a window when Jane and Catherine arrived, another saw Jane set out alone in quest of a priest. Two valets recalled the undisturbed table, the much-disturbed bed. Vital witnesses, however, were missing; Jane Seymour was dead, the priest not to be found, no one knew who he was. Even the deed of conveyance in which Hertford acknowledged Catherine as his wife could not be put in evidence, she could not remember where she left it. The council declared the marriage invalid, sentenced the parties to imprisonment for fornication.

In the following autumn the Queen fell ill of smallpox, and her condition was so grave that her death was expected. As the Scottish claimant, Mary Stuart, was opposed by the Protestants and distrusted as a foreigner Catherine's right to succeed had wide support. Her own conformity to Catholic rites in the previous reign was readily forgiven; many older and wiser than she, Protestants now without reproach, were guilty of a similar lapse. Her sister was revered as a martyr to the Protestant cause, and Hertford himself inherited lustre from the love felt by the people for his father, the "Good Duke." Dignitaries of Church and state might condemn, but common opinion was inclined to think the better of the pair for the strength of their attachment. The Queen herself owed her birth to a union scarcely less irregular; it would not be hard for the council to reverse its judgment, pronounce the validity of a marriage which offered that precious guarantee of security, a male heir.

The lieutenant of the Tower, aware of the prevalence of these feelings, was careful to treat his distinguished prisoners with consideration. He allowed Catherine to keep the pets of which she was fond, dogs, parrots, even monkeys, in her lodgings in spite of the damage done to the furniture. A more important boon was his connivance enabling Hertford to visit her, on condition that he used discretion and paid the watchman a suitable fee. They were able undisturbed to resume their married life.

Elizabeth recovered from smallpox, and the question of the succession ceased to be urgent. She was much displeased to hear of the attention given it, the expectations aroused, and in no mood to restrain her anger when the privilege granted without her knowledge to Hertford and his wife resulted in the birth of a second son, who was christened Thomas. Henceforward they were kept strictly apart, sentenced not only to imprisonment but also to pay a crippling fine. Their too considerate gaoler became a prisoner in his own gaol.

A few months later there was an outbreak of plague in the Tower, and Elizabeth always scrupulous in her sense of duty, ordered the erring pair to be removed from danger of infection. Catherine and the younger boy, Thomas, were sent to live in custody with her uncle, Lord John Grey, at Pirgo in Essex, while Hertford and the elder, Edward, went to his mother at Hanworth. They never saw each other again. Their friends pleaded in vain for them to be released and reunited. Catherine's uncle in whose charge she was put wrote in 1564: "I would I were the Queen's confessor this Lent that I might enjoin her in penance to forgive and forget." His plea had no effect; Catherine remained his prisoner till he died himself in the following autumn, and for the next four years she was moved from house to house in the eastern counties, an unwilling and unwanted guest, whose presence made her host a gaoler. She lived in reasonable comfort, had the company of her younger son; but she pined for her other son and her husband. When she fell ill in January 1568 the cause was an infection of the lungs; but she had no will to resist, she died aged twenty-seven of a broken heart.

While she lay dying in Suffolk the rival heir, Mary Stuart, fell also into Elizabeth's hands. Defeated and forced to abdicate by Scottish rebels, she fled across the Solway to seek refuge in England and was accommodated in one castle after another, nominally a guest, in fact a prisoner. She and Catherine alike were victims of Elizabeth's caution, of her unwillingness to make up her mind. As long as England had an unmarried Queen her successor had to be chosen from another branch of the family, and it suited Elizabeth to leave the choice open so that she could play off the supporters of the one against those of the other. Meanwhile, she kept both claimants under supervision to deter either from forestalling events.

Catherine's early death upset the plan. Her sons having been declared illegitimate carried no weight as an alternative to Mary Stuart. Nevertheless, Elizabeth ordered them to be brought up in a manner befitting high rank, and their father shortly afterwards recovered his freedom and was taken back into her favour. He tried to persuade her to upset the judgment of the council and recognise the validity of his marriage; but she shrank from a decision, fearing the consequences. Catherine's sons growing up in England could become too dangerously popular; Mary's son, crowned James VI in Scotland, was an heir for whose succession public opinion was less likely to be impatient.

Hertford had to wait till King James sat on the English throne to obtain justice for his family. Then he applied for a retrial of the issue; the missing priest emerged from obscurity to give evidence, with the result that the marriage was vindicated, and Edward and Thomas Seymour could be called his lawful sons. The elder inherited his mother's title to the crown, but he allowed it to lapse, preferring a quiet life.

Among the motives prompting Elizabeth's harsh treatment of Catherine the misadventures of the younger sister, the hunchback dwarf Mary, played a part. By provoking derision they brought discredit not only on the girl herself but also on that branch of the Royal Family from which she descended. Catherine's own escapade held much that appealed to popular imagination. Many still alive remembered her grandmother, King Henry's favourite sister, Mary, and her secret wedding in Paris to the Duke of Suffolk. They were ready to extend indulgence to a repetition of this pattern of behaviour when Catherine, the offender, shared her grandmother's good looks. It was another matter when the story was enacted for a third time, and the heroine played by a grotesque. In the eyes of the onlookers it ceased to be a tragedy, became a farce.

The younger Mary was condemned from birth to shortcomings deserving much compassion, but as she grew up she was not unkindly treated by the world. At the age of nine she accompanied her sister to Queen Mary's court, holding rank there as a Royal Princess, and Queen Elizabeth took them both into her service as maids-of-honour. Even when Catherine's marriage led to her disgrace and imprisonment Mary retained her position at court undisturbed. Elizabeth who could not endure the sight of deformity showed a consideration which testifies to the strictness of her principles, if not to the warmth of her heart.

There was an officer who bore the title of serjeant of the Royal water gates. It was a position of some dignity involving attendance on the Queen on the frequent occasions when she embarked from the palace on the river. At this time it was held by Thomas Keyes, a widower in his forties left with a family of half-a-dozen children. He was chiefly remarkable for his stature, a giant standing six-foot-eight and stout to match. No more incongruous partner could have been found for Lady Mary Grey, who was more than twenty years younger and only four feet high. Her sister's example, moreover, already furnished a warning of the punishment incurred for trespass on the line of Royal descent.

Keyes was either very stupid or he had great trust in his luck. His self-importance was nourished by a grand wedding in the family, that of a kinsman, Henry Knollys, who was also related to the Queen, grandson to her aunt, Mary Boleyn; the Queen herself attended the ceremony. When it was over he invited a party of friends including Mary Grey to his lodgings, where they kept up the merriment, dancing and drinking till late in the evening. When the rest departed Mary remained with four others chosen for the purpose. A priest arrived, unidentified like Catherine's, and performed the marriage service by candlelight. Keyes took Mary for his wife with four witnesses to attest to their vows.

Within a week the event was the gossip of the town. Cecil described it in a letter as "the most unhappy chance and monstrous" that "the Serjeant being the biggest gentleman at this court has secretly married the Lady Mary Grey, the least of all the court." Queen Elizabeth swore that she would have "no little bastard Keyes" to succeed her on the throne. Keyes spent five years in the Fleet prison, and Mary was sent into the country, condemned like her sister to the reluctant hospitality of a host who was also her gaoler. More fortunate than Catherine, she survived and in time was released, and her stepfather, Adrian Stokes, her mother's former equerry, who had married again, took her under his protection and showed her much kindness. Even the Queen forgave her at last. There were no children, no "little bastard Keyes," to disturb the succession.

Whatever trouble Elizabeth endured from the behaviour of the heirs of this branch of the family, she had no such danger to fear from them as from Mary Stuart. There was no party in the country committed to put Catherine Grey on the throne; but there were many Catholics at home supported by powerful interests abroad who denounced Elizabeth as a heretic and proposed Mary Stuart not to succeed but to supplant her. They became more active than ever when Mary, having lost her own kingdom, was held in England as Elizabeth's prisoner; effort was needed not only to win her the English crown but to recover the Scottish as well.

Mary's grandmother was Margaret Tudor, her great-grandfather Henry VII, from whom she inherited her place in the English succession; but as the heir and ancestress of a line of Stuart Kings she belongs to the story of the Scottish rather than of the Welsh dynasty. To do her justice it would be necessary to stray far beyond the field of this book, to trace the course of events in Scotland without which no view of her life can be adequate. It is a task more appropriate to the historian of the Stuarts to pass judgment on her character, to decide how far she was Elizabeth's active enemy, how far an innocent victim.

There is room for dispute about the part which she herself played in successive plots, there is none about the danger which they created for the English government. Willingly or unwillingly, she provided a purpose to which all could rally who cherished a grievance whether on religious or political grounds, the earnest advocate of Papal authority, the ambitious nobleman dissatisfied with his share of the spoils. Elizabeth showed unusual forbearance by the standard of her day in refusing for so long to put her rival to death. Her behaviour recalls that of her grandfather towards Perkin Warbeck, the same reluctance to take life, the final exasperation.

She could always count on the loyalty of the bulk of the people; the rebels would have been without importance if they had not received foreign encouragement, chiefly from France and Spain. There was much sympathy in France for Mary Stuart, the widow of a French King; but it was restrained when Elizabeth fostered hopes of her own marriage to a French Prince, and in any case civil war left little time for external adventures. The threat of Spanish intervention was more formidable, aggravated by political and commercial jealousy. The cause of Mary Stuart came as the years passed to be identified with that of Spain. In 1586 English forces were fighting against the Spanish in the Netherlands, supporting the Dutch claim to independence, when a dangerous plot was uncovered in London, an attempt to assassinate Elizabeth, from which she barely escaped with her life.

There was no need to prove Mary's complicity; a recent ordinance imposed the penalty of death on anyone for whose benefit an act of treason was committed. She was put on trial at Fotheringhay Castle near Peterborough and sentenced to be beheaded. It is clear that the proceedings had Elizabeth's full approval, she was angry and badly frightened; but her rage seldom lasted long, her moods changed quickly, it was in her nature to shrink from irrevocable decision. She hesitated for months over the order for Mary's execution.

Meanwhile the King of France, Henry III, sent an ambassador to plead on the prisoner's behalf, he reminded Elizabeth that "she is a princess and your nearest relative." These were arguments present already in Elizabeth's mind; she was well aware that it set a dangerous example to shed Royal blood, and she respected the ties of kinship. Nevertheless the ambassador pleaded in vain; his master, Henry III, was her unwilling suitor in the old days, whose description of herself she remembered: "She is not only an old creature but has a sore leg." The Duke of Guise, Mary's cousin on her mother's side, offered if her life were spared to send his two sons to England as hostages for Elizabeth's safety. He had no success; Elizabeth asked what use the hostages would be to her when she was dead.

More effect was produced by a letter from Mary herself. Leicester found Elizabeth reading it and reported that she was in tears. During the eighteen years that Mary spent in England she and Elizabeth never met face to face. Elizabeth was impulsive, readily susceptible to warmth of feeling. If she had known Mary in person the end could have been very different.

No reprieve for Mary could satisfy Elizabeth's ministers, even if means were found to keep her where she was no danger to the peace of the realm. As long as she lived she was heir to the throne, and they had done too much to injure her to expect to prosper or even to survive after her accession. They urged Elizabeth, therefore, to delay the execution no longer, laid stress on the risk which she took with her own safety till the source of all conspiracy was removed. Their arguments played skilfully on her fears, she knew that the King of Spain was already gathering a great fleet for the invasion of England. Nevertheless she shrank from the responsibility of inflicting sentence of death on a Royal

Princess, a former Queen, her cousin. She complained bitterly that no one was willing to save her from so cruel a decision, to take action on his own by poison or similar means to shorten the prisoner's life. Her complaint went unheeded, not even the most devoted would oblige. It was clear what a relief it would be to her to hear that Mary was murdered, equally clear that the murderer would receive no reward, would probably be sternly punished to convince the world of Elizabeth's innocence.

Her mind changed from day to day, her ministers waited to catch her in a mood favourable to their plans. At last, in February 1587, four months after the verdict of the court, William Davison, the secretary to the council, brought her the death warrant and she signed it. The document was carried in haste before she could recall it to Fotheringhay Castle, and Mary was beheaded. When Elizabeth heard what had been done she expressed great indignation, committed Davison in disgrace to the Tower. She denied that when she signed the order she intended it to be carried out. Writing to Mary's son, the future King James of England, she described his mother's execution as a "miserable accident." Her distress was sincere, she was no hypocrite playing a part. She had genius for self-deception.

CHAPTER 18

Virginia, commemorating Queen Elizabeth, bears lasting witness
to her encouragement of English adventure in the Western Hemisphere. The territory named in her honour was much larger than
that which bears the name today; it extended along the coast from
Newfoundland in the north to the Spanish settlements in Florida.
The first English colony planted on American soil was in Virginia
according to the ideas of the day; but its site, Roanoke Island in
Pamlico Sound, lies within the modern state of North Carolina.

When the bull of Pope Alexander VI gave the King of Spain
sole dominion in lands discovered to the west of the fiftieth
meridian of longitude these northern parts of the new continent
held little attraction for the Spaniards; they were too busy plundering the wealth of the Aztec and Inca civilisations farther south.
Some interest was shown in the north by the English in Henry
VII's reign; but the voyages which it promoted, those of Cabot
and other sailors from Bristol, were undertaken in search of a
northwest passage to China and India, without any purpose of
founding a permanent settlement. In the course of the next half-
century, as it became clear how greatly Spain profited from
American colonies, English envy was aroused; but the monopoly
of the Spanish Main was strictly guarded, and privateers encroached on the trade at heavy risk without protection from the
English government, which preferred to leave Spain alone and
was unwilling to provoke a quarrel. When Mary became Queen
and took a Spanish husband any activity hostile to Spanish interests
was severely forbidden.

Elizabeth's accession at first brought little change. She had enough to do to establish her position at home without seeking foreign conflict, and as long as the French pressed the claims of Mary Stuart to take her place she needed King Philip's balancing influence to check them. In time, however, she became less dependent on him. Her own conciliatory policy in France bore fruit, her encouragement of French suitors, the sons of Catherine de Medici; in addition the bitterness of the religious factions, the civil war between Catholics and Huguenots, was weakening French power in Europe, leaving that of Spain predominant. Cecil, her chief minister, still urged caution; but bolder spirits including Leicester argued that King Philip was a relentless enemy who regarded her as the source of all heresy, and that she should take action at once to prevent him from growing too strong. He would never rest content till he dethroned her.

With characteristic indecision she swung from one policy to the other, too impulsive to discourage adventurers who cherished visions of El Dorado beyond the western ocean, too cautious to support them with her authority at the cost of war with Spain. She had soothing reassurances for the Spanish ambassador, smiles for the sailors who trespassed on Spanish preserves. There was abundant energy in the country demanding an outlet. The curtailment of the power of the nobility by the early Tudor Kings left many young men idle and impoverished who relied for advancement on employment in a noble household. Adventure at sea offered an attractive alternative, a chance to win both honour and wealth, and when it was seen that these exploits enjoyed the Queen's favour there was eager response, especially in Devonshire and neighbouring counties with a seafaring tradition.

Money to equip the ships was readily available from merchants in London. Trade in English cloth was declining, and they needed a new field for investment. American business might be speculative, but it promised a lucrative return. Spanish treasure intercepted on the high seas flowed into England to enrich not only private enterprise but also the Royal exchequer, which claimed a share of the proceeds. Elizabeth had her grandfather's love of a profitable bargain, and her fear of offending Spain dwindled as the gold mounted. When Drake disembarked at Plymouth in 1580 after a voyage circumnavigating the globe, laden with the spoils of Spanish settlements from the Caribbean to Peru, King Philip demanded his surrender as a pirate. Her reply was to knight him.

Walter Raleigh was among those who caught the fever for western voyages. He was a younger son of a landowning family in Devonshire, hard put to it like many of his birth and education to find a career to his taste; but his prospects improved when he obtained an introduction at court through the Queen's old governess, Kate Ashley, to whom he was related. It was a recommendation that carried weight with Elizabeth who was always loyal to old friends, devoted to Mrs. Ashley, and when she saw in addition that Raleigh was a good-looking young man who combined arrogance to the world with deference to herself she was easily persuaded to accept him as a courtier. There is a well-known story of the incident that first earned him her favour, that she was walking on a path after rain, hesitating at a puddle that blocked her way, and he seeing her concern stripped off his new plush cloak and spread it for her in the mud to cross dry-shod.

As her fondness for him increased he took advantage of it to interest her in his dreams of founding a colony in America. He himself had little experience of navigation; but his half-brother, Humphrey Gilbert, was a bold sailor already familiar with the western ocean, and in 1583 she gave consent for an expedition to set out under Gilbert's còmmand for Newfoundland and the coast beyond to find a spot suitable for settlement. Raleigh himself was not allowed to accompany it. She was unwilling to deprive herself of his society at court.

She saved him from active participation in disaster. Gilbert reached Newfoundland, formally claimed it for the English Crown; but when he proceeded on his voyage one of his ships was wrecked, and the two left ran short of food and had to turn home. Soon after passing the Azores they met a violent storm; the weather grew more and more outrageous, and Gilbert's own ship, the smaller of the two, sank with all hands. The other, the *Golden Hind*, sailed on much battered to England to report the failure of the enterprise, the loss of its commander.

Gilbert's death did not deter Raleigh from his ambition; but he took warning to avoid the dangers of the northern crossing and directed his quest thenceforward to the calmer water farther to the south. Soon after the return of the *Golden Hind* he sent two friends, Arthur Barlowe and Philip Amadas, to survey that part of the coast and report on its possibilities. They crossed to the West Indies, then turned north towards the unexplored land beyond the Spanish settlements in Florida. As they approached Cape

Hatteras they found shoal water, and the wind, as they reported, carried a sweet smell "as if we had been in the midst of some delicate garden abounding in all kind of odoriferous flowers." As soon as a suitable inlet appeared they put in, cast anchor and disembarked.

They were on one of the barrier of narrow islands enclosing Pamlico Sound. At first when they saw water beyond them they mistook it for another ocean and were jubilant, believing that this was a passage giving access to the Pacific to enable them to outflank the Spaniards. To their disappointment it proved to be nothing more than a huge landlocked bay, too shallow for navigation except by ships of the lightest draft. Nevertheless they explored the island thoroughly, delighted by its fertility. On the third day a party of Indians came to them in boats, and the leader who was brother to the local chief greeted them with "signs of joy and welcome, striking on his head and breast and afterwards on ours to show we were all one." These Indians paid several visits, exchanging fruits and furs for knives, axes and tinware from the ship's stores, and at last they invited the Englishmen to accompany them to Roanoke Island a short way to the north, where they lived. The reception afforded there was of the friendliest sort, the hospitality effusive. Barlowe reported:

"We found the people most gentle, loving and faithful, void of all guile and treason, and such as live after the manner of the golden age."

He returned to England full of praise for the country, convinced that he had found the right site for Raleigh's colony. Two Indians from Roanoke accompanied him, named respectively Manteo and Wanchese.

The encouraging report filled Raleigh with enthusiasm, the Queen too. A bill was introduced in Parliament to confirm the acquisition of the new territory, which became known from this date as Virginia in the Queen's honour. Funds were raised by a number of prominent investors including Raleigh himself to fit out an expedition, and prospective settlers were chosen to man it. This colony, the first ever planted by the English in America, resembled a military occupation. The recruits themselves invested no capital and acquired no property in their new homes; they were the paid servants of the enterprise, working for a wage and subject to strict discipline.

They sailed from Plymouth in April 1585 under the command

of Raleigh's cousin, Sir Richard Grenville. The exploit destined to earn him lasting fame still lay six years ahead, the battle which he fought to the death in his little ship, the *Revenge*, against a Spanish fleet, "the fight of the one and the fifty-three" described in Tennyson's ballad. He was already among the most daring, however, of the naval commanders who enriched themselves and the Queen with the plunder of the Spanish Main. On this occasion his duty was to escort the settlers on their voyage; when they reached their goal he left them for adventures of his own in quest of treasure, promising to return in the following spring with fresh supplies.

The colony had an unfortunate start; one of the ships ran aground in the shallow passage leading into Pamlico Sound, and water getting into the hold damaged the stores which it carried. Although Grenville left what he could spare when he departed the settlers suffered from grave shortage of provisions, obliged to live as best they could from the produce of the land. This was less available and less abundant than the seeming fertility of the soil encouraged them to hope. They had no experience of the sort of cultivation needed, and they lacked the skill shown by the Indians in catching fish and game. If the Indians had not kept them supplied they could hardly have survived.

It was the intention to found the settlement on the mainland beyond Pamlico Sound, and even before Grenville's departure some preliminary exploration was attempted; but as no suitable site was discovered a temporary base was established for the settlers on Roanoke Island, already known from the survey carried out by Barlowe and Amadas. It was the home of the two Indians taken to England, Manteo and Wanchese, who returning now were able to act as intermediaries and interpreters. Nevertheless there were many disadvantages, not least the lack of a safe harbour deep enough for seagoing ships. As soon as arrangements were completed Ralph Lane, the governor appointed by the Queen, set off with a small party to explore the mainland more thoroughly.

Lane was a soldier fresh from service in Ireland, capable and energetic, stern in asserting his authority over English settlers and indigenous inhabitants alike. He did not share Barlowe's faith in the Indians, that they "live after the manner of the golden age"; in his own report he described them as "savages."

The men whom he led were well armed, and he took care at an early opportunity to seize the paramount chief of the surrounding country and hold him in pledge for the behaviour of the tribe. Success at first rewarded his methods; the Indians had the added motive of fear to persuade them to cooperate, and they told him (he had Manteo to interpret) of a great river beyond their country with deep water at the mouth, probably Chesapeake Bay. The news filled him with hope of finding the site that he needed for his colony.

In his absence, however, trouble was brewing on Roanoke Island. The chief whose friendship dated from Barlowe's visit died, and his brother who succeeded was less ready to favour the strangers. Their military behaviour introduced by Lane offended him, and their helplessness, their dependence on the labour and skill of others strained the scanty resources of the Indian community. The hospitality offered willingly on a short visit became an intolerable burden when the guests outstayed their welcome. Moreover, of the two Indians taken to England, only Manteo returned converted to the English way of life; Wanchese, the other, was less favourably impressed, and now while Manteo went with Lane he remained on the island warning his people against the white-skinned intruders, the power at their command, their insatiable ambition.

Messages travelled between the Indians of the island and those of the mainland, urging the latter to destroy Lane while he was vulnerable, cut off from his main forces. He himself was unaware of anything wrong till he found the country deserted around him; the Indians had vanished, taking all their provisions with them, and as he relied on them for food his men were in danger of starvation. When at last Indians approached calling to him and singing he was much relieved; but Manteo explained that what he heard was a war song, and a volley of arrows confirmed the interpretation. English muskets prevailed, the Indians were put to flight and did not repeat the attack; but before Lane and his men were back at Roanoke they were so hungry that they were thankful to dine on "dog porridge," a soup made by boiling the two mastiffs brought for hunting.

Conditions on their return to the island were little more comfortable than in the wilds. Indian reluctance to supply food increased, ill-will sought all means possible to harass the settlers. At last Lane invited the chief to a conference, and when the Indians came unsuspecting the English set on them and many were killed. The chief himself fled wounded into the woods, where an Irish servant of Lane's caught him and cut off his head. This treachery could plead the excuse of desperate need, but it set an example from which the Indians drew a dangerous lesson.

Meanwhile the settlers waited with impatience for Grenville to return to reinforce them and replenish their stores; he was already long overdue. It was not he, however, whose ships arrived as if in answer to their prayers. Sir Francis Drake, returning home with his fleet from the Spanish Main, put in to see how the settlement fared, and when he heard of its troubles he offered to supply everything needed. He himself had abundance of provisions, the fruit of successful marauding.

Lane accepted the offer gladly, and orders were given to row the stores to land, when suddenly a great storm blew up. Drake's ships, lying in the open roads on a coast with no protecting harbour, were in danger of being cast ashore and wrecked; they saved themselves by putting out to sea, sailing away with many of the settlers who, thoroughly disgusted with Roanoke Island, made haste in the confusion to find places on board. When the storm abated Drake approached again; but Lane's depleted company showed interest no longer in offers of supplies, all that they asked was to be taken off, allowed to return to England. Drake agreed, and the first English colony in America was evacuated.

When Grenville arrived a little later with promised reinforcements there were no settlers to greet him; the fort and houses were empty, and the Indians unable or unwilling to tell him what had happened. After a vain search he left fifteen men on Roanoke Island to retain title of possession, then sailed home to England.

Although the settlement was a failure there were two members of the expedition who returned undiscouraged, refusing to join in the chorus of disgust with which the others described their adventures. These were John White and Thomas Harriot, the former a painter, the latter a naturalist and mathematician. White's water colours, many of which were subsequently reproduced in engravings, are among the earliest sources of evidence of Indian manners. Neither he nor Harriot was content to dismiss the Indians as savages; each tried, the one in paint, the other in words, to understand their way of life, to reveal a new and strange but none the less human community.

Harriot's interest covered not only the people but also the plants of the new continent, especially those whose cultivation could contribute to the welfare of a settlement established there. His report includes the first account published in England of the herb "called by the inhabitants *uppowoc*," already known as tobacco to the Spaniards who observed its use in the West Indies. He describes how the Indians prepare the leaves, drying and bringing them to powder, then they "take the smoke thereof by sucking it through pipes made of clay into their stomach and head, from whence it purgeth superfluous phlegm and other gross humours." He insists on the medicinal virtue of the habit, how it opens "all the pores and passages of the body," with the result that the smokers "are notably preserved in health and know not many grievous diseases wherewithal we in England are oftentimes afflicted." His views, unlike those expressed by medical science today, can be read with comfort and agreement by the tobacconist.

He brought samples of the leaves home with him and gave them to Raleigh. The story has often been told of the servant who entered Raleigh's study with a tankard of ale, and finding his master smoking a pipe, smoke pouring from his lips, thought that he was on fire and emptied the tankard over his head.

Raleigh paid more attention to White and Harriot than to the tales of woe of the others. It seemed to him that he made a mistake in organising the colony on military lines, that the enterprise was more likely to succeed if the settlers themselves were shareholders, who would bring their families with them to create and work farms of their own and would possess the skill to do so. Early in 1587 his plans were ready for a renewed attempt, with a company of 150 or so willing to travel, no desperadoes serving for pay but respectable farmers and tradesmen, who invested a life's savings in the prospect of a new home in the land beyond the ocean. White himself was chosen to be governor, and Manteo, the friendly Indian—evacuated by Drake when he took Lane and his men off from Roanoke—accompanied them.

Dangerous shoals and an exposed coast without shelter for shipping were among the principal causes of the failure of the first colony. White was resolved not to make the same mistake again; he planned to call at Roanoke only to pick up the men left there by Grenville, then to sail on northward in search of a more suitable site, probably on the deep estuary of which Lane had heard from the Indians. On the voyage, however, he fell out with the commander in charge of the ships, Simon Fernandez, a Portuguese whose career owed much to successful piracy. Fernandez was anxious for the expedition to earn profit by holding up and plundering Spanish ships on the way; White objected that this would delay their progress and cause unnecessary discomfort and danger to their passengers, who included women and children. His will prevailed; but Fernandez was ill pleased, impatient to be rid of the settlers as soon as they reached their destination, so that he might make up for missed opportunities by profitable adventure sailing home. When they drew in to the islands skirting Pamlico Sound and a party went ashore he announced that this was as far as he meant to go, that all must disembark and the ships would return to England. White who was himself among those already on land was in no position to argue. The sailors supported Fernandez.

Thus for a second time Roanoke Island became the site of the colony. White made haste to visit Lane's old settlement. He found the fort razed to the ground, the houses still standing; but vegetation—"melons," he calls it—overgrew them and encroached into the rooms, and deer fed there. All was deserted, he saw no trace of Grenville's fifteen men till he came on the skeleton of an English sailor; enough was left to bear witness to a violent death. The fate of the rest became known later, Manteo obtained the story from his friends on the island. It seems that soon after Grenville sailed away the Indians attacked the settlement, and when the Englishmen took refuge in the fort it was set on fire so that they had to come out and fight. One of them was killed, the man whose bones were found; but the others retreated to the water and escaped in a boat. Where they went and what happened to them no one could say. Nothing was ever heard of them again.

Barely three years had passed since the prospecting voyage on which Barlowe described the Indians as "most gentle, loving and faithful, void of all guile and treason." It was a description no longer appropriate since the foundation of Lane's colony at Roanoke. White himself had renewed evidence now of Indian hostility; one of his men going off alone to fish was caught in an ambush and killed. Much of the blame for deteriorating manners lay with changed circumstances. The arrival of the first expedition, that which Barlowe led, was a novelty inspiring wonder, an entertaining diversion which the Indians greeted with pleasure. The strangers lost this advantage when they settled in the country, and their white skins, their exotic clothes and goods became familiar. As association was prolonged it bred friction, and the military measures which Lane adopted, taking hostages and exacting reprisals, aggravated suspicion and resentment. By Indian standards the English were merely a tribe encroaching by force on the tribal territory of others.

An even graver obstacle to cordial relations was the inability shown by Lane's men to supply their own needs. Consisting for the most part of soldiers without farming experience, they lacked the skill to till the soil and catch sufficient game and had to depend on the native population, whose own resources were too scanty to bear the strain without discomfort. When White sent Manteo to approach his people, to persuade them to restore former bonds of friendship, the first request that the Indians made was that their corn should be left untouched. Their demeanour only ceased to be hostile when he assured them that the new settlers were equipped to provide for themselves and would not be a burden on the community.

The settlers owed a great debt to Manteo; it was destined before the story was done to include their lives. Unlike his companion, Wanchese, he returned from his first visit to England with an ardent admiration for English ways, steadfast loyalty to his English patrons, and his second visit did nothing to weaken the effect. With his help the settlers were soon on terms of full confidence with his tribe; they even learnt who was responsible for the death of their comrade, the murdered fisherman. The offenders were a tribe living on the mainland, friends of Wanchese, who kindled their hatred of the English. White sent a force at dawn to punish them, hoping to take them by surprise; but they were warned and fled. Worse still, Manteo's friends from the island following to plunder the deserted crops were mistaken in the dim light for enemies, and several were killed before the sight of a woman among them carrying a child on her back revealed the error, convincing the English that these were no armed warriors but their own allies.

Manteo was much upset by the misunderstanding; but White did his best to make amends, helping the islanders to gather as much as was ripe from the crops, peas, pumpkins and tobacco, growing in the fields, then escorting them including the woman, who was their chief's wife, safely home in their boats. It is evidence of the respect which Manteo enjoyed that he got them to admit that the mishap was due to their own folly, that they ought to have gone to White beforehand to concert plans.

Shortly afterwards a solemn ceremony was performed at the settlement. Manteo received Christian baptism and a warrant appointing him in the name of Queen Elizabeth to bear authority as

Lord of Roanoke. Within a week or so, the christening service was needed again, this time for a baby. White's daughter, Eleanor Dare, wife of Ananias Dare, one of the settlers, gave birth to a girl who received the name of Virginia. She was the first native American of English descent, Virginia Dare.

Meanwhile the stores were all unloaded, the ships caulked and trimmed for the journey home, with fresh water in their tanks, timber for ballast, and a sack of letters from the settlers to be delivered in England. Fernandez was impatient to depart, it was not a coast on which any prudent seaman wished to linger. His fears were confirmed when a northeasterly gale sprang up suddenly, and he had to cut his cables and put out to sea, leaving many of the sailors on land. For six days he was out of sight of the shore, and the settlers believed that he was gone for good; but when the storm abated he was able to bring his ships back into the roads and cast anchor. It would have left him dangerously shorthanded to sail without the missing men.

This experience shook the resolution of the settlers, almost an exact repetition of the events which threatened Drake with disaster when he was here. It was an uncomfortable reminder of the hazards of this part of the Virginian coast, the disadvantage for permanent settlement. White's men, however, were no soldiers of fortune like Lane's; they had too much at stake to give up at this stage, having sold all their possessions in England to invest the proceeds in the enterprise. They did not ask to be taken home; but they demanded that a responsible deputy should travel back on their behalf to explain to Raleigh, even to the Queen herself, how they were forced against their will to land at Roanoke, and to plead for the despatch of a fresh expedition amply supplied to convey them, as was intended, to a more appropriate site.

The difficulty was to choose who should represent them. No one wanted to go, to cut himself off for so long from the work in hand and leave his goods in Virginia unguarded. At last they turned to the governor himself, John White, implored him to accept the duty; his voice would carry more weight than any lesser man's to obtain a favourable answer in England to their request. He was most reluctant, pointing out that his departure would expose him to calumny; the malicious would say that he led others into a country where he never meant to stay himself. They persisted, however, and offered him a signed statement testifying that he left his post only in obedience to their urgent entreaty to promote their interests and obtain satisfaction of their needs. Unable at last to resist their importunacy he consented, and towards the end of August he sailed, having spent little more than a month altogether in Virginia. His daughter and granddaughter remained there. Misadventures delayed his ship. It was November before he reached England, where he found everyone from the Queen downwards preoccupied with the danger from Spain, the huge fleet gathering in Spanish ports ready for invasion. He succeeded, however, in convincing Raleigh of the urgent need to supply the Virginian settlement, and arrangements were made to fit out an expedition under Grenville's command. Winter passed before all was complete, and by then the threat of war was so formidable that Grenville received orders from the council to change his plans and take his fleet to reinforce the Royal navy. The most that could be conceded to White was permission to sail to Virginia with two small ships to relieve the immediate needs of the colonists and assure them that more adequate help would follow as soon as possible.

The concession brought him no benefit. He had the same trouble with the sailors as with Fernandez on the earlier occasion when the colony was planted. In spite of his protests they refused to miss the opportunity to enrich themselves on the voyage by plundering foreign trade, and their victims were not limited to cargoes sailing under the Spanish flag. Their adventures càme to an end when they met a Frenchman who was more than a match for them. Their ship limped home barely seaworthy to Bideford, where soon afterwards its sister ship joined them, having been employed in the same way and with the same result. White was as far as ever from the accomplishment of his mission, the relief of the Virginian settlement.

This was in May 1588, and in July the Spanish Armada put to sea. Everyone's attention was engrossed in preparations to resist it, no one had time to spare for a distant colony of a hundred and fifty souls when England itself was threatened with destruction. The events that followed are among the best-known in English history: the approach of the Spaniards seen from Plymouth where the English fleet was gathered, the skirmishes in the Channel in which English skill and knowledge made up for Spanish predominance in numbers and size, the refuge found by the invaders in the roads of Calais and the success of the fireships used to dislodge them, finally the onslaught of the southwesterly gale which drove them in helpless confusion into the unknown waters of the North Sea. Before the end of August most were either sunk or wrecked, littering the rocks of the Hebrides and the western coast of Ireland.

The defeat of the Invincible Armada left Spain no longer an enemy to be feared. English privateers enjoyed a heyday on the Spanish Main, the Spaniards lacked power effectively to defend their treasure. The result was not to White's advantage; the demand for ships to cross the ocean in quest of Spanish gold exhausted the supply, few were available for his own less remunerative purpose. He persisted, however, urging Raleigh to use his influence, and early in 1590 his arguments were reinforced by the publication of a book in Germany describing the voyages made to America and illustrated with engravings, reproductions of his own paintings. It aroused great interest in England.

In the following year his opportunity came. A venture intending to set out for the West Indies was unable to obtain permission for the voyage. Raleigh persuaded the Queen to lift the prohibition on condition that White and a few friends travelled as passengers, to be conveyed to Virginia. The shipowner agreed with reluctance, and when White and his party came to Plymouth to embark the captain allowed only White on board, turned the others away. It was too late for White to protest. He knew that if he went back on shore to report the breach of contract the ships would sail without him.

Nearly four years had gone by since he parted from the settlers including his daughter and her baby at Roanoke, and it is easy to imagine his anxiety for their fate; but again he had to curb his impatience, endure tantalising delay. The captain had shrewd reason for his refusal to take more than one passenger; he made sure that there would be no volume of complaint if he put his own business first, preferred plunder on the Spanish Main to a troublesome errand. The ships spent the best part of the summer sailing from island to island in pursuit of valuable prizes, and it was not till August that the *Hopewell* carrying White turned north at last towards Virginia.

As they approached the coast outside Pamlico Sound he was much cheered to see a column of smoke rising in the distance from the neighbourhood of Roanoke, clear evidence to his mind of the survival of the colony. The ship cast anchor, and two boats were put out to row through the channel between the islands. There was a dangerous swell, but the first passed safely with

273

White and the captain on board; the second, less competently steered, swamped and overturned, and seven of the crew were drowned. The others were so disheartened that they begged to be taken back to the ship, to leave this unlucky coast without further attempt to find the settlers.

The captain, however, contrite perhaps for his behaviour in the past, refused to give up. He made them rescue the boat which was undamaged, and they rowed on. Darkness was falling, but as they advanced they could see the glow of the fire through the woods, and they announced their approach joyfully with the call of a trumpet and the familiar tune of an English song. Their greeting received no answer, there was no sign of life on the island. It was already night, they could see their way no longer. They disembarked and slept on the shore.

At dawn they scrambled through the undergrowth to the place from which smoke still rose. Flames licked the dry grass and the rotten trunks of dead trees; but no one was there. It was a fire lit spontaneously by the sun.

White pressed on through the woods to the site of the settlement. At the landing-stage a tree caught his eye with letters carved on its bark, CRO. All the houses built by the settlers were taken down; but the palisade surrounding the place was new, and on a post at the corner he found an inscription more explicit than that on the tree, CROATAN. It had been agreed when he left that if the settlers moved elsewhere before his return they should put a notice of this sort to inform him of their destination, adding a cross if they were in trouble. There was no cross either on the post or the tree. Croatan was an island to the south, Manteo's birthplace; the people there were very friendly.

Inside the palisade there were a few weapons, crowbars and similar gear lying among the weeds as if dropped by pilferers who found them too heavy to carry. A party of sailors searching in a ditch came on five buried chests partly disinterred, with their contents—White's books, maps and pictures—torn and scattered. Nevertheless he was easy in his mind, convinced that the Indians looted these goods after the site was abandoned, that the settlers themselves departed peacefully of their free will. The houses had been dismantled without violence; the missing cross on the notice reassured him.

They rowed back to the ship, and the captain agreed to sail down the coast to Croatan so that White could rejoin his friends;

but a storm rose, and in the effort to save themselves from the lee shore they lost three of the anchors that they carried. Only one remained, insufficient for safety, and the captain insisted that they should make for some port in the West Indies. The weather was growing worse, it was too late in the season to take chances. White had to submit; but he thought ruefully of the months wasted on the Spanish Main earlier in the summer, and in his report of the expedition he recorded that these evils "had not chanced if the order set down by Sir Walter Raleigh had been observed, or if my daily and continual petitions for the performance of the same might have taken place."

Even so, he had no idea of abandoning his purpose altogether. The plan was to spend the winter in the West Indies, then to return to Virginia in the spring and visit the settlers at Croatan. The wind disposed otherwise; it blew consistently from the west day after day, and the *Hopewell* running before it, in no condition to beat against it, was carried not to the West Indies but home to England. White did not try again; he resigned himself reluctantly to "leave off from prosecuting that whereunto I would to God my wealth were answerable to my will."

The mystery of the fate of the lost settlers has never been finally resolved. Long afterwards when Queen Elizabeth was dead, and King James ruled in her place, a fresh attempt destined to lasting success was made to colonise Virginia, and a settlement was founded on Chesapeake Bay. Rumours survived of a white community at Croatan, but when a party was sent to investigate the only inhabitants were Indians. These declared that white strangers lived there for many years, till enemies attacked and killed them. Only a few escaped with the help of friendly Indians, and no one knew where they had gone.

In the course of time facts have become known that throw a new light on the story. They are collected and examined by Professor Stephen Weeks in an article published in *Papers of the American Historical Association* Volume 5, and relate to observations made by eighteenth-century travellers among the Hatteras Indians, a tribe living in Robeson County in the southern part of North Carolina. These people, already established when the first recorded immigrants arrived, claimed to be of partly English descent. Many were fair-skinned, some of the men bearded. Their way of life and methods of agriculture were not those of other Indians; they were well-to-do, kept Negro slaves. The English that they spoke

275

was unlike that of their neighbours, white or black; in vocabulary and pronunciation it was nearer the language spoken in England under Queen Elizabeth. The most remarkable evidence is that of their family names, of which forty-one common among them are those of settlers who accompanied White. They include Dare, the name of his son-in-law.

No proof is available; but a persuasive light is thrown on events at Croatan by the story told by the Hatteras Indians themselves, that when enemies attacked their ancestors a friendly guide, Manteo perhaps, led them up the valley of the Neuse, then south to this distant refuge where they settled and prospered. No explanation of their origin fits the evidence so well as the surmise that these were the lost colonists left by White at Roanoke.

Shakespeare's play, *The Tempest*, was not produced till the following reign, but its spirit is that of the Elizabethan explorers. Barlowe's first impression of the Virginian coast as "some delicate garden abounding in all kind of odoriferous flowers" finds an echo in Prospero's haunted island

full of noises,
sounds and sweet airs that give delight and hurt not.

His successors learnt that Caliban also inhabited the paradise, and not all escaped the consequent danger. It is pleasant to be able to believe that among those who did was Miranda's prototype, Virginia Dare.

CHAPTER 19

Queen Elizabeth was fifty-five when the Spanish Armada was defeated. She had fifteen years more to live and reign. It was the period when her name earned its glory. The blow delivered to Spanish ambition raised English prestige to a height which it had never enjoyed before in Europe. The war with Spain dragged on, there were even renewed threats of invasion; but the power behind them was no longer formidable, and the English were even able to turn the tables with the capture and sack of Cadiz. In France, also, changes brought advantage to England. Henry III, Elizabeth's reluctant suitor in the old days and more often an enemy than a friend in later years, was murdered by a Dominican friar in 1589. His younger brother, her "frog," was already dead; no heir was left to the House of Valois, and the King of Navarre, leader of the Huguenots, succeeded to the throne as Henry IV, founding the Bourbon dynasty. The Catholic party opposed his accession, and the civil war continued for another five years, during which he owed much to English financial and military support. Even when he restored peace in France by accepting conversion to the Catholic Church—with the famous comment, "Paris is worth a Mass"—he persisted in a foreign policy jealous of Spain, benevolent to England.

In this afternoon of Elizabeth's life her sun shone in splendour. Shakespeare's plays appeared in the theatre, *A Midsummer Night's Dream* in 1591, *Romeo and Juliet* in 1592; the output flowed uninterrupted through the last decade of the century. Meanwhile

Spenser's epic poem attached a name to the Queen echoed not only by poets and courtiers but also in the hearts of her people:

Upon a great adventure he was bound
that greatest Gloriana to him gave.

Success, charm and longevity transformed her into a legend in popular imagination, the Faerie Queen.

In real life Gloriana was an old woman, hook-nosed and haggard, whose complexion was a layer of paint, whose red hair a wig which she had worn since a severe illness at the age of thirty left her almost bald. When one looks at the portraits that survive of her, the hieratic figure adorned with voluminous tiers of gorgeous clothes, the impression is rather that of an idol than of a human being. Yet her admirers were too diverse to be dismissed lightly as obsequious flatterers; they include old and young, high and low, men and women. She was especially beloved by her servants, with whom she often lost her temper, striking them with violence in her irritability, but who knew that she would always stand up for them, that she repaid loyalty with loyalty. It was a quality inherited from her mother.

Even the ambassadors of nations least sympathetic to her policy bore witness to the liveliness and intelligence of her mind, the charm of her high spirits and sense of humour. Many stories are told that illustrate her wit, but she was equally capable of appreciating another's. A suitor, for instance, came to ask a favour little to her liking. He was dressed for the occasion in a smart pair of boots; but she had a fastidious nose and could not bear the smell of new leather.

"Williams," she told him, "your boots stink."

"Not my boots, madam," he replied. "What stinks, I'll be bound, is my suit."

His suit was granted.

In addition to loyalty she inherited her mother's vanity. Even so it is hard to believe that any woman past sixty could be deceived by the rhapsodies of young men who professed to be dazzled by her beauty, least of all a woman as intelligent as Elizabeth. The truth seems to be that the part of Gloriana was a game of pretence which she played to amuse herself, and in which it was no more relevant to ask what relation the speeches bore to reality than in a play acted on the stage. The very extravagance of the language used helped to foster the illusion of the court of the Faerie Queen. She could be aware, like Prospero, of "the baseless fabric of this vision," and at the same time leave her emotions free to enjoy it.

Most of those who shared the pageant were of a new generation. Leicester was dead. His marriage had been forgiven, her favour restored, and as commander of the troops on land he played a part in the events of the Armada, ready to repel an invader who failed to invade; but he survived the victory by little more than a month, succumbing to what was described as a "continual fever." She mourned his death with great sorrow, and it was in part in tribute to his memory that among the rivals aspiring to succeed him she favoured his stepson, Robert Devereux, Earl of Essex, whom he himself had introduced.

Essex, however, could not really fill his stepfather's place. She and Leicester were of an age, he the elder by about a year; they had known each other from early youth when he was in love with her, and she in her own way with him. Other motives intruded on the relationship as time went by, but neither of them forgot the glow that lit its origin. In contrast, Essex was young enough to be her son, only twenty-one to her fifty-five when his step-father died. There was much indeed that was maternal in her feeling for him, but it pleased her vanity to encourage him to adopt the manners of a lover. When she heard of his secret mar-riage to Sir Philip Sidney's widow she was angry at first as in similar circumstances with Leicester; but on this occasion her ill-humour passed quickly, and Essex resumed his place among her adorers. Married or single, he could play his part as gracefully in make-believe courtship.

The trouble was that he himself took the game in earnest, saw in it a road leading to the fulfilment of his most extravagant ambitions. Behind the Queen's back he indulged in unguarded comment merciless to her ageing charms, but he was convinced that her own feeling for himself was that of a woman passionately enamoured. It did not occur to him that she too was capable of playacting. He had reason indeed to believe that she was fond of him; he was bold and handsome, the type of man that she always admired, and there was much in his character that deserved ap-proval, generosity, easy good nature. She was too shrewd, how-ever, to be blind to his faults, to the danger in which his hot tempered rashness could involve her.

He was not content to enjoy precedence at court; he craved for military glory, urging her to employ him on active service. When much against her will she consented, putting him in command of the forces sent to support Henry IV in the French civil war, his personal courage failed to make up for the incompetence of his tactics, and he returned from a fruitless campaign with heavy loss of men and money. It was not the end of his military career; his entreaties prevailed over her judgment, and she entrusted him with further commissions. In 1596 he shared the command with Raleigh of the expedition which besieged and sacked Cadiz. The exploit earned great applause in England, a punishment inflicted on Spain for the despatch of the Armada, and Essex became a popular hero. He was less inclined than ever to listen to the friends who advised him that his talents were better suited to the court than to war.

His popularity was displeasing to the Queen. She saw how it went to his head, was afraid of the adventures into which ambition could lead him. There were more frowns than smiles when she received him on his return from Spain; but she was too fond of him, too unwilling to be deprived of his company to persist long in rebuffing him, even for his own good. Raleigh, his chief rival among the courtiers, an older man, lacked his exuberance, the charm of youth. The court was a dull place for her when Essex was absent.

He retained his influence there, but not without occasions of friction. His hopes flared too high in good fortune, he was too easily mortified, too impatient of rebuke. A crisis came in 1598 with the death of the Lord Deputy of Ireland and the outbreak of a dangerous rebellion in Ulster which gave urgency to the appointment of a successor. The Queen was disposed to choose Sir William Knollys, who was uncle to Essex and a close friend; but Essex himself, anxious to keep his reliable supporters close at hand, would have preferred one of his enemies to be chosen for banishment to Ireland. There was fierce argument in the council; the Queen stuck to her choice, Essex opposed it, and when she spoke sharply to him he lost his temper, turned his back on her in contempt. She rewarded his insolence with a resounding box on the ear.

The blow took him by surprise, he laid his hand in the heat of the moment on the hilt of his sword; but those nearest intervened to restrain him before he could draw it. He told her that if it had been her father, King Henry, he would not have stood for the insult, then he left the room grumbling about a "King in petti-coats."

Everyone waited for an order committing him to the Tower, even for his execution; but he retired to his house to sulk un-molested, the Queen was silent. Other matters claimed her at-tention. Her old minister, William Cecil, Lord Burghley, lay dy-ing, one of her few remaining links with the past. During his long term of office she had often quarrelled with him, called him an "old fool"; but now she visited him with tears in her eyes. His son sent him partridge from the country; the dish lay untouched, he was too weak to feed himself. When she saw this she took the spoon and fed him with her own hand. After his death she was so distressed that she could not bear anyone to mention his name.

Essex too was a subject of which she did not wish to be re-minded. She was waiting for his apology, eager to accept it and be reconciled; but his pride refused it, he preferred to nurse his grievance. At last his depression brought on a fever, a weakness to which he had been liable from boyhood. He fell gravely ill, and when the Queen heard of it she was all compassion, sent her own doctor to attend him. On his recovery he returned to court, as high in her favour seemingly as before.

In fact, however, there was a difference. He had not apologised, and she did not forget it. Her confidence in him remained shaken. Bad news arrived from Ireland; the rebels were advancing on Dublin, and the post of Lord Deputy was still unfilled. When Essex boasted of his own qualifications she took him at his word, sent him off to Ireland to prove himself, earn forgiveness by the value of his services.

His friends were right who warned him that he had no aptitude for a military profession. At Cadiz he won glory by the reckless gallantry with which he led his troops to storm the town; but other qualities were needed in Ireland in a Lord Deputy, talent for organisation, careful strategy. Essex had neither the temperament nor the experience to prosecute a successful campaign. He wasted time and men suppressing small disorders elsewhere while the main body of the rebels gathered strength in the north. At last when he was ready to advance against them his own forces were so much reduced that he courted defeat. The rebel leader, the Earl of Tyrone, proposed a truce, and Essex was glad to agree to his terms. It was an outcome that suited the rebels admirably, leaving them free to fight another day.

There were rumours of a secret agreement when Tyrone and Essex met, a plot to share the spoils, the former to become Viceroy of Ireland, the latter King of England. Whatever the design may have been, Essex hastened to return to see the Queen and make his peace with her, to give her his own account of events. He crossed the sea, rode with a party of friends to London, where he heard that she was at Nonesuch in Surrey. He galloped on, reached the palace, rushed muddy as he was to her room, found her just getting up. She was undressed, unpainted, not even wearing a wig.

He threw himself on his knees at her feet and kissed her hands. Her first thought seems to have been to avoid any irrevocable word or action till she knew more and had time to think. She laughed at his disreputable appearance, reproaching him lightly for disturbing her at such a time, then sent him away to wash and change his clothes. He did as he was told, and when he returned for a more seemly interview their conversation was friendly.

After dinner she saw him again; but her humour had changed, less inclined to forgive his intrusion on her privacy. She was in fuller possession of the facts, asked him a number of awkward questions, and when his answers failed to satisfy her she insisted on his explaining his behaviour to the council. The upshot was that he was placed in custody in Sir Thomas Egerton's house in the Strand, where he was destined to remain for almost a year. It did him no good that he had the support of the common people, to whom he was still the hero of Cadiz. Vociferous crowds demonstrating on his behalf and execrating his enemies served only to alarm the Queen and embitter her the more against him. She had an idea to send him for trial in the Star Chamber, then changed her mind and relented, shrinking from the verdict.

She still clung to the hope that he would learn his lesson, mend his ways, so that he could come back to court on the old terms of familiarity and affection. In the spring of 1600 he was transferred still a prisoner to his own house, and in the summer all restriction was removed, he was a free man. He professed the most humble submission, exuberant gratitude; but suspicion of his intentions persisted when letters were intercepted which he wrote to friends in Ireland, and still more dangerously to King James of Scotland, Elizabeth's expectant heir.

At Michaelmas the lease expired which she had granted to him at the height of her favour to farm the revenue from customs on the import of sweet wines. He depended on it for a considerable part of his income, and as he was heavily in debt already he implored her to renew it for another term of years. She was undecided, kept him anxiously waiting for an answer. When at last it came it was to tell him that the revenue would be reserved for the Crown.

The decision left her free to restore the privilege later if he amended his behaviour; but that was little comfort to him, he needed money at once. Despair and resentment combined to overcome his remaining scruples of loyalty; he filled his house with armed adherents, encouraged preachers to incite the mob. A troupe of players in the Globe Theatre at Southwark was bribed to put on a performance of Shakespeare's *Richard II*, to give topical force to its theme, the deposition of a monarch. The council no longer hesitated; four dignitaries came to his house to summon him to give an account of himself. He let them in, turned the key on them and left them locked up while he rushed with a party of bravos out into the street, shouting to the citizens to rise in his favour, to follow him to the court.

He overestimated his popularity. No one joined him, no one was prepared. All shrank from embroiling themselves in treason. Most fled indoors; the few whom he met tried to bar his way. His heart failed, he returned crestfallen to his house to find that his hostages had been released. Soon afterwards a strong force of soldiers arrived to arrest him. He surrendered and was taken to the Tower.

At his trial the full story of his dealings both in Ireland and with King James came to light; they were enough to condemn him even without the evidence of his last act of folly. He was pronounced guilty of treason and sentenced to death. Elizabeth, like her grandfather, hated to put her name to a death warrant. Her reluctance to order the execution of Mary Stuart has already been described; she behaved in the same way, procrastinating, changing her mind, on the few earlier occasions in her reign when the headsman's axe was needed. With Essex alone there was little delay. She intervened once to postpone the execution, but countermanded the postponement on the following day, and within a week of his sentence he was beheaded. It was as though she could not trust herself to wait longer.

She had indeed reason enough to make her inexorable, having forgiven him so often before only to find that he took advantage of her leniency. Boldness was a quality that she admired in men, and when she was younger she was not afraid of the ambition that it inspired; she kept Leicester strictly in order. In her old age, however, she could not afford the risk of a favourite who coveted the throne for himself.

It can only have strengthened her resolution when she read his intercepted correspondence, contrasted the flowery compliments which he paid to her face with such phrases from a letter to a friend as that she was "no less crooked in mind than in body." Nevertheless, when a servant to whom he had entrusted incriminating documents of this sort tried to use them to extract money from his widow it was the blackmailer who felt the Queen's anger. She had him prosecuted in the Star Chamber, sentenced to stand with his ears nailed to the pillory and to pay in addition an enormous fine, two-thirds of which she handed over to his victim.

She rarely spoke of Essex after his death; but when occasion demanded it, as in an interview with the French ambassador, she insisted that his punishment was deserved and expressed no regret. Those intimate with her had a different impression, less from her words than her behaviour. She would shut herself up in her room to weep in secret, and her temper, always capricious, became more uncertain than ever, terrifying the women who waited on her when in an access of fury she would pick up an old sword and lunge at the arras. The poor health from which she suffered in youth, and which she seemed to throw off after the menopause, returned to trouble her. She lost appetite, her arm was crippled with rheumatism, and in the autumn of 1601 when she opened Parliament she—who prided herself on standing upright for hours on end without tiring—staggered and would have fallen fainting to the ground if two attendants had not caught and saved her.

Yet in this Parliament she had to deal with the most formidable opposition of her reign, a protest against the grant of monopolies to favoured courtiers. Abuses arising from the practice were responsible for great hardship, for the mounting cost of living. The speeches denouncing it were more violent than any known before in a Tudor Parliament, foreshadowing the conflicts destined to break out under the Stuarts; but unlike her successors Elizabeth knew when to yield and how to do so without loss of dignity. Her spirit rose to the occasion; she was no longer an ailing old woman, she was the Queen, listening with sympathy to the troubles of her people, demanding at the same time their confidence, submission

284

to her authority as the only source of relief. She promised stricter control of monopolies and stern action against anyone guilty of abuse, confirming the promise later by proclamation. Her demeanour no less than her words transformed discontent into passionate loyalty, and when the House of Commons sought an opportunity to thank her she received no mere deputation but all the members led by the Speaker at the palace, one hundred and forty in all. The speech that she made to them proved not only her skill in human relations, in its conclusion she spoke from her heart:

"It is not my desire to live and reign longer than my life and reign shall be for your good, and though you have had and may have many mightier and wiser princes sitting in this seat you never had nor shall have any that love you better."

Many wept as they went up in long procession to kiss her hand and take their leave. It was as if they knew that this was their last farewell.

Through the year 1602 it became evident, in spite of all her efforts, that her strength was failing, and there was much surreptitious contact between the leading men in the realm anxious to insure their careers and the King of Scotland. Even now his right to succeed lacked official acknowledgment; Elizabeth was as unwilling as ever to name her heir, she remembered too well how she herself was courted by ambitious place-seekers towards the close of her sister Mary's life. Her caution, however, was unable to avert what she feared, premature homage to her successor. Her ministers were in tacit agreement that when the time came the throne would be filled promptly, James VI of Scotland crowned James I of England.

This was in fact what she herself had in mind. She would endure no rival while she lived, but it was far from her wish to leave anarchy after her death. Unlike her father she could not hope for the continuation of the dynasty; she would still be the last of the Tudors even if she married. It was her consolation that Tudor England, their achievement, would survive. Less than two centuries had passed since Owen Tudor and Catherine de Valois fell secretly in love, little more than a century since their grandson was crowned Henry VII. In the short time available the dynasty did more than any other in English history to impress its image on the land, a pattern of strong monarchy, prosperous trade, peace and order. The seed was sown by Henry VII and Henry VIII: it was brought to flower by the genius of Gloriana, for whom adventurers sailed in quest of El Dorado, poets sang. Pope Sixtus V expressed his regret that Elizabeth and he could not marry; "Our children," he said, "would have mastered the world."

There was a spell of bitterly cold weather in the early months of 1603; but when her attendants pressed her to wrap up in furs she rejected the advice with contempt, she hated to be reminded of her age. Nevertheless she was unwell, and towards the end of February she consented to move to Richmond, her "warm winter-box," as she called it, where she could live more snugly than at Westminster. The change of quarters failed to restore her health; she was in low spirits, unable to sleep, and in great pain from a sore throat which impeded her speech. In March the symptoms grew worse, but she refused to let her doctors examine her or to go to bed. When Sir Robert Cecil, Burghley's son and successor in office, told her that she must for the sake of her people she was indignant:

"Little man, little man," she replied, "must is no word to use to princes."

She had not the same regard for him as for his father, she held it against him that he was a hunchback. In addition she knew that already he stood high in favour with King James.

Her refusal of medical care was not due entirely to obstinacy. In her last speech to Parliament she told the members that she did not wish "to live and reign longer than my life and reign shall be to your good," and now that she was dying she was unwilling to prolong the agony, anxious only that the disturbance to the government of the country should be over as soon as possible.

The time came, however, when she could hide her weakness no longer. She was put to bed, where she lay for a fortnight, almost speechless from an abscess in her throat. On the 23rd of March her condition was so low that the Archbishop of Canterbury was brought to pray at her bedside. His prayers lulled her, she fell into a deep sleep from which she never awoke. In the early hours of the morning she was dead.

She died five months before her seventieth birthday. The story of the Tudors was ended. The red dragon of Wales, added by Henry VII, was removed from the Royal coat of arms.

EPILOGUE

A short list of books used in compiling this story of the Tudors will be helpful to the reader who seeks fuller information than space allows here. It gives me the chance too to acknowledge my debt to the authors from whom I have borrowed. The first among these is Agnes Strickland, whose *Lives of the Queens of England*, published in the middle of the last century, remains a source without rival; no successor has covered so wide a field in such scrupulous detail. I have drawn on Miss Strickland to fill out the image of every Queen, whether consort or regnant, portrayed here, from Catherine de Valois to Elizabeth I. Another work of similar stature that deserves mention is Froude's *History of England* covering the period from the fall of Wolsey to the defeat of the Spanish Armada.

My account of the origin of the Tudors is founded on an article by J. Williams, "Penmynydd and the Tudors," published in *Archaeologia Cambrensis*, third series, vol. 15 (1869); but further light is added by recent research, notably in an article by Professor Glyn Roberts, "Wyrion Eden," published in *Transactions of the Anglesey Antiquarian Society* (1951), and by Professor David Williams, "The Welsh Tudors," in *History Today* (1954). The scanty knowledge available of the doings of Owen Tudor in England, and subsequently of his sons Edmund and Jasper, is collected by Howell T. Evans in *Wales and the Wars of the Roses* (Cambridge, 1915). Other authors who illuminate this period are K. H. Vickers in *Humphrey Duke of Gloucester* (Constable, 1907), Mabel E. Christie in *Henry VI* (Constable, 1922), and J. R. Lander in *The*

Wars of the Roses (Secker and Warburg, 1965). A contemporary source for the childhood of Catherine de Valois is Jean Juvenal des Ursins in his *Histoire de Charles VI*. Two lives of Margaret Beaufort, mother of Henry VII, have been published, the one written by Caroline Halstead in 1839, the other by Charles Henry Cooper in 1874.

The events leading up to the battle of Bosworth are covered by Eric N. Simons in *The Reign of Edward IV* (Muller, 1966), S. B. Chrimes in *Lancastrians, Yorkists and Henry VII* (Macmillan, 1964), and Paul Murray Kendall in *Richard the Third* (Allen and Unwin, 1955). A contemporary source is Polydore Vergil, whose *Historiae Angliae libri XXVI* have been published in an early English translation edited by Sir Henry Ellis (Camden Society, 1844). Shakespeare's story of the murder of the Princes in the Tower is re-examined by Horace Walpole in *Historic Doubts* (republished by the Folio Society in 1965) and in recent times by Josephine Tey in *The Daughter of Time*.

The reigns of the first two Tudor kings are covered by A. E. Pollard in *The Reign of Henry VII* (Longmans, 1913) and *Henry VIII* (Longmans, 1905), and by J. Gairdner in *Henry VII* (Macmillan, 1889). Particular incidents receive fuller treatment in *Mary Tudor, Queen of France* by Mary Croom Brown (Methuen, 1911), *Anne Boleyn* by Paul Friedmann (London, 1884), and [for a fresh view of Anne Boleyn's death] *The Divine King in England* by Margaret Murray (Faber, 1954). An examination of the physical health of Henry VIII, on which I have greatly relied, is to be found in an essay, "Henry VIII, a medical study," in *The Plague of the Philistines* by Professor J. F. D. Shrewsbury (Gollancz, 1964).

My main sources for the reign of Edward VI are *The Last Tudor King* by Hester Chapman (Cape, 1958) and, for contemporary evidence, *The Chronicle and Political Papers of King Edward VI* edited by W. K. Jordan (Allen and Unwin, 1966). The reign of Mary I is treated by Hilda Prescott in *Mary Tudor* (Eyre and Spottiswoode, 1952) and by E. Harris Harbison in *Rival Ambassadors at the Court of Queen Mary* (Princeton, 1940), that of Elizabeth I in the outstanding work of J. E. Neale, *Queen Elizabeth I*, first published in 1934, to which may be added *Elizabeth and Leicester* by Elizabeth Jenkins (Gollancz, 1961), *Elizabeth and Essex* by Lytton Strachey (Chatto, 1928), and *The Private Character of Queen Elizabeth* by Frederick Chamberlin

(Bodley Head, 1921). The story of Lady Catherine Grey is told in detail by Richard Davey in *The Sisters of Lady Jane Grey* (Chapman and Hall, 1911) and more succinctly and carefully by Hester Chapman in *Two Tudor Portraits* (Cape, 1960). My account of the Elizabethan colonists in America is based chiefly on *Raleigh and the British Empire* by David Quinn (Hodder, 1947), and the contemporary evidence found in *Early English and French Voyages, 1534 to 1608* by Henry S. Burrage (Barnes and Noble, New York, 1959).

Finally I wish to express my thanks to Mrs. Helen Ramage of Beaumaris for her help in obtaining information about the early history of the family, to the Reverend E. Orwig Evans of Penmynydd for showing me the Tudor monuments including the effigy of Goronwy ap Tudor in his church, to my sister-in-law, Mrs. Renée Tickell, for her researches in the British Museum library to elucidate the fate of the lost colony of Roanoke, and to my wife for drawing the pedigrees of the Tudors and Plantagenets.

GODFREY TURTON

Oxford

Index

INDEX

crowning of, 285, 286
death of, 135, 136
economy and, 105–6
Edward IV and, 56–57, 70, 75–78, 105, 106
explorations under, 261
family deaths and, 125–26
family marriages and, 127–35
foreign wars and, 106–10
great-grandfather of, 7
Jasper Tudor and, 69–72, 85, 88, 97–98, 100–1
legitimacy of, 33, 34
Henry VIII (King of England), 58, 125, 150–94, 285
affair with J. Seymour of, 174–75
A. Boleyn and, see Boleyn, Anne
Catherine of Aragon and, 128–38, 136
Catherine Parr and, see Parr, Catherine
characteristics of, 152
Cromwell's support for, 184
death of, 194
death of Catherine of Aragon and, 173–74
failing health of, 192
at "Field of Cloth of Gold," 151–52
1536 rebellion against, 182–83
first gout attack on, 179
foreign wars of, 138–43
heirs of, 153
line of succession established by, 246
marriage annulment of, 156–60, 164, 166–71
marries Anne of Cleves, 185
marries Catherine Howard, 187
marries J. Seymour, 177
Mary Tudor and, 146–49
meets Francis I, 165
policy in Wales of, 100, 181–82
reforms of, 179–81, 216
Scotland's war against, 189–90
Henry VIII, a Medical Study (Shrewsbury), 179
Herbert, Henry (Earl of Pembroke), 247
Herbert, Sir William (Earl of Pembroke), 105
Henry VII and, 56–57, 60–61
Warwick and, 61–66

Hereford, Duke of (later Henry IV), 8–9
Hertford, 1st Earl of, see Somerset, Duke of (Edward Seymour)
Holbein, 184
Hopewell (ship), 274
Hotspur (Sir Henry Percy), 9–10
Howard, Catherine (5th Queen to Henry VIII), 185, 187
Elizabeth I and, 229
execution of, 188
Howard, Thomas, see Norfolk, 3rd Duke of
Howard, Thomas III, see Surrey, Earl of
Howell ap Llewelyn, 29
Huntley, 2nd Earl of (George Gordon), 118

Innocent VIII (Pope), 109
Isabel (Queen to Richard II), 20–21, 24
Isabella of Castille (Queen of Spain), 113, 128–29
Isabeau of Bavaria (Queen of France), 17–24
appearance of, 24
Duke of Orleans and, 17–21
Insurrection
Cade's, 41–42
Glendower's, 8–15, 35, 57, 99
peasant's revolt, 7
"Pilgrimage of Grace," 182–83

Jacqueline de Hainault, Countess, 31–32
Jacqueville (captain), 22
James I (King of England, earlier James VI of Scotland), 256, 260, 275, 282, 283
as successor to Elizabeth I, 285
James I (King of Scotland), 31
imprisonment of, 25–26
set free, 26–27
James II (King of Scotland), 52
James III (King of Scotland), 104
James IV (King of Scotland), 122
death of, 139, 140, 189
marriage of, 127–28
Warbeck and, 118–19
James V (King of Scotland), 139
war against Henry VIII of, 189–90
James VI (King of Scotland and later James I of England), 256, 260, 275, 282, 283
as successor to Elizabeth I, 285

301

in politics, 42–43
York and, 45, 46, 49
Tudor, Owen, 3, 41, 47, 48, 101, 285
  arrest, of, 34–35
  Catherine of Valois and, 27–34
  death of, 53–54
  escape of, 35–36
  in Henry V's wars, 16, 17
  Henry VI and, 36–37
  as upstart, 14
Tudor of Penmynydd (Sir Tudor),
  4–5, 6, 8, 99
Tudor, Sir (Tudor of Penmynydd)
Tudors
  origins of, 3
  senior branch of, 13–14
  See also specific members of Tudor
  family
Tunstall, Sir Richard, 58–59, 63
Tyler, Wat, 7–8
Tyrell, Sir James, 126–27
Tyrone, Earl of, 281–82

Vaudemont, Louise de, 242
Vergil, Polydore, 62, 69, 88–89, 94,
  95, 107–8

Wales, Prince of, origin of, 4
Walpole, Sir Horace, 71, 127
Walsingham, Sir Francis, 240
Walshe, Sir Walter, 161–62
Wanchese (Indian), 265, 266, 270
Warbeck, Perkin, York impersonated
  by, 110–24, 237, 258
Warham, William Archbishop, 166,
  169
Wars of the Roses, rival claims in,
  39–40
Warwick, Earl of (Richard Neville)
  Herbert and, 61–64, 65, 66
  Margaret of Anjou and, 65–66, 69–
  70
  restoration of Henry VI and, 65–
  69
  Wars of the Roses and, 43, 50–55,
  59–63, 74
Warwick, Earl of (son of Duke of
  Clarence), 124, 126
  Simnel's impersonation of, 102–4,
  110–12

Warwick, Earl of, *see* Northumberland, Duke of (John Dudley)
Weeks, Stephen, 275
Weston, Sir Francis, 175
White, John, founding of American
  colony and, 267–75
William the Conqueror, 3
William of Hatfield, 40
Wingfield, Lady, 176
Wolsey, Thomas Cardinal, 61, 134,
  178
  ambitions of, 151–52
  annulment of Henry VIII's mar-
  riage and, 156–59
  arrest of, 161–62
  A. Boleyn and, 155–56
  Brandon and, 147–49
  Cromwell and, 184
  crumbling power of, 160
  death of, 163
  policy of balance of power of,
  153
  rise of, 137
  succeeded by T. More, 164
Woodville, Anthony (2nd Earl Riv-
  ers), 78
Woodville, Catherine, 98
Woodville, Elizabeth, *see* Elizabeth
  Woodville
Wyatt, Sir Thomas, 223, 232
York, Duke of, *see* Edward IV

York, Duke of (son of Edward IV),
  Warbeck's impersonation of, 110–
  23
York, 1st Duke of (Edmund of
  Langley), 40
York, 3rd Duke of (Richard Plantag-
  enet), 61
  battle of St. Albans and, 46, 47
  beheaded, 52, 53
  Cade's rebellion and, 41–42
  claim to throne of, 39–41, 50–52
  Jasper Tudor and, 45, 46, 49
  as Protector, 45, 46
  Tudors and, 43
Young, Bishop of Bangor, 14

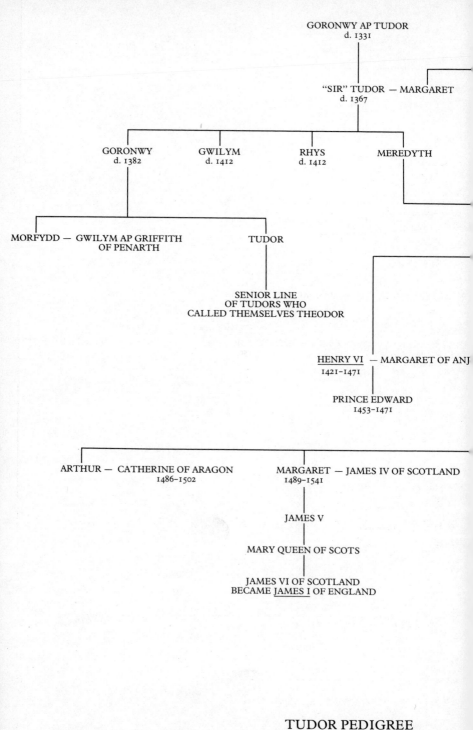

GORONWY AP TUDOR
d. 1331

"SIR" TUDOR — MARGARET
d. 1367

GORONWY
d. 1382

GWILYM
d. 1412

RHYS
d. 1412

MEREDYTH

MORFYDD — GWILYM AP GRIFFITH
OF PENARTH

TUDOR

SENIOR LINE
OF TUDORS WHO
CALLED THEMSELVES THEODOR

HENRY VI — MARGARET OF ANJ
1421-1471

PRINCE EDWARD
1453-1471

ARTHUR — CATHERINE OF ARAGON
1486-1502

MARGARET — JAMES IV OF SCOTLAND
1489-1541

JAMES V

MARY QUEEN OF SCOTS

JAMES VI OF SCOTLAND
BECAME JAMES I OF ENGLAND

TUDOR PEDIGREE
NAMES UNDERLINED ARE THOSE
OF KINGS AND QUEENS OF ENGLAND